ATM Technology and Services Delivery

M. R. Karim

Prentice Hall PTR
Upper Saddle River, NJ 07458
www.phptr.com

Library of Congress Cataloging-in-Publication Data
Karim, M. R.
    ATM technology and services delivery / M. R. Karim.
      p. cm.
    Includes bibliographical references and index.
    ISBN 0-13-085122-1
    1. Asynchronous transfer mode. I. Title.

  TK5105.35 .K37   1999
  621.382′16 — dc21   99-047686

Editorial/Production Supervision: *Joan L. McNamara*
Acquisitions Editor: *Bernard Goodwin*
Marketing Manager: *Lisa Konzelmann*
Editorial Assistant: *Diane Spina*
Cover Design Director: *Jerry Votta*
Cover Designer: *Alamini Design*
Manufacturing Manager: *Alexis R. Heydt*
Composition: *G&S Typesetters*

To the loving memory of my father

Table of Contents

Preface   xiii

Part 1   Fundamentals of the ATM Technology   1

1   Introduction   1

1.1 Evolution of ATM   1
1.2 What is ATM?   3
1.3 Advantages of ATM   5
1.4 Some Examples of ATM Applications   8
    1.4.1 High-Bandwidth ATM Backbone   8
    1.4.2 ATM Switch in a Central Office   8
    1.4.3 ATM in Mobile Communications Systems   10
    1.4.4 Video Conferencing over ATM   13
    1.4.5 Internet Application — Rebroadcast of High-Quality
         Full-Motion Video Clippings   14
1.5 Summary   15
1.6 References   15

2   The ATM Protocol   17

2.1 Introduction   17
2.2 The ATM Protocol Stack   17
2.3 The ATM Layer   18
    2.3.1 Generic Flow Control   19
    2.3.2 Virtual Path and Virtual Channel   21
    2.3.3 Payload Type (PT) Field   22
2.4 ATM Adaptation-Layer Protocol   23
    2.4.1 Service Types   24
    2.4.2 AAL Type 1   24
    2.4.3 AAL Type 2   26

2.4.4 AAL Type 3/4   26
2.4.5 AAL Type 5   29
2.5 Physical Layer   30
2.6 Summary   31
2.7 References   32

3   Call Control Procedures in ATM Networks   33

3.1 Introduction   33
3.2 General Procedures   33
3.3 Point-to-Point Signaling   36
   3.3.1 Outgoing Call from a Terminal   36
   3.3.2 Incoming Call Control Procedures   37
   3.3.3 Call Clearing Procedure   38
   3.3.4 Restart Procedures   39
   3.3.5 Status Inquiry   40
3.4 Message Construction   40
3.5 Point-to-Multipoint Signaling   42
   3.5.1 Setting Up the First Party   43
   3.5.2 Adding Another Party   43
   3.5.3 Dropping a Party   44
3.6 End-Point Addressing in ATM   45
   3.6.1 Address Format of an End-Point   45
   3.6.2 Address Registration   46
3.7 Signaling for Voice and Telephony Over ATM (VTOA)   46
   3.7.1 N-ISDN Signaling   47
   3.7.2 Channel-Associated Signaling   48
3.8 Example of Call Control Message Coding   49
3.9 Summary   51
3.10 References   52
Problems   52

4   ATM Switching Systems   53

4.1 Introduction   53
4.2 Cross-Point Switch   55
4.3 Self-Routing Switches   59
   4.3.1 Banyan Network   59
   4.3.2 Omega Network   60
   4.3.3 Blocking in a Self-Routing Switch   62
   4.3.4 Replicated Banyan Network   64
   4.3.5 Tandem Banyan Network   64
   4.3.6 Cascaded Banyan Networks   65

4.4 Batcher-Banyan Networks   67
4.5 Time-Division Switches with Common Memory   69
4.6 Buffering   71
    4.6.1 Input Buffering   72
    4.6.2 Output Buffering   76
    4.6.3 Completely Shared Buffering   79
    4.6.4 Input Bus and Output Buffering   80
4.7 Summary   81
4.8 References   82
Problems   84

5   Traffic Management in ATM Networks   87

5.1 Introduction   87
5.2 Some Definitions   88
5.3 Quality of Service   89
5.4 Service Categories   90
5.5 Congestion Control in ATM Networks   91
    5.5.1 Early Work   93
    5.5.2 Preventive Controls   95
    5.5.3 Reactive Controls   97
    5.5.4 The ATM Forum's Congestion Control Scheme for ABR Services   98
5.6 Delay/Throughput Characteristics   102
    5.6.1 The Simulation Model   102
    5.6.2 Unspecified-Bit-Rate (UBR) Services   105
    5.6.3 Available- and Variable-Bit-Rate Services   108
5.7 Summary   114
5.8 References   115
Problems   117

6   ATM Network Management   119

6.1 Introduction   119
6.2 General Network Management Functions   119
6.3 The Interface between the Network and Network Manager   121
6.4 The Simple Network Management Protocol (SNMP)   123
    6.4.1 An Overview   123
    6.4.2 The Way an MIB is Organized   128
6.5 ATM Network Management   130
    6.5.1 The ATM Interface MIB   132
    6.5.2 The Protocol Stack in ILMI   135
    6.5.3 Auto-Discovery   136
    6.5.4 System Requirements   137

6.6 Summary   137
6.7 References   138
Problems   138

Part 2 Delivery of ATM Services   **141**

7   Circuit Emulation over ATM   141

7.1 Introduction   141
7.2 Functions to Emulate   143
7.3 Emulation Procedure   145
    7.3.1 64-kb/s Service   145
    7.3.2 N × 64 kb/s Structured without CAS   145
    7.3.3 N × 64 64 kb/s with CAS   148
7.4 An Example of Circuit Emulation — Voice and Telephony
    Over ATM (VTOA)   150
7.5 Generating Source Clock Information   151
7.6 Clock Recovery at the Receiving End   154
7.7 Summary   154
7.8 References   155
Problems   155

8   LAN Emulation over ATM   157

8.1 Introduction   157
8.2 Emulated LAN Types   161
    8.2.1 Ethernet LAN   161
    8.2.2 Token Ring LAN   162
8.3 Functions Performed in Emulation   164
8.4 Protocol Stack   167
8.5 Emulation Procedure   168
    8.5.1 Overview   168
    8.5.2 Control Frames   171
    8.5.3 Initialization   171
    8.5.4 Data Transfer Procedures   177
8.6 Connection Management   179
8.7 LAN Emulation Version 2   180
8.8 Summary   180
8.8 References   180
Problems   181

9   IP over ATM   183

    9.1 Introduction   183
    9.2 Packet Transmission Procedure with IP over ATM   185
    9.3 ATMARP   187
    9.4 Inverse ATMARP   189
    9.5 Performance of TCP/IP over ATM   189
    9.6 Summary   194
    9.7 References   194
    Problems   195

10   Multi-Protocol Over ATM (MPOA)   197

    10.1 Introduction   197
    10.2 Some Definitions   199
    10.3 MPOA Components   199
    10.4 Next Hop Resolution Protocol   201
          10.4.1 Procedures   203
          10.4.2 Data Formats   205
    10.5 MPOA Overview   205
          10.5.1 Configuration   205
          10.5.2 Discovery   205
          10.5.3 Address Resolution   208
          10.5.4 Connection Management   208
          10.5.5 Data Transfer   208
    10.6 Summary   211
    10.7 References   211

11   Switched Multimedia Services   213

    11.1 Introduction   213
    11.2 Standards Supporting Multimedia Services   214
    11.3 Multimedia Services over Narrow-Band ISDN   214
          11.3.1 Network Configuration   214
          11.3.2 H.320 Terminal Architecture   216
          11.3.3 Connection Procedures for a Point-to-Point Call   217
          11.3.4 MCU   218
    11.4 Narrow-Band Multimedia Services over LANs   220
          11.4.1 LANs with Guaranteed Quality of Service   220
          11.4.2 LANs without Guaranteed Quality of Service   220
    11.5 Multimedia Services over ATM   223
          11.5.1 Terminal Architecture — H.321 Terminal   223

11.5.2 ATM Cells for User Data in H.321 Terminals   224
11.5.3 Call Control   226
11.6 Interworking of Multimedia Terminals   226
11.7 Summary   226
11.8 References   229
Problems   230

12   Wireless ATM   233

12.1 Introduction   233
12.2 WATM Networks   235
12.3 Wireless ATM Interface   236
12.3.1 Limitations of the Wireless Medium   236
12.3.2 Desired Features of the Wireless MAC Protocol   237
12.3.3 MAC Protocol for WATM   238
12.3.4 Other Access Protocols   241
12.4 Summary   241
12.5 References   241

13   Multi-Protocol Label Switching (MPLS) in ATM   243

13.1 Introduction   243
13.2 Some Definitions   244
13.3 Principles of Operation   246
13.4 Hierarchical Labels   248
13.5 Label Assignment   249
13.6 Label Distribution in ATM   250
13.7 Routing Table Construction   252
13.8 Summary   255
13.9 References   255
Problems   256

Appendix A. An Overview of T1 and E1 Interfaces   259

A.1 T1 Overview   259
A.2 E1 Overview   263
A.3 References   263

Appendix B. An Overview of DS3   265

B.1 Introduction   265
B.2 Bit Stuffing at DS2 Level   265
B.3 DS2 Multiplexing   265
B.4 DS3 Multiplexing   267
B.5 C Bit Parity Format   268
B.6 References   269

Appendix C. An Overview of SONET   271

C.1 Introduction   271
C.2 SONET Rates   271
C.3 STS-1 Frame Structure   271
C.4 Sub-STS-1 Payloads   275
C.5 Multiplexing Multiple STSs   275
C.6 References   275

Appendix D. ADSL   277

D.1 Introduction   277
D.2 ADSL Data Transfer Capability   277
D.3 Functional Description of ADSL Transceiver   280
D.4 References   283

Appendix E. Abbreviations   285

Index   291

Preface

Currently, a number of books on Asynchronous Transfer Mode (ATM) are available in the market. While each book presents the subject matter with a varying degree of thoroughness, most of them deal with the pure ATM technology. For example, they begin with Broadband Integrated Services Digital Network (B-ISDN) configurations and reference models, then introduce the basic ATM protocol, follow it up with the ATM adaptation layer, and then present a discussion of the common congestion control mechanisms in ATM networks and ATM switching systems. Also, considerable research has been done in the last ten to fifteen years on congestion control mechanisms for ATM networks and their performance in terms of throughput, average delay, etc. Publications and literature abound on these subjects, and in fact, many books describe these particular topics to great lengths.

While those books provide a very good description of ATM, and may in some cases be very useful to researchers, they do not describe how ATM can deliver useful services in the real world. Consider, for example, the case where existing local area networks (LANs) — Ethernets, IBM token rings, etc. — are to be connected to a high-bandwidth backbone network. The ATM protocol, because of its low delays and label-switching capability, appears to be ideal for this backbone network. In this case, the ATM protocol must interwork with TCP/IP. To this date, there are not many books that describe how exactly this interworking should take place. Similarly, as far as multimedia services involving data, voice, image, and video are concerned, there are few books that describe how an ATM network should interoperate with existing, circuit-switched, narrow-band ISDNs that are now providing these multimedia services from public networks. The ATM Forum and other standards organizations are presently addressing some of these topics, and have recently come out with a number of specifications. However, these specifications are generally very detailed, and are not available as a single, comprehensive document. The purpose of this book is to fill the void in this area and provide the reader with an understanding of how useful services can be delivered over ATM. To this end, we have included such topics as circuit and LAN emulation over ATM, IP over ATM, and multi-protocol over ATM, among others.

This book is organized in two parts. The first part, consisting of Chapters 1–6, deals with the basic ATM technology. The second part, Chapters 7–13, describes how ATM delivers services to end-points. We begin with a description of the benefits of ATM and a few examples of its application. The details of the ATM protocol are presented in Chapter 2. For the sake of completeness, we provide an overview of commonly used physical layers — T1, CEPT, DS3, SONET, and ADSL in Appendix A through D. Call control procedures form the subject matter of Chapter 3. The next three chapters present an overview of ATM switching systems, traffic management in ATM networks, and network management, in that order.

We begin the second part of the book with a description of circuit emulation and voice telephony over ATM. The traditional LAN emulation over ATM, IP over ATM, and the somewhat related multi-protocol over ATM are presented in the next three chapters. Audio-visual multimedia services over ATM are described in Chapter 11. Here, by way of introduction, we describe how multimedia services are currently being delivered over narrow-band ISDNs and traditional LANs, and then indicate ways of providing them over ATM. Currently, considerable research is going on in the area of wireless ATM. This rapidly evolving field is briefly described in Chapter 12. Multi-protocol label switching (MPLS) and its use in ATM form the subject matter of Chapter 13. At the end of some chapters, we have added a few problems representing real applications and illustrating design issues. We hope that they will be equally useful to students and practicing engineers.

In writing this book, I have received help from a number of sources. First, my thanks go to Martin Taylor, formerly of Madge Networks, who read the outline of the book and made valuable suggestions about its organization. Thanks are also due to Ken Smolik who took time to read most of the book, and suggested relevant, additional material at appropriate places. Joe Wilkes reviewed many chapters more than once and made suggestions that improved the quality of the book. Arun Viswanathan reviewed the chapter on multi-protocol label switching and offered corrections. Kazem Sohraby commented on the chapter on the traffic management of ATM networks. Razi Karim read parts of the book and provided comments from the perspectives of students and engineers.

I had to write the book on my own time without letting it interfere with my work at Lucent Technology. As such, many times I was on the verge of despair and wanted to abandon it. My appreciation goes to my family, and in particular, my wife, who constantly encouraged me to finish the book, and gladly accepted many lonely months while I was working on it. Without her support and understanding, I could not have completed the book.

Introduction

1.1 Evolution of ATM

With the advent of high-speed telecommunications technology, many new services began to emerge in the 1980's [1]—[3]. These generally consisted of voice, data, image, and video, and varied in bandwidth from 56/64 kb/s all the way to broadband rates of 155 Mb/s or higher. While much of the user traffic (such as voice and video) in these services was traditional in nature and required constant bandwidth for the entire duration of a call, there were many services where the traffic was bursty. In other words, the user remained inactive for quite some time, and then suddenly emitted bursts of data at a high speed for a short duration. Thus, even though the bandwidth, when averaged over a long time, did not vary much, the user may have required a much higher bandwidth for a short duration. In some cases, the applications were connection-oriented, where a connection had to be established before the user information exchange could take place. In this case, for a multimedia service, a single user might have required multiple channels simultaneously. In other instances, applications were connectionless, such as *email* and other LAN-type data communications.

As the high-speed technology began to develop, the CCITT Study Group XVIII undertook the task of defining a standard that would provide all these different services from a public or private network over a single, integrated interface. While information transfer across any interface may involve many functional layers, e.g., service modules, the transfer mode, the physical transmission, etc., Study Group XVIII concentrated on the transfer mode that included only switching and multiplexing — functions similar to those of a link-layer protocol.

In the early stages, the standards group considered the possibility of using a synchronous transfer mode (STM) [1]. Here, the transmitter sends out its data in periodic frames, each consisting of a number of time slots, and each slot being allocated to a particular application for the entire duration of a call. A generic frame format is depicted in Figure 1-1, where each frame is shown to be preceded by a distinct synchronizing pattern.[1] In STM, frames with

---

1. In some cases, as in T1, the synchronizing pattern may be distributed on a bit-by-bit basis over the full length of a frame.

Figure 1-1 A repetitive frame structure in STM.

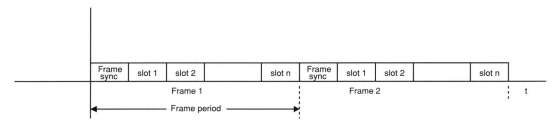

all their time slots appear periodically on a link, even if there is no information to send over a slot.

Narrow-band-ISDN (N-ISDN) is an example of STM where the frame structure is 2B + D for the Basic Rate ISDN (BRI) interface, 23B + D for the Primary Rate ISDN (PRI) interface for North American countries, and 30B + D for the PRI interface for European countries. Here, each B and D channel is 64 kb/s. In N-ISDN, while an application is usually allocated a single B channel, the PRI standard allows for higher bandwidths to be allocated to a user by defining new bandwidth structures such as $H_0 = 6B$, $H_{10} = 23B$, and $H_{11} = 30B$. Thus, at a PRI interface, in a general case, bandwidths are assigned according to the following expression:

$$n_1B + n_2H_0 + n_3H_{10}$$

where the numbers n_1, n_2, and n_3 are such that the available bandwidth of the PRI interface is never exceeded. Thus, for example, a user can be assigned up to four H_0 channels, a single H_{10} channel, or four B channels together with a single H_0 channel. In fact, Study Group XVIII initially considered a frame structure of this type, but one that would allow a much wider bandwidth and a more general and flexible allocation. For example, two new channel types were defined: H_2 with a bandwidth of 32.768 Mb/s, and H_4 with a bandwidth of 132.032 − 138.240 Mb/s. Bandwidth allocation schemes were considered whereby the variable bandwidth requirement of an application could be met by assigning an appropriate number of these channels or fragments thereof in some predetermined combinations. It was observed that with ATM, even if the requested bandwidths remained constant throughout the life of a call, there would be situations, depending on the user demands, where fractions of the bandwidth available on an interface would be unusable, thus resulting in inefficient utilization of the bandwidth. More importantly, with STM, it would be very difficult to meet the bandwidth requirement of bursty traffic by dynamically assigning a variable number of time slots.

In view of these limitations, a new transfer mode — known as the Asynchronous Transfer Mode (ATM) — was suggested. In this transfer mode, there is no concept of a periodic frame of the type illustrated in Figure 1-1. Instead, data is sent out in fixed-size blocks called cells. Whenever a user has information to send, it transmits as many cells as needed according to its bandwidth requirement at any instant, thus enabling an ATM switch to avoid the complexity that is inherent in dynamic allocation of time slots in an STM protocol. Each cell contains in its header portion a virtual channel identifier (VCI) that can be used as a label to identify a logical channel in much the same way as the position of a time slot indicates a specific channel in STM. Many of these logical channels may be multiplexed at an interface point, and as the information is transferred from one end-point to another, a given VCI may be mapped to different VCIs.

Even though the advantages of ATM were obvious, a number of issues were raised about its suitability. First, it was argued that delay-sensitive, constant-bit-rate services such as voice and high-bandwidth video could not be switched over ATM, and as such, might require STM with its circuit-switching capability to coexist with ATM in the same interface. Second, it was thought that even if ATM were suitable for all broadband services, hybrid switches consisting of both STM and ATM fabrics might still be needed in the early stages of ATM deployment to provide a transition from existing STM-based networks. Notwithstanding these problems,[2] there was general agreement among the participants in the standards organizations to proceed with the ATM approach. In 1989, CCITT Recommendation I.121 accepted ATM as the transfer mode solution for Broadband-ISDN (B-ISDN) [4]. Subsequently, a number of other CCITT recommendations were published on different aspects of the ATM protocol [5]—[8].

In 1991, an international organization called the ATM Forum was established to promote the understanding and development of the ATM technology. Since then, the Forum has developed a number of technical specifications on various aspects of the ATM protocol, and has produced white papers and computer-based training courses. For example, specifications have been developed on circuit and LAN emulation over ATM, the integrated layer management interface, physical, medium-dependent interfaces for ATM, etc.[3]

1.2 What is ATM?

The Asynchronous Transfer Mode is a packet switching and multiplexing technique. Even though the word "asynchronous" appears in its description, it *is not in any way an asynchronous transmission procedure*. Because of the way it has been designed, it is particularly suitable for high-bandwidth and low-delay applications. As indicated before, with ATM, information is sent out in fixed-size packets or cells, each containing in its header a VCI that provides a means for creating multiple logical channels and multiplexing them as needed. Because the cells have a fixed size, they may contain unused bits.

---

2. As we shall see later in this book, these problems were successfully tackled by CCITT Study Group XVIII, and subsequently by the ATM Forum. For example, the latter has standardized procedures for circuit emulation over ATM, which, in essence, provide constant bandwidths for delay-sensitive voice and video for the entire duration of a call. Similarly, procedures are being developed to support different applications using a single ATM switching fabric.

3. For a complete list of the approved ATM Forum Specifications, see the Technical Specifications section of the ATM Forum Web site.

Figure 1-2   The ATM protocol layers.

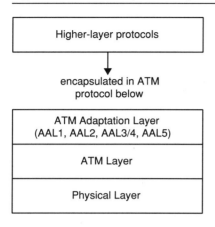

ATM is actually a very simple protocol: it merely transfers data from one point to another, and does not, by itself, provide any error recovery. However, ATM has been designed to interoperate with other, existing protocols. In fact, it can accommodate almost any upper-layer protocols that support end-to-end error recovery.

The complete ATM protocol stack is shown in Figure 1-2. The higher-layer protocols shown in the top-most box are application-specific. For example, they could be the standard file transfer protocol at the application layer with transmission control protocol (TCP) at the transport layer and Internet protocol (IP) at the network layer. Or, they could be simply the network-layer protocol for call and connection controls with a suitable application layer on top. As the name implies, the ATM adaptation layer (AAL) "adapts" the upper-layer packets to the ATM layer below. While the details might vary from one service to another (e.g., connectionless data services, connection-oriented data services, constant-bit-rate data services, variable-bit-rate data services, etc.), this adaptation is achieved by adding a header, a trailer, and some fill octets to the upper-layer packets and segmenting them into fixed-size ATM cells. Below this layer is the so-called ATM layer. This layer can be thought of as a link-layer protocol. However, in some respects, it is different from other link-layer protocols. For example, with the high-level data link control (HDLC) or Q.921 link access procedures on the D channel (LAPD) protocol, the length of a frame varies — it may vary from 2 octets to 256 octets. With the IEEE 802.3 protocol, the length of a packet, excluding the preamble and sync bits, may be anywhere from 64 octets to 1518 octets. In ATM, cell length is fixed at 53 octets. Also, unlike the link-layer protocols, ATM does not provide for acknowledgment procedures at the receiver. Errors can be detected in a cell, but not corrected. It is assumed that the transmission medium is highly reliable.

Blocks of user data of variable lengths from upper layers are passed to the ATM Adaptation Layer (AAL), which adds headers, trailers, padding octets, and/or cyclic redundancy

Figure 1-3 Label switching in an ATM network. Router R1 gets a packet with Label L1 in its header. It uses L1 to route the packet to R2, replacing L1 with Label L2.

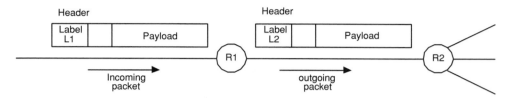

check (CRC) bits according to some rules that depend upon the service type. Each resulting data block is segmented into smaller blocks, which are then encapsulated into 53-octet cells in the ATM layer. It is these ATM cells that are transmitted to the destination. Many different media-dependent, physical-layer interfaces can be used for ATM.

1.3 Advantages of ATM

There are many advantages of an ATM network. Some of them are listed below.

- *Label switching*— The ATM protocol, like the frame relay protocol, is ideally suited for label switching. It works in the following way: In a traditional packet-switched network, when a packet arrives at a router, it examines its layer 3 header and routes the packet to the next hop along an appropriate route based upon the destination address. Since the network layer address generally contains much more information than would be required in making the routing decision, the layer 3 routing process is relatively complex. In label switching, the layer 3 address is mapped to a shorter identifier, which is called a label. It is important to emphasize here that a label is not an explicit address of an endpoint. When the packet is routed to the next hop, the label is sent along with it as part of the header so that the router at the next hop can use it to derive subsequent routing information (see Figure 1-3). In ATM, labels are formed with the 24-bit virtual path identifier (VPI) and virtual channel identifier (VCI) fields.

    Label switching offers a number of advantages. First, since packets can now be routed using a label as an index into the switch memory to determine the next hop, and since labels are shorter than IP addresses, it is easier to build a label-switching router. Second, if IP packets are to be routed between any two end-points in an ATM network in the traditional way, either virtual circuits must be connected in a full mesh configuration among ATM switches, or cut-through switched virtual channels (SVCs) must be established using an appropriate protocol.[4] Label switching obviates the need for such mesh connections and reduces the number of peer routers that need to communicate

---

4. For example, the Next Hop Resolution Protocol (NHRP).

Figure 1-4   Illustration of service delays in a packet-switched network. (a) Fixed cell packets, as in ATM. (b) Variable-size packets, as in Ethernets.

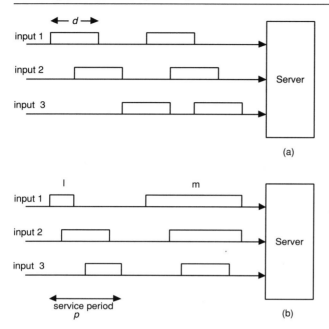

(a)

(b)

with each other. Consequently, a label-switching network is cheaper and faster. Third, label switching in an ATM environment is similar in many respects to label switching in other protocols [9], [10]. It may, therefore, be possible to use common methods for packet forwarding and even network management.

- *Low latency* — An important feature of the ATM protocol is its low latency and seamless capacity to span LANs and wide area networks (WANs). ATM's low latency results from the fact that all packets in the ATM layer have a fixed length. To see this, consider Figure 1-4(a), which shows a server with three inputs. Assume that all packets have a fixed size, *d*. The packets on any input link may arrive randomly with respect to the other input lines. If the server scans the inputs every *d* seconds, which is the length of a packet, then the average service delay for any packet on any input is *d*/2 seconds. Perfect scheduling is possible here because the packet size is known *a priori*. For example, if the data rate on each input line is 25 Mb/s, then for 53-octet ATM cells, the service period is 16.96 microseconds, and the average delay is 8.48 microseconds.

   Next, consider the case where the size of a packet varies from some minimum value, say *L,* to a maximum value, *M*. This is shown in Figure 1-4(b) and is applicable to Ethernet. In this case, the server must scan the inputs frequently enough to match the length of the shortest packets; otherwise, these packets will be subjected to long delays. For example, if the packet size varies from 2 octets to 100 octets, the server should scan the inputs every 640 ns, which may be an excessive burden on the CPU. If the service period is increased to 16.96 microseconds, the average delay is about 13 times the size of the shortest packet. If all packets are fixed-length, scheduling of network resources is much easier.

- *High-speed and high-bandwidth* — Because of its low latency, ATM is particularly suitable for applications that require high-speed transport and high bandwidths. For example, one can use ATM in a network backbone that interconnects traditional LANs such as Ethernets and token ring LANs. Currently, there are many high-speed LANs such as gigabit Ethernets and metropolitan area networks (MANs) covering tens of kilometers in diameter using such protocols as fiber-distributed data interface (FDDI) and dual queue distributed bus (DQDB). ATM could very well form the basis of the new generation of high-speed LANs and MANs. Furthermore, ATM is equally suitable for applications that do not require high speed or high capacity. For example, currently, vendors are offering ATM switches at 25.6, 44.736, 51.84, 155, and 622 Mb/s bandwidths with various cabling types — two- or four-wire category 3 unshielded twisted pair (UTP), multi-mode and single-mode fibers, DS3, and T1/E1 copper circuits.

- *Integrated network* — Normally, a packet protocol is only suitable for bursty, variable-bit-rate services, and would not be able to transport information that is sensitive to delays. For example, the public-switched telephone network (PSTN) can only transport circuit-switched information. An X.25 or frame relay network can handle only packet-switched data. The ATM protocol has been designed such that it can carry not only bursty, variable-bit-rate services, but also delay-sensitive information such as voice and video that would normally be carried by circuit-switched networks. In fact, over the last few years, a rich set of procedures and protocols that enable ATM to support many different services have been developed by the ATM Forum — connection-oriented as well as connectionless, constant-bit-rate as well as variable, and they provide different qualities of service according to the application and customer needs. Thus, with ATM, it is possible to provide all different services with a single, integrated network.

- *Integrated access from customer premises* — ATM provides a means for achieving integrated access to broadband services from public or private networks. Services such as compact disc (CD)-quality music, pay-per-view movie channels, high-definition TV, high-speed Internet data downloading, etc. can all be combined with traditional, circuit-switched voice and low-speed data services and then presented over a single ATM pipe to the customer premises, where a set-top box would demultiplex these services. The user could even request special services from a network provider using an upstream control channel.

- *Interworks with existing protocols and legacy LANs* — There are many instances where new applications would almost certainly require the bandwidth and speed of an ATM network. One such example involves collaboration among different research organizations with high-resolution, high-bandwidth imaging data. The ATM network, if installed, would still be able to interwork with traditional data networking protocols and legacy LANs such as Ethernet, token ring, and FDDI. Thus, the existing network infrastructure needs to be augmented only when or where necessary, leading to a graceful but less expensive evolution to the new technology.

- *Bandwidth-on-demand*—Bandwidth-on-demand is another innate benefit of ATM. In private networks, higher bandwidths can be requested by users. However, generally, they must be provisioned through network managers, and cannot be assigned dynamically at connection setup time. With some private networks that are equipped with inverse multiplexing capability at both ends, it may be possible to request and obtain increased bandwidth dynamically. Even then, the range is rather limited. With ATM, users may request a desired bandwidth when originating a call, and the network would attempt to dynamically allocate the requested bandwidth only if the customer had subscribed to this feature at subscription time. Furthermore, for ATM networks, there are traffic and congestion control mechanisms in place which, in the event of congestion, allow the network to maintain the quality of service for each customer with minimum degradation. Thus, initially, one could install a network with only a minimum amount of reserve capacity, and add to the network only when the demand for bandwidth has grown to a point where it is no longer possible to provide each customer with the subscribed quality of service.

1.4 Some Examples of ATM Applications

Many different applications of ATM will be discussed in relevant chapters of this book. For the time being, however, we will present a few examples of common applications.

1.4.1 High-Bandwidth ATM Backbone

Because of its low latency, ATM is inherently suitable for a high-bandwidth backbone network. This is shown in Figure 1-5. The legacy LANs are connected to the ATM network through bridges and routers. Integrated data, voice, and video can now be delivered to desktops. This is possible because ATM is capable of supporting diverse, upper-layer protocols so that the existing network infrastructure can be connected to an ATM network without any modification. ATM servers and high-speed ATM workstations can also be directly connected.

1.4.2 ATM Switch in a Central Office

In the post-divestiture era, a local exchange carrier must provide interfaces between its local switches and any inter-exchange carrier that wants to provide inter-exchange service between two Local Access Transport Areas (LATAs) or between two points of the same LATA separated by a second LATA. Currently, a special type of switch, called an access tandem, is used for this purpose. It takes the inter-exchange traffic from the local switches in a central office, multiplexes them, and routes them to each destination inter-exchange carrier. Because these

Figure 1-5 ATM is used in a backbone network, inter-connecting different types of traditional LANs. Conversion to/from the ATM takes place at the bridge and router as shown.

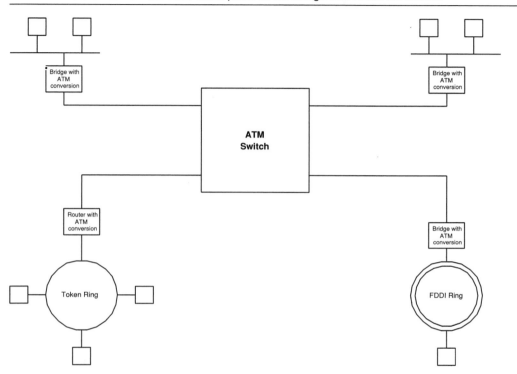

tandem switches have a fixed capacity, as the traffic grows with time, they must either have large spare capacity to start with so that they meet the growing demand with time, or they must be replaced by larger systems when the traffic exceeds their capacity. ATM switches, because of their efficient bandwidth management and inherently low delays, are ideal for this application. This is shown in Figure 1-6. The ATM network can similarly handle inter-exchange signaling information, data for operations and maintenance, exchange of data to or from advanced intelligent networks, etc. Thus, in essence, ATM provides a multi-service platform for public networks. The system has the following features:

- AAL Type 1 or 2 — constant-bit-rate, connection-oriented, with timing relation between source and destination required.
- Dynamic routing based on real-time routing criteria.
- Low latency.
- High bandwidth.

Figure 1-6   An ATM switch in a central office provides interfaces to inter-exchange carriers, acting as a high-speed tandem switch of an inter-exchange carrier at the point of connection with a local exchange carrier.

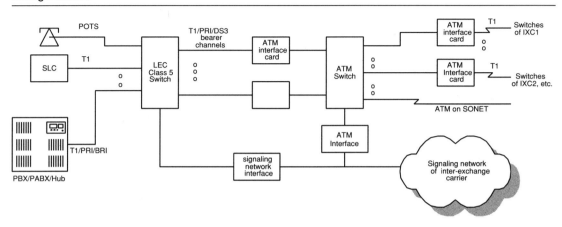

Figure 1-7   A simplified functional block diagram of a mobile communications network.

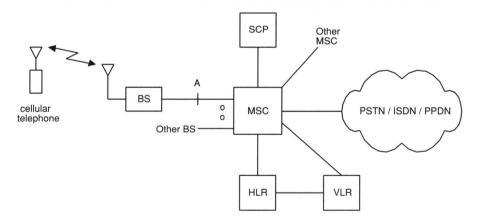

1.4.3 ATM in Mobile Communications Systems

A mobile communications system is another interesting application of the ATM technology. ATM is currently being used in TIA/EIA standard IS-634-A, which defines an interface between a base station (BS) and a mobile switching center (MSC) [13]. A simplified version of the network reference model for this interface is shown in Figure 1-7. Base stations, which provide radio communications with mobile stations, form a wireless network. Calls to or from a mobile station are switched by an MSC via the base stations. An MSC is usually connected to a PSTN, an ISDN, a Public Packet Data Network (PPDN), or any combination thereof, and may also be connected to other MSCs as well. The home location register (HLR) contains a database of the phone numbers and services for all subscribers to the home system. The visitor location register (VLR) contains a database of the phone numbers and services for all visitors to the system. The entity SCP (service control point) is a database system that performs the so-called intelligent network (IN) functions such as translation of the destination number for 800-type calls, credit card validation, voice mail and voice recognition systems, etc.

IS-634-A defines the interface at reference point A between an MSC and a BS. While it specifies the interface requirements for all types of user traffic and signaling information exchanged over this reference point, ATM is used to transport only the following information:

1. The coded user traffic (e.g., user data, or 64-kb/s PCM voice packetized to lower bit rates) and signaling information between an MSC and a BS. The purpose of the signaling information is to allocate the radio channels that transport the user traffic. Separate logical channels carry the user traffic and signaling information. These interface functions are designated as the A3 interface.
2. The signaling information between the source BS that initially serves a call and any other BS that supports the call (i.e., the target BS). This interface function is designated as the A7 interface.

Figure 1-8 shows the protocol stack for these interfaces. Notice that at the ATM adaptation layer, AAL5 is used for the signaling information and AAL2 for the user traffic.

The use of ATM for the next generation of mobile communications systems has been proposed by a number of authors [11], [12]. A possible architecture for such a network that would be able to support different mobile communications systems, e.g., AMPS, CDMA,

Figure 1-8   The protocol stack for the A3 and A7 interfaces.

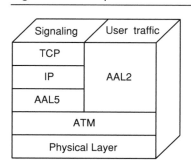

Figure 1-9   Architecture of the next-generation, mobile communications network.

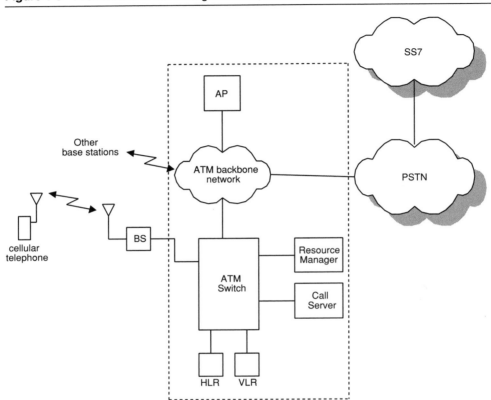

TDMA, and GSM,[5] and at the same time provide interoperability among them, is shown in Figure 1-9. In this architecture, ATM is the underlying technology of the interconnection network. It supports multimedia services using both the native-mode ATM and existing TCP/IP protocols according to service needs, and it provides bandwidth-on-demand with guaranteed quality of service. Each BS contains multiple radios and operates over either a subset of channels available to a system, as in AMPS, or all channels, as in the CDMA system. The block designated as the Resource Manager manages the radios and channels via the ATM switch. The Call Server implements call-associated functions and interacts again through the ATM switch with the Resource Manager whenever a mobile has to be connected to a radio, disconnected from a radio, or reassigned to a new channel.[6]

---

5. AMPS — Advanced Mobile Phone Service; CDMA — Code Division Multiple Access; TDMA — Time Division Multiple Access; GSM — Global System for Mobile Communications.

6. As a mobile moves from one sector of a cell to another sector, or from one cell to another, it is necessary to switch the mobile from one channel to another. This is called a hard handoff. In a CDMA

Figure 1-10 Video conferencing in a private network using an ATM switch. ATM multimedia conferencing is based on ITU standards H.310 and H.321. Copyright 1995 ATM Forum.

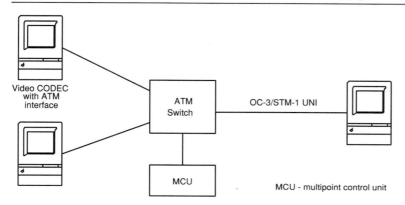

The ATM backbone network permits multiple base stations in a mobile service area to be connected together, provides interoperability among various access networks (e.g., AMPS, CDMA, TDMA, and GSM), and connects the mobile serving area to the existing PSTN. New services and features are added to the network via the entity marked AP (adjunct processor) on a per-need basis. Since the APs are connected to the ATM backbone network, the same services are uniformly available throughout the system at increased efficiency and reduced cost. The network marked SS7 (Signaling System 7) forms the basis of the advanced intelligent networks (AINs), and provides such services as 800-type calls, credit card validation, home location register for mobile communications systems, voice mail and voice recognition systems, etc.

1.4.4 Video Conferencing over ATM

Because of its low latency and high-bandwidth capability, ATM is ideally suited for video conferencing. In fact, ATM switches that provide full-motion, high-quality video conferencing over OC-3/STM-1 user network interfaces are available in the market. They support the use of a multipoint control unit (MCU) to control both conferences and broadcasts of audio and video signals. A generic network configuration for video conferencing is shown in Figure 1-10. Similarly, some commercial switches provide multimedia services, integrating high-resolution, bi-directional video, stereo-quality audio, and high-speed (48 kb/s) data.

---

system, there is another type of handoff that does not involve switching the channels; as a mobile moves from one location to another, a new BS may begin to serve the mobile using the same frequency band as the old BS. This is known as a soft handoff. During the life of a call, a mobile may go through a number of handoffs.

1.4.5 Mass Distribution of Multimedia Information in Real Time

Because of its high bandwidth and low latency, ATM is ideal for distributing high-quality multimedia programs in real time. Figure 1-11 shows how a cable TV provider or news service organization can deliver multimedia services in real time to its customers. The analog signal is converted into digital form with an MPEG-2 (Motion Pictures Expert Group) encoder. Higher layer protocols such as ITU Recommendations H.310 or H.321 are used to convert the encoder output into a form suitable for transmission over ATM. This ATM signal is transported over an OC-3 link to the internet, or one or more cable TV networks where it is first converted into an analog form so that it can be broadcast over a network. The encoded signal is stored on a server so that it can be broadcast at a later time, or locally reviewed and edited. This system has the following advantages:

- Because ATM can support different qualities of service according to customer needs, the system can serve a much larger number of users.
- Since the system is capable of large bandwidths, it can provide multiple programs of high quality videos simultaneously.

Figure 1-11   The use of ATM to provide multimedia services over the Internet or cable TV networks.

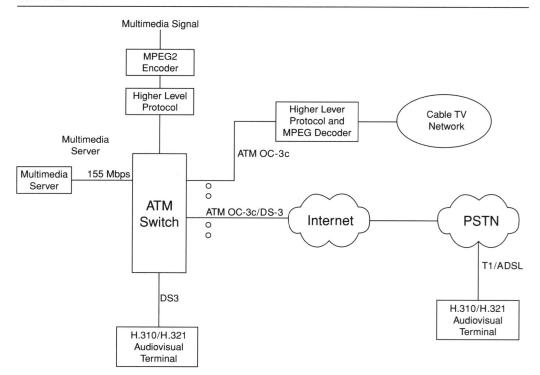

- Since delays caused by ATM switches are inherently low, events can be broadcast in real time using digital techniques for high quality videos.

A number of other applications for ATM are described in Reference [14].

1.5 Summary

In this chapter, we traced the evolution of ATM and presented a brief description of the protocol. ATM offers a number of advantages. For example, it is capable of label switching, provides low latency, and supports not only traditional, variable-bit-rate data services but also delay-sensitive voice and video. As such, it can be used to provide integrated access from customer premises to a broadband network. A number of supporting protocols have been developed for ATM that allow it to interwork with traditional data networking protocols and legacy LANs. Thus, the existing network infrastructure requires augmentation only when necessary, leading to a graceful and less expensive evolution of the ATM technology. Another important aspect of ATM is the provision of bandwidth-on-demand and quality of service. Congestion control mechanisms have been developed that guarantee the quality of service requested by each user. We discussed these advantages in detail and closed the chapter with a number of examples that illustrate the benefits of ATM.

1.6 References

[1] S. E. Minzer, "Broadband ISDN and Asynchronous Transfer Mode (ATM)," *IEEE Commun. Mag.*, Sept. 1989, pp. 17–24.

[2] J. S. Turner, "New Directions in Communications," *IEEE Commun. Mag.*, vol. 24, no. 10, Oct. 1986, pp. 8–15.

[3] G. Hayward, L. Linnell, D. Mahoney, and L. Smoot, "A Broadband ISDN local access system using emerging-technology components," *Proc. of Int'l Switching Symp. '87,* vol. 3, 1987, pp. 597–601.

[4] CCITT Recommendation I.121, "Broadband aspects of ISDN," Blue Book, Geneva, Switzerland, 1989.

[5] ITU-T Recommendation I.150, "B-ISDN Asynchronous Transfer Mode Functional Characteristics," Nov. 1995.

[6] ITU-T Recommendation I.361, "B-ISDN ATM Layer Specification," Nov. 1995.

[7] ITU-T Recommendation I.363, "B-ISDN ATM Adaptation Layer (AAL) Specifications," Mar. 1993.

[8] ITU-T Recommendation I.413, "B-ISDN User-Network Interface," Mar. 1993.

[9] R. Callon, et al., "A Framework for Multiprotocol Label Switching," Internet Engineering Task Force, Network Working Group, *Internet Draft*, Nov. 1997.

[10] E. Rosen, et al., "Multiprotocol Label Switching Architecture," Internet Engineering Task Force, Network Working Group, *Internet Draft*, July 1998.

[11] G. E. Fry, et al., "Next generation wireless networks," *Bell Labs Tech. J.*, Vol. 1, No. 2, Autumn 1996, pp. 88–96.

[12] E. Ayanoglu, et al., "Mobile information infrastructure," *Bell Labs Tech. J.*, Vol. 1, No. 2, Autumn 1996, pp. 143–163.

[13] TIA/EIA/IS-634-A MSC-BS Interface (A-Interface), July 1998.

[14] ATM Forum: ATM Application Notes, NetWorld+Interop 97, Las Vegas, May 6–8, 1997.

The ATM Protocol

2.1 Introduction

As we saw in the last chapter, ATM is a packet protocol, where data from different sources is sent over the same physical channel using asynchronous transfer mode procedures. The protocol has been designed to meet the needs of different user applications. For example, not only is it suitable for connectionless data services at variable bit rates, as in traditional LANs, it also supports the transfer of connection-oriented, circuit-switched data or even 64-kb/s PCM speech signals. Similarly, one can use it to transport user data as well as call control messages to set up a connection. The purpose of this chapter is to present the basics of the ATM protocol [1]–[4].

2.2 The ATM Protocol Stack

To handle different services efficiently, a layered architecture has been built into the protocol, each layer performing specific functions. Figure 2-1 shows the generic protocol stack. The higher-layer protocols include, among others, the application layer, the transport layer, and the network layer. Examples of the application layer protocols are the file transfer protocol (FTP) for transferring files, simple mail transfer protocol (SMTP) for transferring electronic messages, the telnet protocol that provides virtual terminal services, etc. The transmission control protocol (TCP) and Internet protocol (IP) are the transport- and network-layer protocols, respectively.

The ATM adaptation layer (AAL), as we will show shortly, is service-dependent. The purpose of the adaptation layer is to format the data from the application layer in a way that best meets the needs of a given service and then present it to the layers below. More specifically, it takes the variable-length packets from the higher layers, adds a header, a trailer, and if necessary, some fill octets, depending upon the application, segments the resulting packets into smaller packets so that they fit the fixed-size ATM cells, and then passes the segments to the ATM layer. Based on these functions, the adaptation layer can be divided into two sublayers: the convergence sublayer (CS) and the segmentation and reassembly sublayer (SAR). The CS itself consists of two sublayers: the service-specific convergence sublayer (SSCS) and

Figure 2-1   The generic protocol stack used in ATM applications.

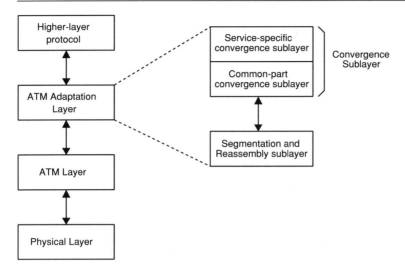

the common-part convergence sublayer (CPCS). The SSCS, as the name implies, performs only those functions that relate to the particular service in question, while the CPCS performs the functions that are common across all services.

The ATM layer is somewhat similar to the data link-layer protocol of Narrow-band ISDN. For example, it allows user data from different sources to be multiplexed over multiple virtual channels on the same physical link, and provides for the simple flow control and framing that are necessary for identifying the start of a frame. However, as we shall see later, unlike the link access procedures on the D channel (LAPD) of narrow-band ISDN, it does not provide acknowledged data transfer or error recovery. To understand the features of this protocol, we shall begin with a description of the ATM layer.

2.3 The ATM Layer

An ATM cell consists of 53 octets: the first five are the header and the remaining 48 are the information field. The various fields of a cell at a user network interface (UNI) are shown in Figure 2-2.

Briefly, the first four bits of the header constitute the generic flow control (GFC); it provides a simple flow control mechanism at the ATM layer. The next eight bits are the virtual path identifier (VPI), followed by a 16-bit virtual channel identifier (VCI). These two fields specify a logical channel in an ATM connection. The payload type indicator (PTI) field is three bits long, and describes what type of data is being carried in the information field of the cell. The cell loss priority (CLP) bit indicates to the receiver if this particular cell can be discarded in the event of network congestion. The header error control (HEC) field is the eight-bit par-

Figure 2-2 The ATM cell structure at a B-ISDN UNI. An NNI has the same structure, except that it does not contain the GFC field. Instead, it has a 12-bit VPI field.

Octet 1	8	7	6	5	4	3	2	1
1	GFC				VPI			
2	VPI				VCI			
3	VCI							
4	VCI				PT			CLP
5	HEC							
6–53	48 Octets of Information							

GFC - Generic Flow Control
PT - Payload Type (indicator)
VPI - Visual Path Identifier
CLP - Cell Loss Priority
VCI - Virtual Channel Identifier
HEC - Header Error Control

Table 2-1 Pre-assigned Cell Headers for Use at the Physical Layer

Header (4 octets in hex)	**Cell Type** (for use at the physical layer)
00 00 00 01	Idle cell
00 00 00 09	Cell for OA&M functions at the physical layer

ity on the first four octets of the header. Its purpose is to enable the receiver to detect errors that might have occurred in the header during transmission. The cell format at a network-to-network interface (NNI) is similar, except that for the NNI, there is no GFC field. Instead, it uses a 12-bit VPI field.

In B-ISDN, some pre-assigned header values have been reserved for operation, administration, and maintenance (OA&M) purposes at the physical layer. At the receiving end, cells with these header values are not passed on to the ATM layer. Table 2-1 is a partial list of these header values.

We now give a more detailed description of the header fields.

2.3.1 Generic Flow Control

In ATM, an important concept is the quality of service (QoS) [6]. Consider, for example, a constant-bit-rate application such as 64 kb/s voice. In this case, the application, during the life of a call, must have a guaranteed bandwidth — the same in both the forward and backward directions. It can tolerate some delays, but no significant variations in those delays. The application may also stipulate that there be no loss of cells. So, that would be one class of QoS.

For data applications, the requirements are different. For example, when transferring a file from an ATM server to a PC, one can tolerate significant delays, or even significant delay variations. The user may specify the maximum bandwidth — perhaps very little in one direction, but significantly higher in the other, and accept some cell loss because the higher-layer protocols in the application have built-in error-recovery procedures.

Clearly, there can be many other classes of QoS. The user of a virtual channel (VC) or virtual path (VP) can request and be granted a desired QoS from the network. The QoS descriptors include such parameters as average and peak cell rate, cell loss ratio, average delay, and so on. These parameters may be fixed at subscription time, or they may be negotiated during call setup. Once negotiated, they must not change during the life of a call; however, they can be renegotiated in a subsequent call. The network monitors the parameters associated with a VCC and tries to ensure that no user uses the network resources more than its share so that each gets the QoS it requested. In the event of congestion, networks should have some means of controlling the traffic generated by an offending user [7]. While higher-layer protocols on a network may use a sophisticated congestion control mechanism, the four-bit generic flow control (GFC) field provides a simple flow control at the ATM layer.

To see where the GFC mechanism is applicable, consider, for example, Figure 2-3, which shows B-ISDN reference points [5]. B-ISDN devices B-TE1 and B-TE2 are connected to B-NT2 at S_B. B-NT2, in turn, is connected to the ATM network at reference point T_B. To control the traffic that is locally generated by B-TE1 and B-TE2, B-NT2 can apply the GFC mechanism. In this case, the GFC will only control the traffic that is coming into B-NT2.

A public network may or may not use the GFC field to control a terminal; but if it does, similar rules will apply. For example, a B-TE2 that is directly connected to either the network

Figure 2-3 Physical configurations of terminals in B-ISDN. The GFC mechanism is used to control traffic from the terminals toward the network. The letter "B" in the terminal designations indicates their broadband capabilities. Terminals marked B-TE′ are connected in a bus configuration.

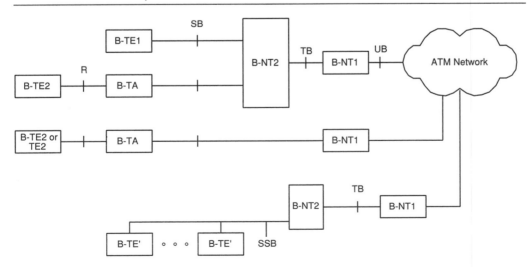

Table 2-2(a)   The GFC Field in the Network-to-Terminal Direction

GFC Field	Functions Performed
Bit 1 (lsb)	When set to 1, it indicates a HALT command from the network, asking the terminal to stop transmitting, assuming that controlled connection procedures are being used.
Bit 2	In the default mode, the network sets it to 1 to indicate a controlled connection, and 0 otherwise. When it is 1, the terminal should monitor the GFC field for a HALT command.
Bit 3	In the default mode, this bit is set to 0.
Bit 4	Always set to 0.

Table 2-2(b)   The GFC Field in the Terminal-to-Network Direction

GFC Field	Functions Performed
Bit 1 (lsb)	Unused and always set to 0.
Bit 2	In the default mode, the terminal sets this bit to 1 to indicate that this cell is from a controlled connection, and 0 otherwise.
Bit 3	In the default mode, this bit is unused and is set to 0.
Bit 4	Set to 1 if the terminal is controlled, and 0 otherwise.

or a B-NT2 may be controlled by the network using the GFC. Here, the network is called the controlling equipment. It should be remarked, however, that supporting the GFC is not mandatory. For example, a TE may choose not to implement the flow control mechanism at all, in which case, it is called an uncontrolled device. Thus, there are two types of ATM connections: controlled and uncontrolled. Devices connected to a network at reference points S_B and T_B may be either controlled or uncontrolled, whereas those connected at SSB of the bus configuration should be controlled.

The values of the GFC field depend on the direction of transmission. When it is not used, it must be set to zero. Thus, for example, an uncontrolled device sets this field to zero in all ATM cells that it sends. Table 2-2(a) describes how the four bits of the GFC field are used from a network to a terminal. The use of the GFC field in the opposite direction is shown in Table 2-2(b).

When the power is first turned on, all terminals start in the uncontrolled mode. They must then monitor the GFC field in the incoming cells. If this field is set to a SET value, the terminals change to the controlled mode.

2.3.2 Virtual Path and Virtual Channel

As we indicated before, the ATM layer provides for a VC for each user application and one or more VPs. A VP consists of a group of VCs that have some common attributes. For ex-

Table 2-3 Pre-assigned VPIs and VCIs

Specific Use	VPI (in hex)	VCI (in hex)
Unassigned cell	00	00 00
Meta-signaling	xx	00 01
General broadcast signaling	xx	00 02
Q.2931 (point-to-point) call control procedures	xx	00 05
ILMI protocol	00	01 00

ample, if some VCs have to be routed to the same node or destination, they can be assigned the same VP so that they can all be switched together. Thus, VPs are generally used at a cross-connect or switching system.

At the UNI, the VPI-VCI field consists of 24 bits. The number of bits in this field that are actually used for routing purposes may vary and is generally decided at subscription time. While each VC in a VP must have a unique VCI, two different VCs with the same VCI may be contained in two different VPs. In ATM, a user application may require the data to be transmitted in one direction only, or it may require transmission in both directions. In the latter case, at any interface point, whether it is a UNI or NNI, the same value of the VPI or VCI field is used in both directions. Similarly, the bandwidth for a given VC may be identical in each direction, as in a symmetrical communication, or different in the two directions. Also, notice that a VPI or VCI has only local significance and is valid only at a given interface. In other words, the same VPI / VCI value may exist at two or more interface points.

Although the assignment of a VCI to a VC configured at different interfaces is rather arbitrary, VCs that perform the same functions should be assigned the same VCI at all interface points. The same applies to VPIs. Some VCs and VPs have been reserved by standards committees for specific purposes. Table 2-3 is a list of some of the more commonly used ones. In this table, "xx" means any value is permissible. The same VCI must be configured and used in each VP to perform the specific functions for which it has been pre-assigned. For example, in all VPs that are configured at an interface, VCI = 5 should be used for Q.2931 call control procedures.

2.3.3 Payload Type (PT) Field

This field indicates whether or not a cell is carrying user data, OA&M information, or information related to resource management. The permissible values of the PT field are given in Table 2-4. Another important application of this field is in AAL Type 5, as described in Section 2.4.5. When a packet is too long to be contained in a single ATM cell,[1] it is broken into smaller segments. A header and a trailer are added to each segment, indicating whether a par-

---

1. That is, a CS-PDU is too long for an ATM cell.

Table 2-4   The PTI Field in the ATM Cell Header

PTI		Meaning
00|0	0	User data, no congestion, AUU = 0
00|1	1	User data, no congestion, AUU = 1
01|0	2	User data, congestion, AUU = 0
01|1	3	User data, congestion, AUU = 1
10|0	4,5	OAM cell
11|0	6	Resource management
11|1	7	Reserved

ticular segment is the first, the last, or a continuation segment. In some applications, it is not possible to add this header or trailer. In these cases, the PTI field is used to indicate the segment. The ATM layer user-to-user (AUU) bit of the PT field is set to 0 for the first or any middle segment, and set to 1 for the last segment. If, on the other hand, the convergence sublayer protocol data unit (CS-PDU) contains just one segment, then that bit is set to 1. The congestion bit of the PT field continues to be used in the message mode and has its usual meaning — 0 if there is no congestion and 1 otherwise.

The cell loss priority (CLP) bit of the ATM cell header is 0 for high-priority cells and 1 for low-priority cells. Thus, if this bit is set to 1 in a cell, a network experiencing congestion may discard the cell.

The HEC bits are generated by polynomial multiplication and division modulo 2. A polynomial corresponding to the first four octets of the header is multiplied by x^8, and the result is divided by the generator polynomial:

$$x^8 + x^2 + x + 1$$

The remainder gives the HEC bits.

2.4 ATM Adaptation-Layer Protocol

The purpose of the ATM adaptation layer is to take protocol data units (PDUs) from the higher layers (e.g., the application layer) and convert them into a format that is suitable for transmission over ATM cells. In other words, the ATM adaptation-layer protocol provides an interface between the application layer and ATM layer. Since the application-layer protocols are service-specific, the ATM adaptation layer must be designed to meet the needs of the specific services. For example, the user may require a constant-bit-rate service for transferring circuit-switched information across an ATM network with minimum delay. For proper operation, it may need to transfer the timing information as well to the destination. Here, occasional errors in the data can be tolerated. In another case, the user may have an application where a large file has to be transferred across the network. Reasonable delays are acceptable, but there must be no errors in the received information. The AAL protocol, as it were, adapts the

Table 2-5   Service Class Types that Determine the Functions of the CS

Service Class	Attributes
A	Connection-oriented, constant-bit-rate, and needs to transmit timing information over the ATM cells. An example is the circuit emulation of a T1/PRI interface.
B	Connection-oriented, variable-bit-rate, and needs to transmit timing information over the ATM cells. An example is a multimedia service with variable-bit-rate video and audio.
C	Connection-oriented, variable-bit-rate, but does not need to transmit timing information over the ATM cells.
D	Connectionless, variable-bit-rate, and does not need to transmit timing information over the ATM cells.

ATM protocol to these and other, diverse applications without sacrificing its inherent advantages — low delay and fast transport.

Recall that in many applications, a higher-layer service data unit (SDU) may be as many as several thousand octets, whereas the payload of an ATM cell is only 48 octets. As such, there is a need for segmentation and reassembly of an upper-layer SDU. Thus, one very basic function of the AAL protocol is to provide segmentation and reassembly. Other functions at this layer include error recovery, handling of cell delay variation, recovery of the source clock frequency at the receiving end, etc.

The adaptation layer is broken down into two sublayers: the CS that performs service-dependent functions, and the SAR sublayer that performs segmentation and reassembly. As we mentioned before, the CS is further divided into two layers: the SSCS that is defined by the particular service, and the CPCS that is common to all services.

Based on different types of services, the adaptation-layer protocol has been classified into five types as discussed below.

2.4.1 Service Types

For the purpose of defining the functions of the CS, we can define services broadly into four classes. They are shown in Table 2-5.

2.4.2 AAL Type 1

An example of an application that requires this type of ATM adaptation layer is circuit emulation for the connection-oriented, constant-bit-rate services of Service Class A. There are a number of functions that the CS is required to perform in circuit emulation. For example:

- It provides a means for tracking lost and misinserted cells.
- It allows timing information to be transferred so that the data can be delivered to the user at a constant bit rate.[2]

---

2. This is an essential feature in DS1 equipment.

Figure 2-4 The format of an SAR-PDU with an even-numbered sequence count in AAL Type 1 for circuit emulation. This is called the P format.

Bit 8	7	6	5	4	3	2	1
CSI		SC			CRC		P
0		Pointer to First Octet, say *M*					
Fill Data - Octet 1							
Fill Data - Octet 2							
o							
o							
Fill Data - Octet *M*							
First Octet							

Figure 2-5 The format of an SAR-PDU with an odd-numbered sequence count in AAL Type 1 for circuit emulation. This is called the non-P format.

Bit 8	7	6	5	4	3	2	1
CSI		SC			CRC		P
Payload Octet 1							
o							
o							
Payload Octet 47							

The function of the SAR layer, for this application, is to take this rather large block of data (called the AAL-SDU), segment it into a number of smaller blocks, and then send the blocks out in a sequence. These smaller blocks are called SAR-PDUs, each of which has a total length of 48 octets.

At the transmitting end, the CS delivers a CS-PDU of 47 octets to the SAR sublayer, which adds one octet of header to it. The header is actually a sequence number (SN), which consists of a one-bit convergence sublayer indication (CSI), a three-bit sequence count (SC), a three-bit CRC, and one bit of parity (see Figures 2-4 and 2-5). The SC is modulo 8, starts with 0, and increments by 1 for each sequence. Normally, the 47-octet SAR-PDU payload, along with this header, would be passed on to the ATM layer as an ATM-SDU. However, in the structured data transfer (SDT) method that is used here, there is a slight variation of this normal procedure.

In this method, the first octet is still the SAR-PDU header, and every even-numbered sequence count (i.e., SC = 0, 2, 4, 6) uses a pointer in byte position 2 to indicate the start of the structure block. In the standards document [3], this is known as the P format, and it is shown in Figure 2-4. Every odd-numbered sequence count (i.e., SC = 1, 3, 5, 7), on the other hand, contains a 47-octet payload. The format of this SAR-PDU is called the non-P format, and it is shown in Figure 2-5.

As shown in Figure 2-4, the pointer value M indicates an offset in bytes between the pointer field and the first octet of the structured block. Normally, M ranges from 0 to 92, inclusive. Clearly, the first octet of the user information (of this or the next SAR-PDU) will be positioned in this SAR-PDU if $M < 46$, and in the next SAR-PDU payload (i.e., in the next odd-numbered sequence count) if $M > 46$.[3]

The CSI bit of the P format in every even-numbered cell (i.e., SC = 0, 2, 4, and 6) is set to 1. Bit 8 of the pointer field octet is reserved for future use and is set to 0. Following the CS specifications of AAL Type 1, a Structure Data Transfer (SDT) pointer is inserted at the first opportunity in a cell with an even sequence count value. The fill octet is generally all 1's.

The CSI bit in the odd-numbered cells may be used to transfer information about the data structure or timing information. In the latter case, the synchronous residual timestamp (SRTS) is used to indicate the frequency difference between a common reference clock derived from the network clock and a service clock.[4]

2.4.3 AAL Type 2

An example of a service handled by AAL Type 2 is Service Class B and above — variable-bit-rate, circuit-switched applications where the source timing information may have to be transmitted to the receiving end. For instance, it may be an H.321 multimedia application with G.723 speech coders and variable bandwidths on a call-by-call basis. Functions of AAL Type 2 are the same as those of AAL Type 1. It is possible that this class of service would be supportable simply by extending the features and rules of AAL Type 1. However, work on this has not been completed.

2.4.4 AAL Type 3/4

AAL Type 3/4 is used for connectionless or connection-oriented, variable-bit-rate services that do not require timing information to be sent from the source to the destination (Service Class C). Two modes of service are possible: the message mode and the streaming mode. The first is suitable for transferring framed data (for example, an LAPD frame) and the second for low-speed data requiring low transport delay. In the message mode service, an AAL-SDU is passed in one or more CS-PDUs. In the SAR sublayer, a CS-PDU is segmented in a straight-forward manner. Thus, it is only the last segment that may contain some unused bytes. This is

---

3. If the pointer action is not needed for delineating a structured block contained in this SAR-PDU payload or the next SAR-PDU payload, then the 7-bit pointer field is set to all 1's.

4. The details of how this SRTS information is transmitted and used at the receiving end are given in the chapter on circuit emulation (Chapter 7).

Figure 2-6   AAL Type 3/4. (a) The message mode. (b) The streaming mode.

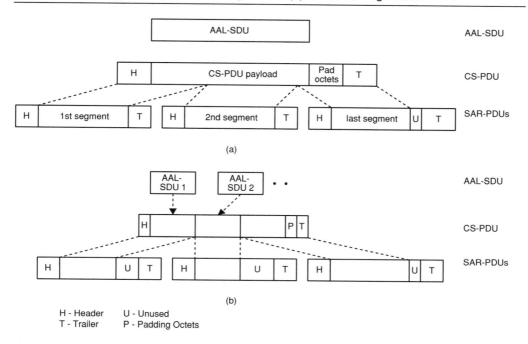

H - Header   U - Unused
T - Trailer   P - Padding Octets

clarified in Figure 2-6(a). In the streaming mode, a CS-PDU may consist of one or more fixed-size AAL-SDUs. However, when a CS-PDU is segmented, an SAR-PDU must carry exactly one AAL-SDU. Thus, each AAL-SDU, together with any adjacent header or trailer of the CS-PDU, must be sufficiently small. For example, an AAL-SDU that goes into the payload portion of a CS-PDU may be as small as one octet. For clarification, see Figure 2-6(b). Obviously, in the streaming mode, segments can be pipelined since a transfer can be initiated as soon as a single AAL-SDU is available. This mode also provides a means for aborting the transmission of an AAL-SDU.

Convergence Sublayer Format

In many cases, the SSCS is null so that AAL-SDUs will map directly into a CPCS-PDU. The format of the CPCS-PDU is shown in Figure 2-7. Currently, the CPI field is set to an all-zero octet; other values are being reserved for future use. At the sending end, for a given CPCS-PDU, the Btag and Etag fields are set to the same value, thus providing a way to correctly associate the header and trailer with a given CPCS-PDU. Their values are then incremented by one for each successive CPCS-PDU.

BASize indicates to the receiving end the maximum buffer size required to hold the CPCS-PDU. For the message mode, it is set to the length of the CPCS-PDU payload; while in

Figure 2-7   The CPCS-PDU format for AAL Type 3/4.

CPCS-PDU Header			CPCS-PDU Payload	PAD	CPCS-PDU Trailer		
CPI 1 octet	Btag 1	BASize 2	Variable-length	0, 1, 2 or 3	AL 1	Etag 1	Length 2

CPI - Common Part Indicator   Btag - Beginning tag   BASize - Buffer Allocation Size
AL - Alignment   Etag - End tag   Length - Length of the CPCS-PDU payload

the streaming mode, it is equal to or greater than this length. One use of the CPI field would be to indicate the BASize.

The purpose of the PAD field is to align the CPCS-PDU trailer on 32-bit boundaries. Thus, it may be necessary to add up to three octets of padding to the CPCS-PDU. The pad octets may be set to 0, and are ignored at the receiving end. The AL field, together with the PAD field, provide 32-bit alignment of the CPCS-PDU trailer. This octet is just a filler and does not convey any information to the receiver. The length field indicates the length in *counting units* of the CPCS-PDU payload.

SAR Sublayer Format

Notice that while a CS-PDU may have a variable length, each SAR-PDU is always 48 octets long, of which 2 octets are header, 2 octets are trailer, and the remaining 44 octets form the payload. Figure 2-8 shows the format of an SAR-PDU.

As shown in the above figure, the ST field of any segment indicates whether it is the only segment of a message, or the first, middle, or last segment of a multiple-segment message. The purpose of the MID field is to multiplex a number of SAR connections on a single ATM-layer connection. An example of its use is the following: Suppose that a user with multimedia services (e.g., audio, video, and data) is assigned a single VCI and VPI. In this case, to multiplex all services of that user on the given VCI and VPI, each SAR-SDU corresponding to a given

Figure 2-8   The format of an SAR-PDU.

SAR-PDU Header			SAR-PDU Payload	SAR-PDU Trailer	
ST 2 bits	SN 4 bits	MID 10 bits	44 octets	LI 6 bits	CRC 10 bits

ST - Segment Type   01 - Last segment
11 - A single segment message   SN - Sequence Number
10 - First segment of a message   CRC - Cyclic Redundancy Check
00 - Middle segments   LI - Length Indication

service must use a unique MID value. The same value is then used in all SAR-PDUs of that SAR-SDU.

The 44-octet payload field of an SAR-PDU may have some unused octets. These octets are set to 0 and are ignored by the receiver. The LI field indicates the number of information octets of an SAR-SDU contained in the SAR-PDU payload. The CRC covers the header, payload portion, and LI field.

2.4.5 AAL Type 5

Connectionless, variable-bit-rate services that do not require timing information to be transmitted to the remote end (Service Class D) include by far the largest number of applications. Common applications in this category are ILMI, LAN emulation, call control procedures, etc. AAL Type 5 is used in these applications.

Actually, AAL Type 5 is similar to AAL Type 3/4, except that it is simpler and more efficient. Like AAL Type 3/4, AAL Type 5 also supports both the message and streaming modes. Two operational procedures are available: assured and non-assured. In the first, each AAL-SDU is delivered to its destination error-free using retransmission and flow control if necessary. In the second, there is no guarantee that a given AAL-SDU will be delivered correctly.

There are, however, some differences between AAL Type 5 and AAL Type 3/4. They are discussed below.

Convergence Sublayer Format in AAL Type 5

The CPCS-PDU format is shown in Figure 2-9. Notice, first of all, that its payload portion is not preceded by a header. Second, the PAD field may contain up to 47 octets. The reason is that at the SAR sublayer, the CPCS-PDU is broken into 48-octet segments. Each segment consists only of the payload, and no header or trailer. Hence, it is necessary that the CPCS-PDU, before it is passed on to the SAR sublayer, be an integral multiple of 48 octets.

The CPCS-UU field allows user-to-user information to be transported across the network transparently. Currently, only one function has been defined for the CPI field, and that is to align the CPCS-PDU trailer to 64-bit boundaries. The length field indicates the number of octets contained in the CPCS-PDU payload. When it is set to zero, the receiver should interpret it as a request to abort. The 32-bit CRC is computed using the rest of the CPCS-PDU as the message polynomial.

Figure 2-9 The CPCS-PDU format for AAL Type 5.

CPCS-PDU Payload (CPCS - SDU)	PAD	CPCS-PDU Trailer			
Variable-length	0–47 octets	CPCS-UU 1 octet	CPI 1 octet	Length 2 octets	CRC 4 octets

SAR Sublayer and ATM Layer

As mentioned earlier, in AAL Type 5, an SAR-PDU has neither a header nor trailer. Thus, in the SAR sublayer itself, there is no way to indicate a segment type. This is done in the ATM layer by means of the three-bit payload type (PT) field of the cell header. See Section 2.3.3.

2.5 Physical Layer

The physical-layer protocol deals with the actual transport of information over a chosen medium, and includes such things as line coding to provide timing recovery at the remote end, signal conditioning to protect against amplitude and phase distortion, and a mechanism to provide some maintenance capabilities remotely. The physical layer also specifies interfaces over which a user device connects to a network, or one network connects to another network. The medium may be two-wire twisted pair, four wires, fibers, or even a wireless communication channel. The common physical-layer protocol used in ATM networks is SONET over fibers. In some cases, DS3, T1/CEPT, and even ADSL (asynchronous digital subscriber line) are used.

There are two types of interfaces in ATM: the user-to-network interface (UNI) and network-to-network interface (NNI). These interfaces are shown in Figure 2-10. The UNI may be public or private. If the ATM network is private, the interface is a private UNI. If it is a public network, it is a public UNI. Similarly, an NNI may be public or private.

For some interface types, the physical-layer protocol can be divided into two sublayers: the physical medium-dependent (PMD) sublayer and the transmission convergence (TC) sublayer. The PMD sublayer includes such transmission functions as bit transfer and bit alignment. The TC sublayer, on the other hand, provides functions that are not dependent on the physical medium, and includes, for instance, cell delineation and possibly ATM cell header error checking.

Figure 2-10   Interface points in an ATM network.

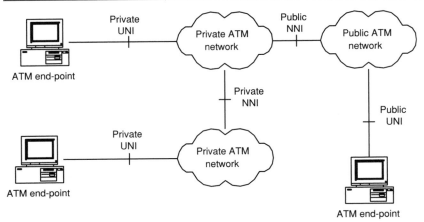

Table 2-6   Physical-Layer Protocols for UNI and NNI

UNI	NNI
622.08 Mb/s SONET STS-12c	622.08 Mb/s SONET STS-12c
155.52 Mb/s SONET STS-3c	155.52 Mb/s SONET STS-3c
44.736 Mb/s DS3	44.736 Mb/s DS3
100 Mb/s multimode fiber	
1.544 Mb/s T1 /2.048 Mb/s CEPT	
Variable-rate ADSL	

The physical-layer protocols that are currently being used by UNI and NNI are shown in Table 2-6.

The PMD sublayer of the DS3 interface is responsible for bit timing, line coding, and conditioning for the physical medium. The media-independent TC sublayer is responsible for header generation and verification, framing and cell delineation, path overhead utilization, and bit stuffing.

SONET STS-3c is obtained by concatenating the synchronous payload envelopes (SPEs) of three synchronous transport signals − 1 (STS-1). In STS-3c, the signals are not byte-interleaved. Rather, its SPE is one continuous payload. Hence, it must be passed on as one composite payload.

The physical-layer functions of SONET are similar to those of DS3. Among other things, the protocol provides

- Overhead bytes.
- B-ISDN-specific operations and maintenance.
- Performance management.
- Fault management.
- Facility testing.

These physical-layer interfaces are briefly described in Appendixes A through D.

2.6 Summary

In this chapter, we provided the details of the ATM protocol stack. More specifically, we looked at the various fields of the ATM layer, which is comparable to a data link layer. This was followed by a description of the ATM adaptation layer. Since this layer provides an interface between an application layer and the ATM layer, its functions are service-specific. Also, since a higher-layer packet may consist of several hundreds or thousands of octets, whereas the payload of an ATM cell is only 48 octets, one of the functions of the AAL is to provide segmentation and reassembly. Thus, the AAL consists of two sublayers: the service-dependent CS and the SAR sublayer. Depending on the services, there are four AAL types. We discussed them in this chapter in some detail. The common physical-layer protocol in ATM is SONET over fibers. In some cases, T1, DS3, and ADSL are also used.

2.7 References

[1] ITU-T Recommendations I.150, "B-ISDN Asynchronous Transfer Mode Functional Characteristics," Nov. 1995.

[2] ITU-T Recommendations I.361, "B-ISDN ATM Layer," Nov. 1995.

[3] CCITT Recommendations I.363, "B-ISDN ATM Adaptation Layer (AAL) Specification," March 1993.

[4] R. Handel, M. N. Huber, and S. Schroder, *ATM Networks — Concepts, Protocols and Applications*. New York: Addison-Wesley, 1994.

[5] ITU-T Recommendations I.413, "B-ISDN User Network Interface," Mar. 1993.

[6] ITU-T Recommendations I.350, "General Aspects of Quality of Service and Network Performance in Digital Networks, Including ISDNs," Mar. 1993.

[7] ITU-T Recommendations I.371, "Traffic Control and Congestion Control in B-ISDN," Aug. 1996.

Call Control Procedures in ATM Networks

3.1 Introduction

There are two types of virtual channels (VCs) in an ATM network: permanent and switched. A permanent virtual channel (PVC) is configured and assigned by the user at network configuration time, and as the name implies, it is permanently available to the user. The user can send data over the channel anytime. These PVCs are automatically activated as the system is powered up. It is only when the configuration profile of the network (or the user device) is lost or corrupted that there is a need to reconfigure the PVCs. A switched virtual connection (SVC), on the other hand, is dynamically assigned by the network when the user wants to use network resources. At the end of a call, the SVC is taken down so that it can be assigned to another user. The use of SVCs is the preferred approach since it allows network resources to be used efficiently among a larger number of users than is possible with PVCs. The purpose of this chapter is to describe call control procedures for establishing SVCs.

3.2 General Procedures

Broadly speaking, there are three procedures for establishing a VC:

1. Meta-signaling — First, a signaling VC is established using meta-signaling procedures on a known virtual channel connection (VCC) with VCI (virtual channel identifier) = 1. This signaling VC is then used for connecting desired VCCs. Meta-signaling procedures are described in ITU-T Recommendations Q.2120 [2].

2. Out-of-band signaling on a user-to-network interface (UNI) — As in N-ISDN, where the well-known D channel is used for signaling, a dedicated VC with VCI = 5 is used to originate a call. The procedures used are defined in ITU-T Recommendations Q.2931 [1], which are really extensions of the Q.931 call control procedures for N-ISDN. Q.2931 standards provide for point-to-point signaling only and do not support broadcast signaling. A point-to-point connection is defined to be a connection between two end-points over one or more VCs or virtual paths (VPs). In a point-to-multipoint connection, on the other hand, an end-point may be connected to more than one end-point

over one or more VCs. In ATM, there is no native broadcast or multicast mode as there is in, say, an Ethernet LAN. Nevertheless, it is still possible for a user to connect to more than one end-point using point-to-multipoint signaling procedures. To do this, the calling party first establishes a VCC to one of the desired end-points and then adds the other parties one at a time to the established connection.

3. User-to-user signaling — Using a known VCC as an initial signaling channel, a VCC is established within a virtual path connection (VPC) between two UNIs. The latter VCC is then used for signaling.

In this chapter, we will be concerned only with Q.2931 call control procedures. However, both point-to-point and point-to-multipoint signaling procedures will be described.

Q.2931 procedures allow a user to make a call request with desired bearer capabilities, provide for error recovery, indicate the cause in the event of a call failure, resolve call collisions, and support re-initialization of an interface when the network finds it impossible to communicate with the end-point attached to the interface. In B-ISDN, an end-point may request a desired transit delay, the AAL protocol to be used, the desired bit rate in a constant-bit-rate (CBR) service type, etc. The errors could be of various types. For example, a message might be badly constructed, contain an invalid end-point destination address, or include a bearer capability that either does not exist or is not subscribed to by an end-point. Call failures may be caused by a number of reasons. For example, the network may deliver a correct call origination request to a terminal, but the latter may be out of order and thus never respond to an incoming call. Similarly, a call may be rejected either by the network or by an end-point. In either case, the call is aborted by sending a message that also includes the possible cause for rejecting the call. A collision occurs when an end-point attempts to originate a call at the same time that the network is presenting an incoming call to the end-point. Sometimes, a network, particularly if it is a public network, may allow two end-points to exchange terminal capabilities so that they would be compatible with each other when they begin to transmit data after a connection has been established between them. Since all of these and other capabilities are built into the protocol, the procedures are generally quite involved. Very often, they are described in terms of SDL diagrams that prove useful to designers.

The ATM protocol stack used in call controls is shown in Figure 3-1. AAL Type 5 is used for call control messages. To see how an ATM cell is constructed for this adaptation layer, refer to Chapter 2. When an end-point sends out a message, it may start a timer to protect against any possible malfunction in the receiving end so that it does not have to wait indefinitely for a response. Since a network must necessarily be more robust than a user device such as a terminal, call control procedures implemented on a network are generally more elaborate than those implemented on a terminal.[1]

Before we describe the details, it is necessary to explain some conventions. A VP consists of a number of VCs, and is associated with a virtual path identifier (VPI). However, these

---

1. There are, however, devices in which symmetrical procedures are used on both sides of an interface.

Figure 3-1   The protocol stack used in ATM call controls.

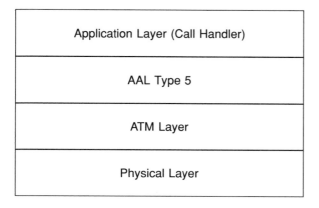

| Application Layer (Call Handler) |
| AAL Type 5 |
| ATM Layer |
| Physical Layer |

Figure 3-2   Definition of virtual paths. (a) An ATM device with a single interface containing two virtual paths with VPI=1, 2. (b) A device with two interfaces. The same VPIs are being used because they reside in different interfaces.

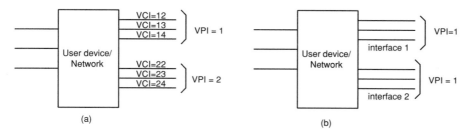

VPIs have only local significance. In other words, if a device has only a single interface, it may contain a number of VPs, each assigned a unique VPI as shown in Figure 3-2(a). But, if there are multiple interfaces on a device, paths in different interfaces can have the same VPI as shown in Figure 3-2(b). In this case, each of the various paths across all interfaces may now be distinguished by a unique virtual path connection identifier (VPCI). Thus, VPIs and VPCIs are identical in a device with a single interface, but not so in a device with multiple interfaces. Also, just as VCs can be cross-connected in a network or a user device, so can VPs.

Point-to-point and point-to-multipoint signaling procedures are described in detail in References [1], [3]. They support the following service classes: (i) connection-oriented, constant-bit-rate services that are sensitive to cell loss and cell delay variations, (ii) connection-oriented, variable-bit-rate services, and (iii) any connection-oriented services where the user defines the traffic type.[2]

---

2. For a description of the service classes available in ATM, refer to Chapter 2.

3.3 Point-to-Point Signaling

3.3.1 Outgoing Call from a Terminal

There are two types of signaling: associated and non-associated. In associated signaling, the signaling VC controls only those VCs contained in the VPC that carries the signaling VC. In non-associated signaling, on the other hand, the signaling VC may control VCs of other VPCs as well. Generally, both types of signaling should be provided in the user device and network.

The user device originates a call by sending a SETUP message and starting a timer called T303.[3] A message may contain a number of information elements, some of which are mandatory, while others are optional. The SETUP message must include the ATM traffic descriptor, broadband bearer capability, called party address, and quality of service (QoS) parameter. If associated signaling is used, the user device must also include the connection identifier information element, and indicate an exclusive VPCI and an exclusive VCI in that VPC, or an exclusive VPCI but any VCI. In other words, the user device would accept, in the first case, only the indicated VC and VP, and in the second case, only the indicated VP but any VC in the VP. In the first case, if the indicated VC/VP is not available, the network sends a RELEASE COMPLETE with cause code 45 ("no VP/VC"). In the second case, if the indicated VP is not available, the network sends a RELEASE COMPLETE with cause code 35 ("requested VPCI/VCI not available"). If the requested VP/VC combination is available, the network reserves it for this call and includes it in the connection identifier information element of the first message that the network sends to the calling party.

If non-associated signaling is used, the user has a third option: not to include any connection identifier information element at all, thereby indicating to the network that it is willing to accept any VPCI/VCI combination. In this case, the network selects an idle VPCI/VCI and subsequently sends it in the first message transmitted to the originating end-point.

The VCs that can be assigned to an end-point lie in the range 32–65535. The network assigns them starting from the lower end of the range. On the other hand, when an end-point wants to request a specific VC, it selects a channel from the upper end of the range. VCs 0–31 are reserved for other purposes.

The calling party may use either the en bloc or overlap sending mode. In the en bloc sending mode, the entire called party address string is sent in the SETUP message, while in the overlap sending mode, the SETUP message contains only partial address digits, or none at all. When using the en bloc sending mode, the user device must also include the broadband sending complete information element. In the overlap sending mode, the network responds with a SETUP ACKNOWLEDGE message and then prepares to collect the dialed digits. The dialed digits are sent via INFORMATION messages. When all digits have been sent, a broadband sending complete information element is sent to the network.

Assuming that the en bloc sending mode is being used, if the network does not reply to the SETUP message before T303 times out, the originating end-point may transmit the

---

3. T303 is a 4s timer.

SETUP message a second time, restarting the timer all over again. If there is no reply by the second expiry of the timer, the user device clears the call.

On receiving a SETUP message, the network checks the bearer capability information element and verifies if the requested bearer capabilities are within the limits subscribed to by the user device. If they are, the network then parses the called party ID in the case of en bloc sending. If it is a valid number, the network sends the originating end-point a CALL PROCEEDING message that may contain, among other things, the connection identifier information element. If the destination end-point is connected to the same switch, the latter simply sends a SETUP message to the end-point. On the other hand, if it is across a transit network, the switch routes the call over a trunk by sending a SETUP message en route to the destination end-point. If the requested bearer capability has not been subscribed to by the user, the network rejects the call by sending a RELEASE COMPLETE with cause code 57 ("bearer capability not authorized"). If the requested capability is not currently available, the call is rejected with cause code 58.[4]

On receiving a CALL PROCEEDING message, the user end-point stops timer T303, and starts another timer, T310.[5] At this time, the originating end-point is in the outgoing call proceeding state.

As T310 is running, the network waits for a response from the destination end-point. This response could be either an ALERTING message followed by a CONNECT message, or it could be just a CONNECT message. The receipt of an ALERTING message indicates that the called party is being alerted, whereas the receipt of a CONNECT message indicates that the destination end-point has accepted the call. In either case, the network passes the message to the originating end-point. If the latter receives the ALERTING message, it stops timer T310, provides, if necessary, a locally generated ring-back tone to the user, and waits for the CONNECT message. When it receives the CONNECT message, it stops timer T310, if it has not been stopped already, and sends a CONNECT ACKNOWLEDGE message to the network. If there is no response from the network before T310 expires, the originating end-point clears the call with cause code 102 ("recovery on timer expiry").

3.3.2 Incoming Call Control Procedures

When the network receives a SETUP message from a user device, it first checks to see if it has sufficient resources to handle the call. If it does, it presents the SETUP message to the destination end-point, starts timer T303, and transitions from the Idle state to the Call Present state. For en bloc receiving, the message contains the complete address of the called party and may also contain the sending complete information element. If the network does not have

---

4. The call is rejected with cause code 63 if a service or option requested by the user is not available or unspecified, and with cause code 65 if the requested bearer service has not been implemented by the network.

5. T310 is a 30–120s timer.

sufficient resources, it rejects the incoming call request by sending the originating terminal a RELEASE COMPLETE message with cause code 47 ("resources unavailable, unspecified").

As timer T303 is running, the network may receive a CALL PROCEEDING, ALERTING, CONNECT, or RELEASE COMPLETE message. If it receives a CALL PROCEEDING message from the called party before T303 expires, it will stop that timer, start timer T310, and change to the Incoming Call Proceeding state. If it receives an ALERTING message, it stops T303, sends the ALERTING message to the calling party, starts a T301 timer,[6] and enters the Call Received state. If it receives a CONNECT message, it will stop T303, send the CONNECT message to the calling party and a CONNECT ACKNOWLEDGE message to the called party, and enter the Connect Request state. Finally, if it receives a RELEASE COMPLETE, it will invoke the call clearing procedure (see below) at the originating interface by sending the calling party a RELEASE message with cause code 18 ("no user responding").

If the network receives a CALL PROCEEDING message, but then does not receive an ALERTING, CONNECT, or RELEASE message before T310 expires, it will invoke the call clearing procedure at the originating interface with cause code 18 ("no user responding") and at the destination interface with cause code 102 ("recovery on timer expiry").

If the network receives an ALERTING message, but then does not receive any CONNECT or RELEASE message before T301 expires, it will invoke the call clearing procedure at the originating interface with cause code 19 ("no answer from user") and at the destination interface with cause code 102 ("recovery on timer expiry"). Notice that in data calls, a user device may skip the ALERTING message and send a CONNECT message right away.

If the network does not receive any response from the called party before T303 expires, it will transmit the SETUP message a second time and restart the timer. If there is no response before the second expiry of this timer, the network will invoke the call clearing procedure at the originating interface by sending the calling party a RELEASE message with cause code 18 ("no user responding"). The stick diagram of Figure 3-3 summarizes the call control message flow.

3.3.3 Call Clearing Procedure

The call clearing procedure is identical on both the user and network sides. If the calling party wants to clear a call, it sends a RELEASE message to the network, starts timer T308,[7] disconnects the VC, enters the Release Request state, and waits for a RELEASE COMPLETE message from the network. The network, in turn, disconnects the VC to the calling user, sends a RELEASE COMPLETE to the calling party, releases the call reference value and the VC that it has been using on the calling interface, and then initiates the clearing procedure toward the called user. When the calling party receives the RELEASE COMPLETE message, it stops timer T308, releases the VC, and enters the Idle state. If the user device does not receive any

---

6. T301 must be set to a minimum of 3 mins.
7. T308 is a 30s timer.

Figure 3-3   Call connection messages in an ATM network.

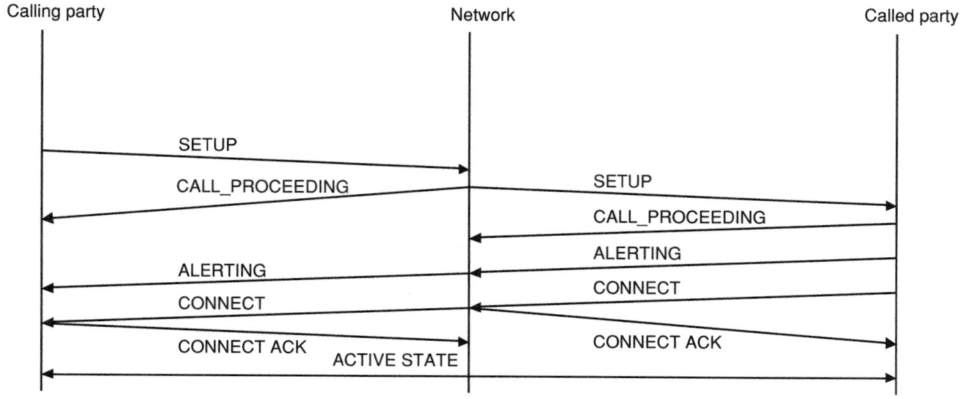

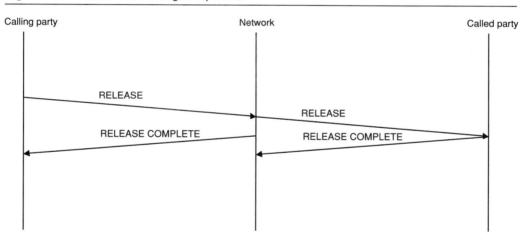

Figure 3-4   Disconnect message sequence.

response from the network before T308 expires, it transmits the RELEASE message a second time, optionally including a second cause information element with cause code 102 ("recovery on timer expiry"), and restarts the timer all over again. If there is no response before the second expiry of this timer, the user device puts the VC in the maintenance mode, releases the call reference value, and enters the Idle state. Figure 3-4 is the disconnect message sequence.

3.3.4 Restart Procedures

When there is a reason to believe that a VC or an interface is not working properly, it may be worthwhile to reinitialize the VC or the associated physical interface. This is done by sending a RESTART message with the proper restart indicator information element and a connection identifier information element indicating the VC or interface to initialize. The sender also starts timer T316.[8] When the sender receives the RESTART ACKNOWLEDGE message, it stops timer T316, clears calls, if any, on the indicated VC or interface, and releases the call reference values. On receiving the RESTART, the receiver should also do the same things. If the sender does not receive the RESTART ACKNOWLEDGE prior to the expiry of T316, it can retransmit the RESTART message and restart the timer one or more times until it gets the RESTART ACKNOWLEDGE message. If all attempts fail, the sender removes all calls from the indicated VC or the interface and puts them in the out-of-service condition. Note that the RESTART message may be sent by either the user or the network, and should use the global call reference value.

3.3.5 Status Inquiry

This message is useful since either end of a connection can use it to inquire about the current state of its peer. The sending end sends this message and starts timer T322.[9] On receiving this message, the receiving end should reply with a STATUS message, indicating, among other things, its current call state. If the sender does not receive a reply prior to the expiry of T322, it can retransmit the message (and restart that timer) one or more times until it gets a reply. If all attempts fail, the sender clears the call using cause code 41 ("temporary failure").

3.4 Message Construction

All call control messages have the generic structure of Figure 3-5. A message consists of a number of information elements (IEs), of which the first four — the protocol discriminator, call reference value, message type, and message length — are common across all messages, while the others are message-specific. The protocol discriminator indicates which protocol is being used (Q.2931), and distinguishes it from other protocols such as Q.931 for N-ISDN.[10] The call reference value is a call ID. It is assigned by the originating side of an interface at the time a call is initiated. Thereafter, it is used by both sides of the interface in all messages exchanged across the interface in connection with the call, and is removed only at the end of the call. The message type identifies the message being sent, and it is followed by the length of the message.

Of the message-specific IEs, only some are mandatory while others may be mandatory in one direction (network-to-user or user-to-network) but optional in the other, or optional in both directions. The mandatory IEs must be provided in the message; otherwise, the call will not go through. The IEs must appear in the order indicated in the table; otherwise, the mes-

---

8. T316 is a 2min timer.
9. T322 is a 4s timer.
10. It is one octet long, and is 0x09 for Q.2931.

Figure 3-5 The generic structure of a call control message for Q.2931.

Protocol Discriminator 1 (octet)	Call Reference Value 4	Message Type 2	Message Length 2	IE 1 Variable-length	IE 2 Variable-length	o o o	IE n Variable-length

Table 3-1 List of Message-specific IEs of Some Frequently Used Messages

Message Type	Mandatory IEs	Optional IEs
SETUP	ATM Traffic Descriptor, Broadband Bearer Capability, QoS Parameter	AAL Parameters, Broadband High-Layer Information, Broadband Repeat Indicator, Broadband Low-Layer Information, Called Party Number, Called Party Sub-address, Calling Party Number, Calling Party Subaddress, Connection Identifier, End-to-End Transit Delay, Notification Indicator, OAM Traffic Descriptor, Broadband Sending Complete, Transit Network Selection
CALL PROCEEDING	End-Point Reference [11]	Connection Identifier [12]
CONNECT		AAL Parameters, Broadband Low-Layer Information, [13] Connection Identifier, End-Point Reference
RELEASE	Cause	

sage will be flagged as a protocol error and the call may not even complete. Table 3-1 lists the IEs of some frequently used messages.

Message-specific IEs have the generic format of Figure 3-6. The message action indicator following the information element ID indicates what action to take if the received IE is invalid. Generally, it is set to all zeros. In this case, the receiver should clear the call if it is an invalid IE.

---

11. Applies to point-to-multipoint connections. This IE is mandatory in the CALL PROCEEDING message if it was included in the SETUP message.

12. This IE is mandatory in the network-to-user direction if the message is the first in response to a SETUP message. When a SETUP message is presented to a user device, it may accept the connection identifier that the network has indicated in the SETUP message. In that case, the CALL PROCEEDING message that the user sends in reply to the SETUP message may not contain this IE. Otherwise, the user device must include it in the first message that it sends.

13. The called end-point may like to send this IE to the calling user. When it does, the network must pass it to the calling user.

Figure 3-6   The generic structure of an information element.

Information Element ID				
Ext.	Coding Standard	IE Instruction Field - 5 bits		
		Flag	Spare	Msg. Action Ind.
1	2 bits	1	1	3
Length of the IE				
Contents of the IE				

3.5 Point-to-Multipoint Signaling

A brief description of point-to-multipoint signaling procedures is presented below. For details, see Reference [3].

In a point-to-multipoint connection, a calling user may set up a connection with more than one called user in the form of a tree configuration as shown in Figure 3-7(a). The calling

Figure 3-7   Point-to-multipoint call controls. (a) The definition of a point-to-multipoint connection. (b) The use of a functional entity called the multicast server that provides the point-to-multipoint connection.

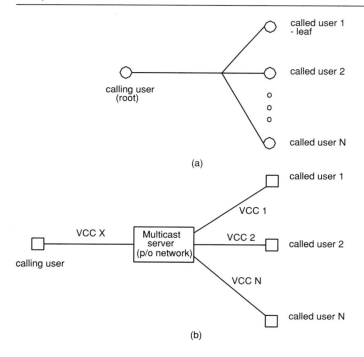

user is called the root and each called user is called a leaf. The signaling channel used is the same as the one used in a point-to-point connection. In the signaling procedures that are currently available, user information is permitted only in one direction, namely, from the root to any leaf.

The call control procedures do not specify or even imply how the multicast or broadcast capability in a network must be implemented. One can, for instance, make use of a functional entity called the multicast server in the network to provide this capability. For clarification of the concept, refer to Figure 3-7(b). Here, the root initiates a call by requesting a connection to be established with User 1. The multicast server, which is part of the network, responds by setting up VCC X between the network and the calling user, and VCC 1 between the network and User 1. The calling user then sends an ADD PARTY message, requesting the network to add Called User 2. In response, the server establishes VCC 2 between the network and User 2. The calling user then repeats the procedure until all desired parties have been added to the call.

3.5.1 Setting Up the First Party

To establish a connection with the first party, the calling user sends a SETUP message containing an end-point reference information element with the end-point reference identifier value set to 0.[14] Furthermore, its broadband bearer capability must be encoded to indicate a point-to-multipoint connection in the user-plane connection configuration octet. If the message contains the end-point reference information element, but its bearer capability does not indicate a point-to-multipoint connection, the network will reject the call with cause code 100 (" invalid information element contents"). Similarly, if the bearer capability is set to a point-to-multipoint connection, but there is no end-point reference information element in the message, the network will reject the call with cause code 96 ("mandatory information element is missing"). Since the bearer information flows in only one direction in a point-to-multipoint connection, the SETUP message must contain a zero backward user cell rate parameter. Otherwise, the network will reject the call with cause code 73 ("unsupported combination of traffic parameters").

3.5.2 Adding Another Party

Assuming that the call to the first party was successful, the root may proceed to add a second party to the call by sending an ADD PARTY message to the network and starting a 14s timer, T399. This message must contain the end-point reference information element with the end-point reference value pertaining to the second party. This value must be non-zero and unique, and can be 1 for the second party. The network checks to see if it can provide the requested QoS and support the user-requested cell rate. If it can, it presents an ADD PARTY (or

---

14. The end-point reference information element identifies the party to be added to the point-to-multipoint connection. It starts with 0 to indicate the first called party in the call.

Figure 3-8   Messages exchanged to set up a point-to-multipoint connection.

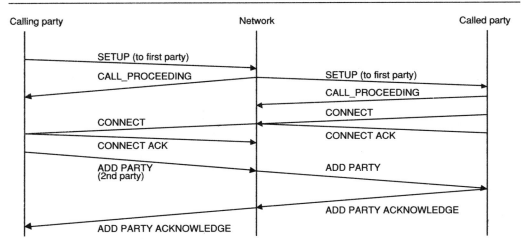

SETUP) message to the called user and starts its own T399 timer. This message must contain both the same VPCI/VCI combination in its connection identifier information element and the same call reference value as in the initial call setup message. If the network cannot provide the requested QoS or support the user-requested cell rate, it sends an ADD PARTY REJECT message to the calling user with an appropriate cause code.[15]

If the called user accepts the request, it sends an ADD PARTY ACKNOWLEDGE message to the network and enters the Active Party state. Upon receipt of this message, the network stops its timer T399, enters the Active Party state for the party, and passes the ADD PARTY ACKNOWLEDGE message to the calling user, whereupon the latter stops T399 and enters the Active Party state for the party. The root can then continue this procedure and add other parties to the call.

If, on the other hand, the called user is not able to accept a call for some reason (e.g., its terminal capabilities are not compatible with those of the root), it may reject an ADD PARTY request by sending the network an ADD PARTY REJECT message with the proper cause code. In this case, the network stops its timer T399 and requests the calling user to clear this party. Messages exchanged to establish a point-to-multipoint connection are shown in the stick diagram of Figure 3-8.

3.5.3 Dropping a Party

Either the network or a user in a point-to-multipoint connection can initiate the dropping of a party. The exact procedures for doing this are rather involved, but the general idea is that, under normal circumstances, a party can be dropped by sending a RELEASE or DROP

---

15. Notice that an ADD PARTY REJECT message can be sent only if no other response to the ADD PARTY message has been sent.

Figure 3-9 Stick diagram showing messages exchanged when a party is dropped from a point-to-multipoint connection.

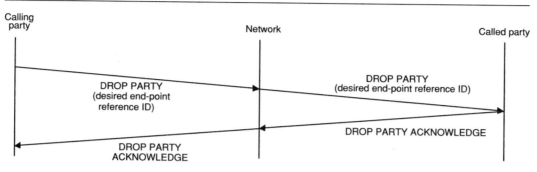

PARTY message. Generally, the RELEASE message is sent to a user when all other users in the call have already been released or are in the process of being released. In this case, normal clearing procedures hold. A DROP PARTY message, on the other hand, is sent to a party when that party as well as one or more other parties in the call, are still in the Active or Non-Null states. Upon receipt of a DROP PARTY message, the network releases the indicated end-point reference, sends a DROP PARTY ACKNOWLEDGE to the sender of the DROP PARTY message, and initiates procedures for dropping the indicated user. Figure 3-9 summarizes the messages used to drop a party from a call.

3.6 End-Point Addressing in ATM

3.6.1 Address Format of an End-Point

Each end-point in an ATM network has a unique ATM address. When a user initiates a call, the address of the called party is included in the SETUP message using the called party number information element. Similarly, the SETUP message may also include the calling party number information element so that when necessary, the switch can deliver the calling party number to the called party as a supplementary service.

The format of this address has been specified by ISO 8348 and CCITT X.213, and is shown in Figure 3-10. The first four fields are called the network prefix since it is the network that supplies their values. The network prefix is the same for all users connected to the same UNI, and is different only for different interfaces. The last two fields — the end system identifier (ESI) and selector (SEL) — are called the user part of the ATM address since they identify a user device uniquely. While variations of the above format are possible, the length of the ATM address remains fixed at 20 octets. Each octet consists of two binary coded decimal (BCD) digits. When an address is an E.164 telephone number, the called party number information element must be constructed with each BCD digit encoded as an IA5 character. If the ATM address has the DCC or ICD format, it must be placed in the information element as shown in Figure 3-10.

Figure 3-10   The ATM address format. The address may follow the E.164 ISDN numbering plan, or it may have a DCC or ICD format. In the latter case, the 8-octet field has 4 subfields as shown in the lower part of the figure.

Authority and Format ID	E.164 ISDN Telephone Number, Data Country Code (DCC), or International Code Designator (ICD)	Routing Domain	Area within a Routing Domain	End System ID (ESI)	Selector (SEL)
1 octet	8 octets	2 octets	2 octets	6 octets	1 octet

DCC or ICD Identifier	Domain-specific Part Format ID	Administrative Authority	Reserved
2 octets	1 octet	3 octets	2 octets

3.6.2 Address Registration

Before it can route a call to an end-point, the network must know the address of the end-point. User devices and the network can exchange addresses using address registration procedures.

Address registration takes place over Integrated Local Management Interface (ILMI) messages. Two MIB tables are used: one to hold network prefixes and the other to hold registered ATM addresses. The user side maintains the network prefix table, creating, updating, or deleting an entry each time the network issues an ILMI *SetRequest* message, requesting the user side to record a new network prefix. Similarly, the network maintains the address table and creates or updates an entry each time the user side sends an ILMI *SetRequest* message to the network requesting the network to add or delete an address. Of course, either side can accept or reject a request.

3.7 Signaling for Voice and Telephony Over ATM (VTOA)

Voice and telephony over ATM will be described later in connection with circuit emulation (Chapter 7). When two end-points of an N-ISDN or traditional PSTN are connected across an ATM network for 64-kb/s voice and telephony, it is necessary to convert their signaling procedures into ATM signaling, and vice versa [4]. For convenience, the network configuration is redrawn in Figure 3-11, where an interworking functional entity marked IWF provides an interface between a non-ATM device and an ATM network. NT2 is the N-ISDN network termination 2 that may provide up to layer 3 functions, and may even perform switching and concentration.

The IWF performs two things. First, it converts the Q.931 or channel-associated signaling of a narrow-band network into ATM signaling, and vice versa. AAL Type 5 is used for signaling. Second, it converts the B-channel circuit mode voice into a format that is suitable for transmission over ATM, and vice versa. This is accomplished through circuit emulation with AAL Type 1. In what follows, we describe only the signaling procedures.

Figure 3-11   Voice and telephony over ATM. Here, two N-ISDN phones connect over an ATM network.

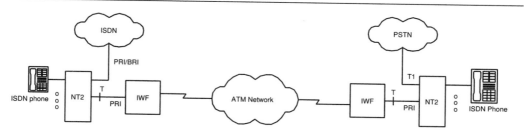

3.7.1 N-ISDN Signaling

The call control message sequence for interworking between an N-ISDN and an ATM network is shown in Figure 3-12. Two separate VCCs are used: one for signaling purposes between the IWFs of the two end-points and the other for bearer channels. If these VCCs do not exist when an ISDN phone originates a call, a signaling VCC is first established between the calling IWF and the ATM switch, and then between the switch and the called IWF, using the standard Q.2931 call control procedures. In the same way, another VCC is then established for the bearer channels between the calling IWF and the ATM switch, and between the switch and the called IWF. Here, the B-ISDN SETUP message must contain, among other things, the following information elements: the ATM traffic descriptor, the broadband bearer capability, and the QoS parameter.

Figure 3-12   Call control messages for voice telephony between two ISDN end-points over ATM.

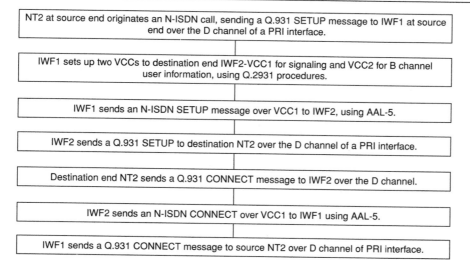

After these VCCs have been established, the calling IWF sends an N-ISDN SETUP message to the called IWF over the IWF-IWF signaling VCC. Next, the called IWF sends an N-ISDN SETUP message to the called station. If the latter responds by sending an N-ISDN CONNECT message, the called IWF forwards it to the calling IWF and then to the calling station. At this point, the two stations are connected end-to-end.

If these VCCs already exist, the calling IWF can immediately proceed to send the N-ISDN SETUP message to the called IWF over the IWF-IWF signaling VCC, and complete the connection procedure as described in the last paragraph.

3.7.2 Channel-Associated Signaling

Channel-associated signaling (CAS) is a form of in-band signaling for T1 interfaces. Here, on-hook/off-hook supervisory functions are performed using the so-called robbed bits, that is, the A and B bits which are the least significant bits of the sixth and twelfth frames of each T1 superframe. The dialed digits are sent in-band over the same channel as the user information.

When a station goes off-hook, the T1 channel assigned to the station is seized. This is indicated to the calling IWF by setting the A bit high. When the associated IWF recognizes it, it sends an acknowledgment to the calling station by setting its A bit high, then low for a certain period, then high again. This is called a wink. The detailed message exchange is shown in Figure 3-13. Notice that ATM signaling for the underlying VCCs is exactly the same as for the N-ISDN case.

Figure 3-13   Call control messages for VTOA between two non-ISDN end-points with CAS.

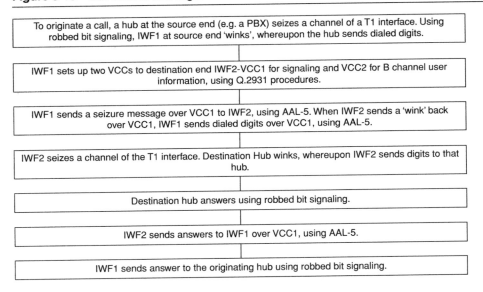

3.8 Example of Call Control Message Coding

In this section, we will describe the message encoding procedure with an example. Suppose that we want to originate a B-ISDN call into an ATM network requesting a connection-oriented, variable-bit-rate, Class C service that does not require any end-to-end timing. The data transfer is taken to be bi-directional, with a desired peak cell rate of 32,000 cells/s in either direction. This corresponds to a bandwidth of 1.536 Mb/s. The cell rates in the source behavior and resource management (RM) cell are expressed as a 14-bit, floating point, binary number with a 9-bit mantissa and 5-bit exponent using the following formula:

$$x = 2^e(1 + \tfrac{m}{512}), \quad 0 \le e \le 31, \quad 0 \le m \le 511$$

where x is the cell rate. In our case, x is 32,000. To represent it as the above floating point number, choose $e = 14$ and solve the above equation for m. This gives $m = 488$ (decimal) = 1E8 (hex). Thus, the peak cell rate is

$$\overset{}{00} \quad \overbrace{01110}^{e} \quad \overbrace{111101000}^{m}$$

or 1D E8 in hex.

When requesting the service, we could indicate to the network that the cell loss ratio (CLR) will be based on the loss of only those cells in which the cell loss priority (CLP) bit is set to zero (i.e., CLP = 0).[16] Alternatively, it could be specified to the network that the CLR value will be determined in terms of any cells lost regardless of their CLP bit setting (i.e., CLP = 0 + 1). In our example, the latter is assumed for both the forward and backward peak cell rates.[17]

As described earlier, there are two types of signaling: associated signaling and non-associated signaling. In associated signaling, the user is assigned a VC from the same VPC that carries the signaling VC. However, the user can indicate to the network that it would accept any VC or only a specific VC of its choice. In non-associated signaling, the network can assign a VC from any VPC and not just from the same VPC that carries the signaling VC. Thus, here, the user can specify a specific VC and a specific VPC of its choice, or agree to accept any VC and any VPC. In this example, we will assume non-associated signaling and no preference for any VPC or VC. This is indicated in the SETUP message by either simply omitting the connection identifier information element or including this information element constructed such that its contents have a zero length.[18] We choose to do the latter in this example.

While a SETUP message may contain many information elements, only some of them

---

16. Normally, the network would drop only low-priority cells in which the CLP bit is set to 1. However, depending upon the congestion level, even those cells whose CLP bit is set to zero may be lost.

17. In this case, the network allocates resources on the assumption that the user may set the CLP bit to zero in all cells.

18. In other words, the connection identifier information element is present, but empty.

Table 3-2   Encoding a SETUP Message

Protocol Discriminator	0000 1001
Call Reference Value (CRV)—Its length is 3 octets. The flag bit is set to 0 since the originating side is being considered. The assigned CRV is assumed to be 1.	0000 0011 0000 0000 0000 0000 0000 0001
Message Type—SETUP message. The flag bit in the second octet is set to 0, indicating that the message action field is to be ignored and errors should be handled in a regular manner.	0000 0101 1000 0000
Message Length (i.e., the total number of octets following this field)—The message contents are 45 octets long.	0000 0000 0010 1101
ATM Traffic Descriptor—The first octet is the information element identifier. The second octet indicates that the ITU-T coding standard is used and that errors are to be handled with regular procedures. Only the forward and backward peak cell rates with CLP = 0 + 1 are specified. Thus, the length of the information element's contents is 8.	0101 1001 - - - - - - - - 1000 0000 - - - - - - - - 0000 0000 0000 1000 - - - - - - - - 1000 0100 0000 0000 0001 1101 1110 1000 - - - - - - - - 1000 0101 0000 0000 0001 1101 1110 1000
Broadband Bearer Capability—The first octet is the information element identifier, and regular error-handling procedures are indicated. The length of the information element's contents is 2. The Class C service category is requested.	0101 1110 - - - - - - - - 1000 0000 - - - - - - 0000 0000 0000 0010 - - - - - - - - 1000 0011 1000 0000
Called Party Number—Its contents are 8 octets long. The unknown numbering plan is assumed. The numbers dialed are 545–1897. These are expressed as IA5 characters.	0111 0000 - - - - - - - - 1000 0000 - - - - - - - - 0000 0000 0000 1000 - - - - - - - - 1000 0000 - - - - - - - - 0011 0101 0011 0100 0011 0101 0011 0001 0011 1000 0011 1001 0011 0111

Table 3-2 *Continued*

Protocol Discriminator	0000 1001
Connection Identifier—This information element is present, but has a zero length. This indicates that the calling party is willing to accept any VC and any VPC.	0101 1010
	1000 0000
	0000 0000
	0000 0000
QoS Parameter—This parameter is not supported by B-ISDN User Part Release 1. Thus, the forward and backward QoS service classes (octets 4 and 5) are both unspecified.	0101 1100
	1000 0000
	0000 0000
	0000 0010
	0000 0000
	0000 0000
Broadband Sending Complete—The information element's contents are only one octet long.	0110 0010
	1000 0000
	0000 0000
	0000 0001
	1010 0001

are mandatory and the others are optional. The mandatory elements are: the protocol discriminator, call reference value, message type, message length, ATM traffic descriptor, broadband bearer capability, and QoS parameter. The optional elements are: called party number and connection identifier.[19] Since all digits of the called party number are included in the SETUP message,[20] the broadband sending complete information element must also be sent. The encoded SETUP message is shown in Table 3-2.

3.9 Summary

In this chapter, we presented the ATM call control procedures based on ITU-T Recommendations Q.2931 for B-ISDN. These Recommendations do not support meta-signaling. The procedures apply to connection-oriented services where bit rates are constant, variable, or user-defined. Call control messages are sent over a dedicated VC with VCI = 5, and use the services of AAL-5. Messages exchanged between two end-points for some call control scenarios with point-to-point signaling were shown using stick diagrams. The generic message structure was described as well. Also discussed was point-to-multipoint signaling. Here, when a

---

19. Notice that it is necessary to provide the information elements in the correct order. Otherwise, the message may be rejected by the network.

20. This is called en bloc sending.

user originates a call, the switch first sets up a VCC to that user. As the calling user adds each party, the switch establishes a separate VCC to the latter. Signaling procedures for voice and telephony over ATM were considered. The need for these procedures arises when two end-points of a narrow-band ISDN or a traditional PSTN are connected across an ATM network for 64 kb/s voice. At the end of the chapter, we gave an example of how a SETUP message is encoded.

3.10 References

[1] ITU-T Recommendations Q.2931, "Broadband Integrated Services Digital Network (B-ISDN)–Digital subscriber Signalling System No. 2 (DSS 2)–User-Network Interface (UNI) Layer 3 Specification for Basic Call Control / Connection Protocol," Feb. 1995.

[2] ITU-T Recommendations Q.2120, "B-ISDN Meta-Signalling Protocol," Feb. 1995.

[3] ATM Forum, "ATM User-Network Interface Specification," *Draft*, Version 2.4, Aug. 1993.

[4] ATM Forum, "Voice and Telephony Over ATM — ATM trunking for narrow-band services," BTD-VTOA-LLT-01.11, Feb. 1997.

Problems

3.1 In Section 3.8, we showed how to construct a SETUP message for an outgoing call request for a VBR, class C service from an ATM end-point. For the same service, encode the following messages: CALL PROCEEDING, CONNECT, CONNECT ACK, RELEASE, and RELEASE COMPLETE.

3.2 For the same service in Problem 3.1, construct a RELEASE COMPLETE message denying a call request because the bandwidth requested by the originating terminal exceeds the subscribed limits.

3.3 Design a software function that an ATM switch would invoke when it receives a point-to-multipoint call request from an end-point. Make the function as general as possible. For instance, assume that the function would allow any number of parties to be added to a call.

3.4 Design a software function that a switch could use to encode any information element of a message by passing proper parameters. Recall that the length of an information element depends on a number of factors, and may vary from one call to another.

ATM Switching Systems

4.1 Introduction

A number of switching architectures have been proposed for ATM networks over the last few years, and many of them have, in fact, been implemented in commercially available systems. See, for instance, References [1]—[8] for a comprehensive survey of these architectures. As the data rate involved in an ATM network is generally very high, the architectures of ATM switches are based on the principles of high-speed packet switching, where much of the switching function is implemented in hardware using the concept of distributed control and parallel processing. With the steady progress in very large-scale integration (VLSI) technology, it is now possible to design these switches as integrated circuits in larger and larger capacities.

A general-purpose switch may be based on a space-division or time-division architecture, or a combination of both. Early telephone switches, which were circuit-switched, were mostly space-division switches. Examples are No. 5 crossbar switches used in PSTNs. These switches can be viewed as a collection of cross-points with a certain number of input and output lines, designed in such a way that any input can be connected to any output. In fact, it is possible to design an elementary 2×2 switching element and connect many of them in multiple stages to form a much larger switching system. We will see later in this chapter that high-speed packet switches for ATM networks are built around space-division switching principles. However, because of high data rates in ATM, there are a few issues here that do not arise in traditional circuit switching. For example, from a given input port to a desired output port, there may be a number of paths through a switch. One can select any specific path by administering a routing function of an entire switch by means of a single, centralized controller. In this case, however, the routing speed would be naturally limited. To overcome this limitation, it may be necessary to use a distributed control mechanism by implementing a multiplicity of controllers throughout the switch such that each individual switching element becomes, in effect, self-routing.

As a second example of the requirements of a high-speed packet switch, since packets may arrive at an input port from many different sources simultaneously, and since a source may occasionally send out packets in bursts, it is necessary to buffer incoming packets. These buffers can be provided at either the input or the output ports, or sometimes at both inputs and outputs. Since they have a finite size, there is always some non-zero probability that a fraction of the total number of packets transmitted by the source might be lost. Similarly, there are other parameters that may determine the performance of a switch.[1] For example, the performance would depend on whether buffers are being used at the input, output, or both, the buffer size, how the input buffers are being serviced, and the overall architecture of the switch fabric itself.

Since packets generally arrive at different inputs asynchronously, it is possible that, at a certain instant, two or more of them may contend for the same resources of the switching system (e.g., the same links in a multi-stage interconnection network), even though the output ports to which they are destined are idle at that instant. In this case, the connections are said to be blocked. While blocking due to insufficient capacity can occur even in traditional circuit switches, a high-speed packet switch is susceptible to another form of blocking. Suppose that two packets that have the same destination address arrive at an input port. If the desired output port does not have sufficient buffers, it may not be possible to transfer both packets to that output port even though two separate paths are available in the switch. In this case, we say that there is an output blocking in the switch.

In a time-division switch, on the other hand, data is sent out in frames of constant periodicity, each frame consisting of a number of time slots. When a call has been established, the calling and called parties are each dynamically assigned a separate time slot for the entire duration of the call, and the switching function is performed by interchanging the contents of the two slots. This switching principle is currently used in most commercial switches these days (e.g., Lucent Technology's No. 5 ESS™, etc.). These switches are not quite suitable for high-speed packet switching because of the relatively long delays involved in setting up or taking down the connections.

The purpose of this chapter is to present a brief overview of the ATM switching architectures. Our goal here is not to describe all possible switching architectures that have been worked upon by various researchers in this field, but rather only those that are popular and are currently being implemented. For example, we have presented architectures that provide only point-to-point connections, and do not discuss how they can be modified to support broadcast or multicast modes. Similarly, packet switches based on the shared medium access mechanism of LANs are only mentioned but not described in this chapter.

This chapter is organized as follows: We begin with a description of the traditional cross-point switches and indicate how they should be modified so that they can work in an ATM environment. In many commercially available, high-capacity, high-speed packet switches, self-routing networks are being used in their interconnection fabric. An overview of these networks, which include, among others, the omega, banyan, and Batcher-banyan networks of the so-called delta class, is presented in Section 4.3. The next section deals with the input and out-

---

1. As we show in Chapter 5, a number of parameters such as the throughput, cell loss probability, and delay describe the performance of an ATM switch.

put buffering strategies that are commonly used in an ATM switch. Wherever possible, the relative performance of the buffering mechanism has been included. It is in the context of the output buffering strategies that we discuss the knockout switch.

4.2 Cross-Point Switch

A space-division switch that is conceptually the simplest and has found wide application in conventional PSTNs is a cross-point switch. A functional description of such a switch is shown in Figure 4-1. Figure 4-1(a) is a 4×4 cross-point switch with 16 cross-points. Figure 4-1(b) is one way of implementing a digital cross-point array. Notice that with this array, it is always possible to connect a given input line to a given output line even though the other three inputs or the other three outputs have already been connected together. Thus, there would never be any blocking in this switch.

In this figure, we show a small, 4×4 cross-point array. Theoretically, one can fabricate an array of $n \times n$ cross-points for much larger values of n. However, since the number of cross-points in such an array is proportional to n^2, this number increases rapidly with larger values of n. Thus, it is worthwhile to investigate whether a switch with a given number of inputs and a given number of outputs can be built with a smaller number of cross-points without sacrificing the non-blocking feature.

This problem was thoroughly studied by Clos in 1953 [9]. He showed that indeed it was possible to build an $n \times n$ non-blocking switch for larger values of n using smaller building blocks and with fewer cross-points than the n^2 cross-points of a square array. In this case, switching is performed in multiple stages. For example, suppose we need a switch with 36 inputs and 36 outputs. If we build a single square array, we would require 1296 cross-points. However, if we build the switch with smaller building blocks, as shown in Figure 4-2, we would require only 1188 cross-points and yet preserve the non-blocking property of the switch.

Figure 4-1 A functional representation of a cross-point switch. (a) A 4×4 array. (b) A possible implementation of a 2×2 digital packet switch.

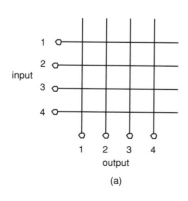

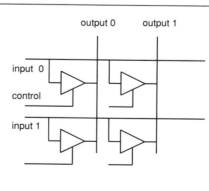

(a)

(b)

Figure 4-2   A three-stage, non-blocking Clos switch with 36 inputs and 36 outputs. This switch has 108 fewer cross-points than a 36 × 36 square array.

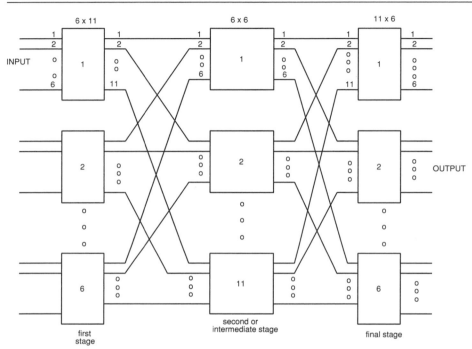

Notice that this switch is built in three stages — the first stage consists of six 6 × 11 switches, the intermediate stage has eleven 6 × 6 switches, and the final stage has six 11 × 6 switches. Clos derives the following general formula for the number of switches required in the intermediate stage:

Suppose that it is desired to build a three-stage $N \times N$ switch such that $N = n^2$. The first stage consists of n $n \times k$ switches, the intermediate stage k $n \times n$ switches, and the third stage n $k \times n$ switches, where

$k = 2n - 1$

For example, in Figure 4-2, $n = \sqrt{36} = 6$ and $k = 2 \times 6 - 1 = 11$. Table 4-1 compares the cross-points of a square array and a three-stage fabric for a few values of N. Notice that for $N < 36$, a three-stage switch actually needs more cross-points than a square array. However, if N is large, say 10,000, there is more than an order of magnitude reduction in the number of cross-points.

Similarly, Clos has also shown that for larger values of N, say $N > 1000$, the number of cross-points required is even further reduced if the number of stages is increased to say, five or seven.

Table 4-1 Comparison of the Number of Cross-points of a Square Array and a Three-Stage Array for a Few Values of the Input and Output Links

N	Cross-Points of a Square Array	Three-Stage Array
16	256	336
36	1,296	1,188
64	4,096	2,880
100	10,000	5,700
10,000	100,000,000	5,970,000

These cross-point switches can also be used for packet switching. However, before they can be used for this purpose, it is necessary to incorporate some buffers and the associated port control circuitry. Clearly, as mentioned before, these buffers can be placed at different points in the switch. For example, they can be integrated within the switch fabric as part of the cross-points themselves as shown in Figure 4-3 [1]. Here, at each cross-point, the destination address of each incoming packet is decoded (in the block marked AD) and compared with the

Figure 4-3 A space-division cross-point switch with modifications to handle high-speed packet switching. Buffers and the associated control circuitry are placed within the cross-points themselves.

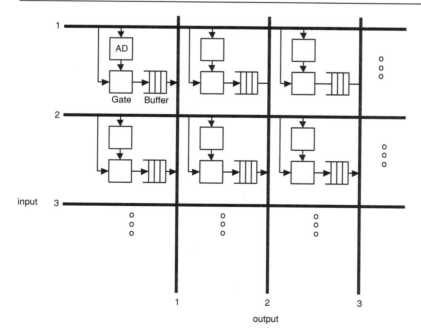

Figure 4-4 A cross-point switch with a buffer at each input port.

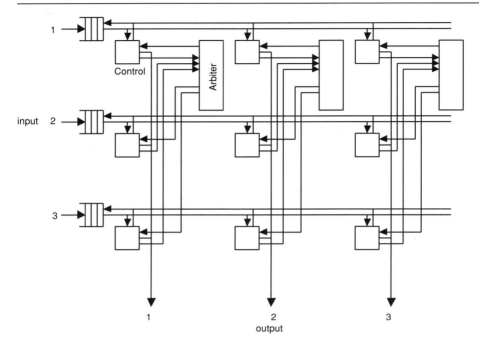

address of the associated output port. If there is a match, the packets are gated into a FIFO, where they are stored temporarily until they can be placed on the output link. Since in an $N \times N$ switch, there are N buffers for each output bus, it is necessary to service the multiple queues associated with each bus in a way that would guarantee some degree of fairness. It is worthwhile to note that even though the buffers are located within the cross-points themselves, in effect an output buffering scheme is being used here, which as we shall show later provides a higher throughput than an input buffering scheme.

Alternatively, these buffers can be placed on the switch inputs as shown in Figure 4-4, where each input port has a FIFO [1]. Associated with each output link is an arbiter, which monitors the FIFOs via the functional block labeled "Control" in the diagram, resolves the contention among multiple buffers whose head-of-the-line packets are destined to the same output, selects only one of those input buffers at a time while stopping the others by means of a control signal,[2] and allows its packet to pass through to the output link. Notice that there is no output blocking in this switch because in the arbitration process, it is necessary to decode the destination addresses of incoming packets, and consequently, packets destined to different outputs are filtered appropriately and then applied to an output link.

2. The so-called back pressure.

Since the complexity of these switches increases as N^2, they are generally not very economical to use except when the switches desired are small with, say, $N \leq 8$. Thus, there is no advantage to using a three-stage array in such cases.

4.3 Self-Routing Switches

4.3.1 Banyan Network

A class of multistage interconnection networks that have been widely researched and found to be particularly suitable for high-speed packet switching is the so-called delta class of networks, which were first introduced in multiprocessor systems for interconnecting memories and processors [10]–[12]. They are characterized with two distinct properties. First, there exists a path between any given input and output. Second, they are self-routing because an incoming packet is routed through each individual switching element entirely on the basis of a single bit destination address that appears at its input ports. Networks that belong to this class are baseline networks, reverse baseline networks, banyan networks, omega networks, indirect binary n-cube networks, and generalized cube networks. The use of buffers in a banyan network was first considered by Dias and Jump [13], and later extended to packet switches by Turner and Wyatt [14] and Turner [15]. We will describe only one of these networks here, the banyan switch,[3] which forms the basis of many ATM switch fabrics.

As the name implies, these networks consist of multiple stages, each constructed with a number of 2 × 2 switching elements. Figure 4-5(a) shows one such element where destination address 0 routes a packet to the upper outlet and one to the lower. When an address bit 0 is applied to the top inlet and a 1 to the bottom as shown in case (i) of Figure 4-5(a), the switch is in the straight connection state — a packet coming to the upper inlet is routed to the upper outlet and a simultaneous packet at the lower inlet is routed to the lower outlet. When an address bit 1 is applied to the top inlet and a 0 to the bottom, the switch is in the crossed connection state as shown in case (ii). Thus, this elementary building block performs an exchange permutation of the incoming lines. A conflict, however, results when the address bits on the two inputs are identical because in this case, the switch tends to route both incoming packets to the same outlet. This is shown in cases (iii) and (iv) of Figure 4-5(a). Consequently, a banyan switch, when used by itself, will experience blocking with an arbitrary destination address at its inputs.[4]

Larger arrays can be built using several stages of this basic building block. An example is shown in Figure 4-5(b), where a 4 × 4, two-stage switching array is constructed with four basic switching elements. In this 4 × 4 array, a 2-bit address field is used to switch a packet to its

---

3. A banyan network is also known as a generalized cube network.

4. As we shall see later, there are ways to overcome this problem. For example, one can precede a banyan switch with a multistage sorter network and transform any arbitrary destination address into a pattern such that the packet can now be routed through the banyan network successfully without any conflict.

Figure 4-5 A banyan switch. (a) A 2 × 2 basic building block. The possible connection states of the switching element are depicted here. (b) A 4 × 4 banyan switch.

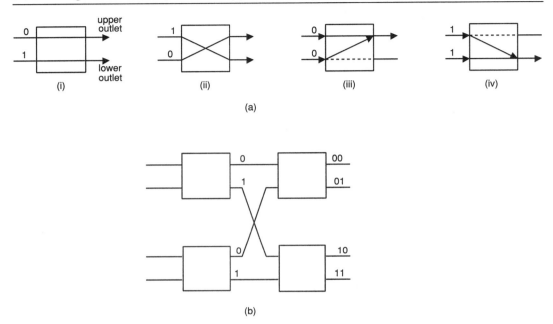

destination. The more significant bit of the address is used to switch the packet through the first stage and the lower significant bit through the second stage. In a general case, the most significant bit of the destination address controls the first stage, the next most significant bit the next stage, and so on.

This procedure of controlling the switching elements of each stage of a multistage network is further illustrated in the 8-input, 8-output, three-stage banyan network of Figure 4-6. Here, we have also traced the routes taken by two packets, one incident at input port x_0 with destination address 000 and the other at input x_6 with address 110. Notice how each stage is being controlled by the corresponding address bit of the destination address.

An examination of the three stages of the banyan network reveals how a larger array can be built using the basic building blocks. For example, a 16-input banyan network is shown in Figure 4-7.

4.3.2 Omega Network

Omega networks, which also belong to the delta class, are used in a sorting network to solve the blocking problem of a self-routing switch. As such, it would be instructive to study them here. A three-stage, 8-input omega network is shown in Figure 4-8. In general, an N-input omega network consists of $\log_2 N$ stages, and is known as an Ω_N network. The inputs to the

Figure 4-6 An 8 × 8, three-stage banyan network. The routes taken by two packets, which are incident at inputs x_0 and x_6 with destination address 000 and 110 respectively, are shown by the heavy lines.

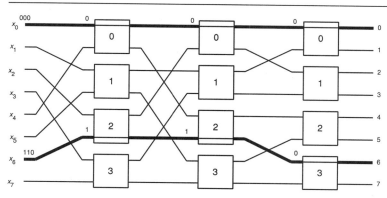

Figure 4-7 A 16-input banyan network.

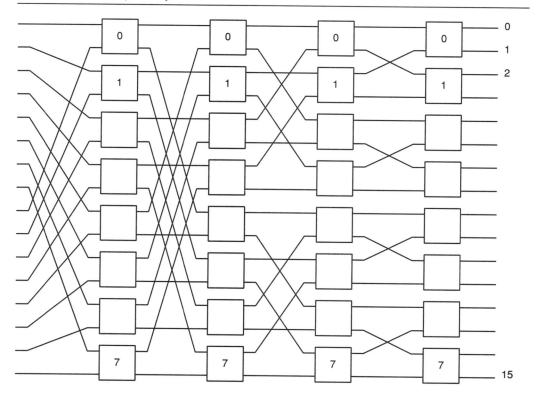

Figure 4-8 A three-stage Ω network.

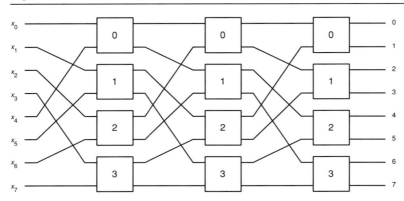

first stage, $x_0, x_1, \ldots, x_7$, are labeled such that x_k is the destination of the k-th input. Notice that the order in which the input lines are connected to a succeeding stage is identical for all stages. For example, the inputs to the switching elements of the first column are x_0, x_4, x_1, x_5, x_2, x_6, x_3, and x_7, and appear, respectively, as outputs 0, 1, 2, 3, 4, 5, 6, and 7. Thus, each stage shuffles an input sequence {0, 4, 1, 5, 2, 6, 3, 7} into an output sequence {0, 1, 2, 3, 4, 5, 6, 7}. In addition, each individual switching element performs an exchange permutation.

Notice that the two networks of Figures 4-6 and 4-8 are similar, except for the connections of the second-stage switching elements. In fact, Siegel and Smith [31] have shown in their paper that a banyan network is topologically (and functionally) equivalent to an omega network, and each can, therefore, be derived from the other by a straightforward rearrangement of the connections of the intermediate stage.

Unlike a square $N \times N$ cross-point switch, a banyan switch has far fewer cross-points. For example, a 16×16 cross-point array has 256 cross-points, whereas a four-stage, 16×16 banyan switch has 128 cross-points. In other words, the number of stages in an $N \times N$ banyan switch is $\log_2 N$, each stage having $2N$ cross-points. Thus, the total number of cross-points required in an $N \times N$ banyan is $2N \log_2 N$. Therefore, the complexity of these switches increases as $N \log_2 N$, and not as N^2 as in a cross-point array. As such, they are more economical to build. Also their modularity makes them particularly suitable for large-scale integration.

4.3.3 Blocking in a Self-Routing Switch

As mentioned before, in a banyan network, there exists exactly one path between any inlet and any outlet. However, since identical control address bits at the inputs of any switching element will cause a conflict, it is evident that blocking may result if packets with arbitrary destinations arrive at two or more input ports. Consider, for instance, Figure 4-9, which shows two forms of blocking — internal blocking and output blocking. In Figure 4-9(a), a connection, shown by the heavy line, has already been established between input port 0 and output

Figure 4-9 Blocking in a banyan switch. (a) Internal blocking. (b) Output blocking.

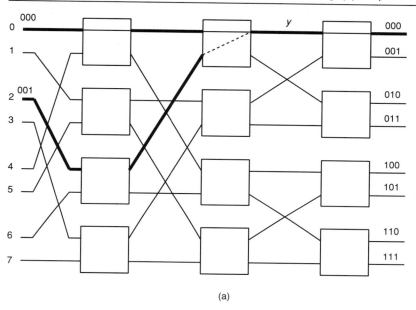

(a)

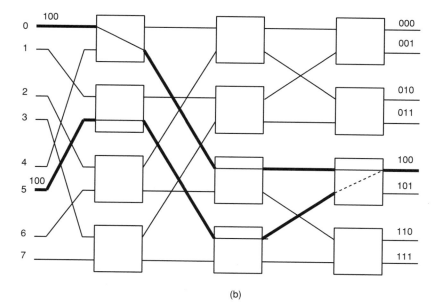

(b)

port 000. A subsequent call from input port 2 to destination 001 is blocked because although there is a path between port 2 and the intermediate stage, the link labeled *y* from the intermediate stage to the destination output is already in use. Thus, even though output port 001 is idle, the connection shown by the dotted line cannot be made.

Figure 4-9(b) illustrates output blocking. Here, two packets with the same destination address, 100, have arrived at two input ports, 0 and 5. Assuming that there is no external buffer at the destination, although two non-overlapping links are available from the originating inputs to the desired destination, only one connection can be established at a time. Thus, the second packet must wait until the transmission of the first is complete. Similarly, it is possible to find other connections that may give rise to blocking between some inlet and outlet pair.

4.3.4 Replicated Banyan Network

Since the probability of internal blocking increases with the offered load on the system, the blocking problem can be alleviated by using, among other things, multiple banyans [12], [16]. For example, to eliminate the internal blocking condition of Figure 4-9(a), one could use, say, multiple banyans, where each input link is connected to the input ports of each banyan through demultiplexers. This is shown in Figure 4-10 for M banyan networks, each with N inputs and N outputs. The outputs of the multiple banyans are connected to the output link through multiplexers. When a packet arrives, the system controller may choose one of the M banyan networks randomly, and apply the packet to its input. When a second packet comes in that tends to conflict with the established links of the first, it is applied to another randomly selected banyan that is idle. Instead of making a random selection, one could, however, use a well-defined algorithm and choose the first banyan for the first connection. When a second packet comes in, an attempt is made to route it through the first banyan anyway. If there is internal blocking in the first banyan, only then would the second banyan be used, and so on.

Since in a general case, more than one banyan network may be active for a given output port, it is possible that cells from multiple connections may arrive at an output link at the same time. Consequently, it is necessary to provide buffers at the output ports.

4.3.5 Tandem Banyan Network

The tandem banyan switch of Figure 4-11, which solves the internal blocking problem in a different way, was suggested by Tobagi, et al. [17]. The switch consists of K $N \times N$ banyan networks connected in cascade. In other words, output i of any stage is connected to input i of the following stage. Furthermore, output 1 of each stage is connected through an address filter to the input of the $k \times 1$ multiplexer. Similarly, output 2 of each stage is connected through a similar address filter to the input of a second multiplexer, and so on. The outputs of these N multiplexers constitute the desired outputs of the tandem banyan network. When two or more packets contend for the same links through the switch, the first one is routed through the first banyan over a connection that is set up in the normal way. All other contending packets are marked as misrouted packets, and are routed through the first banyan via unused input

Figure 4-10 Multiple banyan networks used to alleviate internal blocking in an $N \times N$ banyan switch.

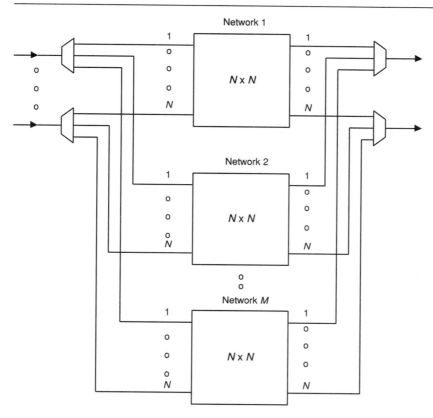

ports. Unmarked packets, i.e., packets which won contention in the first stage, are removed from the first banyan to their appropriate ports by means of the address filters. The marked packets emerging from the first banyan are now unmarked and are considered for routing through the second banyan following the same procedure as in the first stage. This process is repeated through all K stages. If there are any marked packets emerging from the K-th stage, they are dropped.

4.3.6 Cascaded Banyan Networks

Notice in Figure 4-9(a) that when a connection has already been established between input 0 and output 000, packets originating from input 2 and destined for output port 001 will be blocked. However, if they had the same destination address, but had originated from a different input port, say, port 1, there would be no such blocking. Thus, it appears that blocking

Figure 4-11   A *K*-stage tandem banyan network.

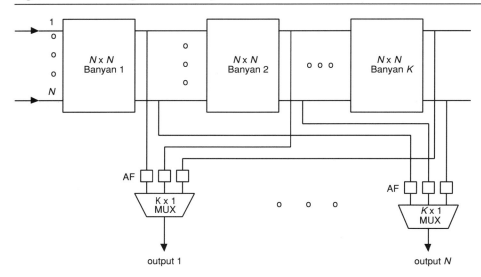

could be avoided if one had used two banyan networks in cascade instead of just one such that an incoming packet on input port 2 of the first banyan would somehow be forced to appear at input 1 of the second banyan. This concept is used in the cascade arrangement of two banyans in Figure 4-12, where the first banyan simply routes the call to an appropriate input of the second banyan so that two connections do not contend for the same links in the switch. The first banyan, as such, is called a distribution network. It actually randomizes the input port appearances on the second banyan. Clearly, this distribution network cannot be self-routing. In fact, while routing packets through this network, the address bits of the destination are ignored, and cells are routed to alternate outlets of each individual switching element. It is worthwhile to note that this cascaded network is very similar to a Benes network [18],[2].

Figure 4-12   A cascade of two banyan networks that avoid blocking. The first banyan is non-self-routing. Here, destination address bits are ignored, and packets are routed to alternate outlets of each individual switching element. Thus, it merely randomizes the appearance of inputs to the second stage, which is self-routing.

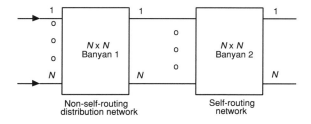

Figure 4-13 A Batcher sorting network followed by a banyan routing network. The combination can realize any arbitrary permutation of the inputs.

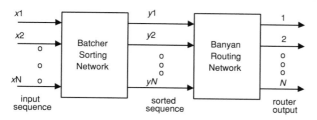

4.4 Batcher-Banyan Networks

We saw before how internal blocking may result in a banyan switch when packets with arbitrary destination addresses arrive at the switch inputs. In Section 4.3.6, it was suggested that blocking could be avoided if the inputs to a self-routing network appeared in a certain order. This particular ordering can be achieved by a Batcher sorting network[5] [19]. Since this sorting network is topologically equivalent to an omega network [20], it can also perform the necessary routing function of a switch. However, if there are any inactive inputs, as there often are in a practical situation, the network does not perform routing correctly. To overcome this problem, Huang and Knauer [21] proposed the use of a self-routing banyan in conjunction with a sorting network as shown in Figure 4-13. Here, the sorting network first orders any arbitrary sequence of active and inactive inputs according to the magnitudes of the destination address tags, and applies the sorted output to the self-routing banyan, which then routes the incoming packets to their proper destinations.

A Batcher network, like an omega network, is also a shuffle-exchange network [23], and consists of multiple stages, each stage made up of the 2×2 switching elements of Figure 4-5. To understand how a Batcher network works, assume that a sequence, $\{c_n\}$, is made up of two monotonic sequences, $\{a_m\}$ and $\{b_r\}$, as

$$\{c_n\} = \{a_1, a_2, \ldots, a_{N-r}, b_1, b_2, \ldots, b_r\}$$

The sequence $\{c_n\}$, constructed in the above manner with two monotonic sequences, one ascending and the other descending, is called a bitonic sequence. Narasimha [20] has proved (i) that a Batcher network can sort any arbitrary input pattern into a bitonic sequence even when some of these inputs are inactive, and (ii) that a bitonic sequence can be properly routed by a banyan network. As the elements of this sequence (in any order) are applied to the inputs of a sorting network, the latter compares their magnitudes and outputs them in a descending or ascending order as shown in Figure 4-14, where a's are the active inputs and b's are the inactive inputs, and

$$a_1 < a_2 < \ldots < a_{N-r}; \quad b_1 < b_2 < \ldots < b_r$$

---

5. Named after K. E. Batcher, who first proposed the use of sorting networks in his paper [19].

Figure 4-14 Sorting by a Batcher network with an arbitrary sequence of inputs. (a) Outputs appear in ascending order. (b) Outputs are arranged in descending order.

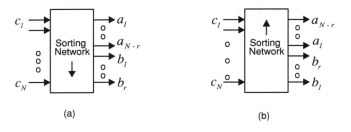

(a)   (b)

Figure 4-15 An 8-input Batcher network. Arrows inside the subnetworks indicate the direction in which inputs with larger tags are routed. © 1988 IEEE.

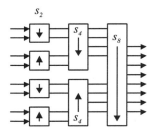

An 8-input sorting network performs sorting in three steps[6] by means of subnetworks and S_2, S_4, and S_8 as shown in Figure 4-15. Each subnetwork is implemented using the basic 2×2 switching elements, which are controlled in such a way that inputs with larger tags are routed in the direction pointed to by the arrows inside the subnetworks. Each subnetwork, S_k, sorts an input sequence of length k, where k is assumed to be a power of 2 and requires $\log_2 k$ stages to implement. Thus, an N-input sorting network requires

$\frac{1}{2}\log_2 N(\log_2 N + 1)$ stages.

The implementation of the 8-input sorting network is shown in Figure 4-16, and the complete cascaded Batcher-banyan network in Figure 4-17. Let us examine how this network resolves the internal blocking problem. Again, we will consider the situation depicted in Figure 4-9, where two packets incident at inputs 0 and 2 with destination addresses 000 and 001, respectively, are internally blocked when routed by a three-stage banyan. In Figure 4-17, these

---

6. Log$_2$ 8 steps.

Figure 4-16   The implementation of an 8-input Batcher network with 2 × 2 switching elements.

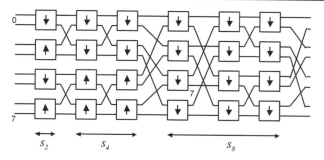

Figure 4-17   The complete, 8-input, Batcher-banyan network, indicating routes taken by two packets as they are sorted by the Batcher and routed by the self-routing banyan network.

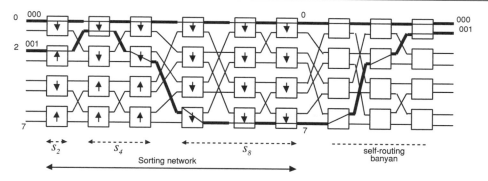

two packets are again assumed to originate from the same input ports and have the same destinations. Remembering that each stage of a Batcher network sorts its inputs in an ascending or descending order of the magnitudes of their address tags (as pointed to by the arrows shown in the switching blocks), it is easy to trace the routes taken by the packets as they are routed through the sorter. The first packet takes the upper path and emerges at output port 0 of the sorter, while the second one follows the lower path and exits the sorter at output port 7. The self-routing banyan now picks up the packets at these ports and routes the first one to its destination, 000, and the second one to its destination, 001, as required.

4.5 Time-Division Switches with Common Memory

It is possible to build a packet switch without using a space-division or time-division switching array. Instead, one can use dedicated hardware with common memories to perform the switching, as well as the routing function. In this case, a control circuitry monitors the inputs,

Figure 4-18   Functional block diagram of an asynchronous time-division switch (e.g., the *Prelude* of Reference [28]).

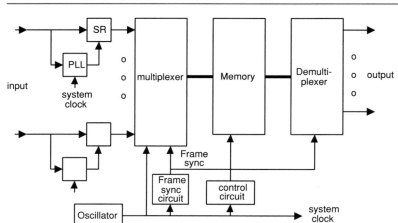

derives the destination addresses from the packet headers for subsequent routing, converts the incoming serial data packets into parallel forms, and writes them, say, on a first-come, first-served basis, into the common memory. A second control circuit reads the memory out, and using the routing information that was derived earlier, writes the packets into the destination port where they are shifted out serially on a bit-by-bit basis.

Switches based on this general concept have been described in References [27] and [28]. An example is the asynchronous time-division switch known as the *Prelude* of Reference [28]. Its functional block diagram is shown in Figure 4-18. The serial incoming data at each input port is clocked into a shift register with a data-derived clock. A synchronous frame is constructed by assigning a time slot to exactly one packet from each input. The output of this slotted frame is then converted into parallel forms and written into the common memory. The control circuitry extracts the header information from the packets, and then uses it sequentially to read the data out of the memory, convert the data into a similar frame, and then write the data of each time slot into the corresponding output port.

A packet switch based on this approach, however, would be generally quite small. For example, the *Prelude* switch has only 16 inputs and 16 outputs and a bandwidth of 280 Mb/s/s.

If a desired switch is relatively small, there are many other ways of designing it. For example, in a variation of the concept of asynchronous time-division multiplexing, one could dispense with much of the hardware of Figure 4-18, and instead use multiple processors to perform the switching function. However, in this case, in addition to the buffering delays, packets would encounter significant switching delays. Similarly, it is possible to design an ATM switch based on the principles of LANs, where a common transmission medium, such as an

Ethernet bus or a token-passing ring, is shared by two or more stations. These systems have been thoroughly analyzed and are well-documented in the literature [29], [30]. However, very often their bandwidth capacity and throughput fall short of the requirements of a typical ATM switch.

4.6 Buffering

Since the packet arrival and departure process is purely random, it is necessary to provide sufficient buffering in an ATM switch. Consider first the input ports. A number of physical links, each with multiple virtual connections, may be multiplexed together and then applied to an input port. Cells from all of these physical or virtual channels may arrive simultaneously at a port, and hence must be buffered, where they wait until they can be serviced by the switch (see Figure 4-19(a)). Also, since cells arriving on different links are completely asynchronous,

Figure 4-19   The external buffers in an ATM switch. (a) Input buffers. (b) Output buffers.

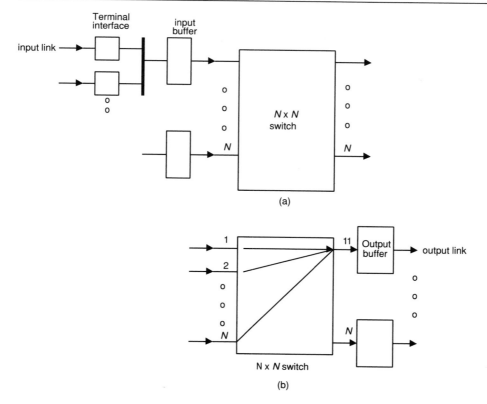

(a)

(b)

it is possible that at the instant when a new cell arrives, the switching element of the input port is routing another cell. As such, even though the switching speed of an ATM switch is much faster than the packet arrival rate, it is necessary to have buffers at the inputs.

Consider now the output ports. As a cell is being shifted from an output port over a serial link en route to its destination, a second cell may arrive at an input port that is bound to the same output. In this case, we could, of course, buffer the cell at the input and switch the cell to the desired outlet only after it is finished transmitting the first cell. Alternatively, we could provide a buffer at the output so that if there is no blocking in the switch itself, the second cell could be transferred to the outlet and saved in the buffer until it is ready to be transmitted. This is shown in Figure 4-19(b).

Finally, we could place buffers inside the switch itself. However, when a switch has multiple paths, an internal buffer may cause the cells to be delivered out-of-sequence. Furthermore, if each switching element is to have a buffer, routing and the overall switch design become complex. Thus, our discussion will be restricted to the simple case, where a switch has only input and output buffers as shown in Figure 4-19.

4.6.1 Input Buffering

To understand the various input buffering strategies that one can use for an ATM switch, consider Figure 4-20. In this figure, the switch is assumed to be a non-blocking, space-division switch such as the ones described in the last section. For each input port of the switch, the input links from multiple sources are terminated by terminal interface cards, where the incoming data is converted into parallel forms and applied to the input of a FIFO. The length of a FIFO is specified in terms of ATM cells. For example, a FIFO at an input port may be 1024 cells long. At the beginning of each time slot, a controller monitors all FIFOs, and based

Figure 4-20   Buffering ATM cells on the input side of a switch.

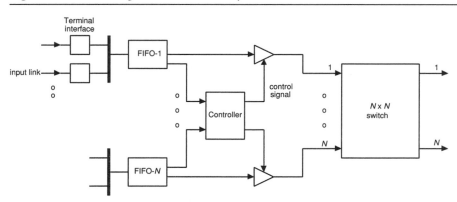

on some algorithm, selects them one at a time, reads the ATM cell from the head of the FIFO, and applies it to the desired inlet of the ATM switch, assuming that its destination port is idle. The ATM cell is then transported through the switch on a bit-by-bit basis by the self-routing switching element according to the destination address contained in the header portion of the cell. In this case, there is no output buffer.[7]

Many selection strategies and their performance ratings appear in the literature. Some of the common ones are:

1. The system controller monitors each input FIFO in a round-robin fashion, and when it finds that there is a packet at the head of the input queue whose destination port through the switch is idle, it reads that packet and writes it into the temporary buffer.
2. The controller services the input FIFOs on a first-come, first-served basis. To be more specific, if there is just one FIFO where packets are waiting to be serviced, it selects that FIFO, reads the packet from the head of the queue, and writes it into the corresponding buffer provided the destination output port is idle. If there is more than one input queue, it selects the one that has the earliest packet arrival and then moves to the next, and so on.
3. The controller monitors all FIFOs and makes its decision on the basis of the queue length, selecting the input that has the longest queue.
4. The controller selects an input FIFO randomly.

Karol, et al. [24] and Hluchyj, et al. [25] have studied the performance of a particular input queuing scheme for a high-speed packet switch. As before, a non-blocking, space-division switch is considered. Packets, which are assumed to be fixed lengths, arrive on all inputs synchronously. In other words, all incoming packets occupy fixed time slots, which are synchronized across the entire system by a common clock and thus can be represented as in Figure 4-21. Each input is provided with a separate FIFO, where incoming packets are held until they are allowed to access the switch fabric. At the beginning of each time slot, exactly one packet at the head of each FIFO is allowed to pass through the switch, provided its destination port is idle. If, however, head-of-the-line packets in k of these input buffers are all destined to the same output port, only one is selected and switched to the output, while the remaining $k - 1$ packets must wait their turn until the next time slot. Notice that in this case, all other packets that are queued behind the $k - 1$ packets are blocked, even though their destination ports may be idle. Obviously, then, the throughput that one would be able to achieve with this scheme would be limited. Here, the term "throughput" is defined as the number of packets that can pass through the switch in the steady state, normalized to N, where N is

---

7. Nevertheless, we might still need a buffer as part of the outgoing link circuit to interface the high-speed packet switch to the link. However, for the purpose of this analysis, this buffer is not considered necessary for the input buffering scheme.

Figure 4-21   An $N \times N$, non-blocking, space-division packet switch, where packets arrive at the input ports in a synchronized, time slot fashion. The numbers shown within the incoming packets are the destination ports [24] [25]. © 1987 IEEE.

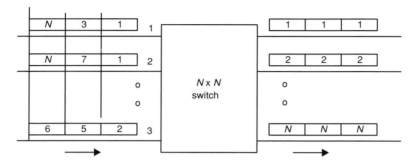

the number of input or output ports on the switch. In fact, the maximum throughput is shown to be

$$\rho_0 = 2 - \sqrt{2} \quad \text{as} \quad N \to \infty$$

For other, finite values of N, the maximum attainable throughput is plotted in Figure 4-22.

Figure 4-22   The maximum attainable throughput with the input buffering scheme for some finite values of N, where N is the number of input or output ports of an $N \times N$ switch. © 1988 IEEE.

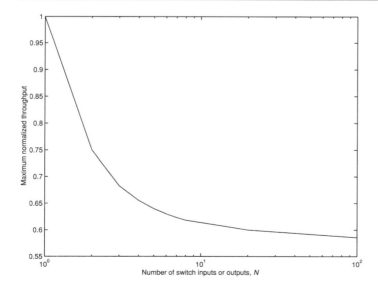

Figure 4-23 The average queuing delay with the input buffering scheme as a function of the of-fered load for the limiting case of $N \rightarrow \infty$, where N is the number of input or output ports of an $N \times N$ switch [25]. © 1988 IEEE.

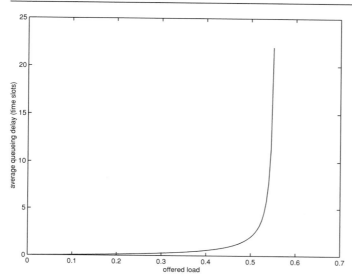

Figure 4-23 gives the average queuing delay encountered by buffered packets as a function of the offered load for the limiting case of $N \rightarrow \infty$. In fact, the average delay can be approximated by this curve for all values of $N \geq 16$. In this figure, it is assumed that packets arrive independently in each time slot with a Bernoulli distribution, choosing any one of the output ports with an equal probability, $1/N$. Notice that the delay increases indefinitely when the offered load is about 0.57.

A number of variations of this basic scheme that can improve the maximum achievable throughput are possible. For example, Reference [24] suggests the following modification of the strict FIFO service strategy: As before, in any given time slot, each input is allowed to send at most one packet. However, for each input buffer, this packet is now chosen in the following way: At the beginning of each time slot, the first w packets, instead of just one, in each FIFO sequentially attempt to access the switch fabric. If the destination port of the packet at the head of the queue is idle, that packet is allowed to pass through the switch. Otherwise, the second packet in the queue is considered as a possible candidate for accessing the switch. If its destination port is idle, that packet is selected. Otherwise, the third packet in the queue is examined to see if its destination port is idle. This process is repeated until all w packets have been considered for the input. Figure 4-24 gives the throughput as a function of the switch size, N, for $w = 2$ and $w = 4$. For larger values of w, the maximum throughput increases, as expected, since packets that are waiting in a queue behind an output-blocked packet at the head of the queue can now pass through the switch to an idle output. Notice that if $w = 1$, the ser-

Figure 4-24 Throughput as a function of the switch size, *N*, for a few values of *w* [25]. © 1988 IEEE.

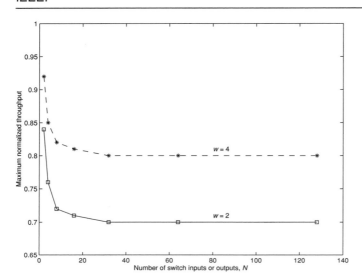

vice discipline reduces to the simple case of the input buffering scheme that was considered before. Here, *w* is referred to as the window size.

It is important to mention here that one can achieve the same or even a higher throughput by dispensing with the input buffers altogether and simply dropping the packets if the destination port is busy with a packet from an earlier time slot. However, this is not a very desirable way to improve the performance of a system because the high packet losses that would inevitably result from this service strategy may not be acceptable to the upper-layer protocols as they tend to further aggravate the congestion problem.

For the random selection scheme 4, discussed on page 73, assume that ATM cells are arriving at an input port in a given time slot with probability *p* and they form a Bernoulli distribution process. If the destination ports of the incoming cells are also random, but uniform, that is, if the destination is any one of the *N* output ports with equal probability, the delay, *D*, is given by [22] as follows:

$$D = \frac{(2 - p)(1 - p)}{(2 - \sqrt{2} - p)(2 + \sqrt{2} - p)} - 1, 0 \le p \le 2 - \sqrt{2}$$

4.6.2 Output Buffering

In this scheme, each output port of an $N \times N$, non-blocking, space-division switch is assumed to have a FIFO of length, say, *b*, such that unlike the input buffering scheme, it is now possible to transfer more than one packet destined to the same output in each time slot. More specifically, packets arriving in any given time slot at *k* input ports, with $k = 1, \ldots, N$, with the same destination address, can be allowed to pass through the switch to the associated out-put buffer by making the switch N times faster. However, once they arrive at the output port, exactly one of them is sent out per time slot over the output link. Reference [24] gives the mean waiting time as a function of the offered load, and the cell loss probability as a function of the buffer size for different values of the switch size, N. For example, the average waiting time, D, as a function of the offered load, p, for $N \rightarrow \infty$ and $b \rightarrow \infty$ can be modeled by an $M/D/1$ queue, and is given by the following relation:

$$D = \frac{p}{2(1 - p)}$$

where p, as before, is the packet arrival rate. The traffic is assumed to be uniform. In other words, the probability that an arriving packet is destined to a given port, n, is the same for all values of n, and is equal to $1/N$. The average waiting time as a function of the offered load is plotted in Figure 4-25 for buffer size $b = 1, 2,$ and ∞. As the buffer size decreases, the waiting time in the queue also decreases. However, in this case, as we will see below, the probability of packet loss also increases.

Because of the finite buffer size, some packets will be lost as a result of buffer overflow. Figure 4-26 shows the packet loss probability in the output buffering scheme as a function of the buffer size for the limiting case of $N = \infty$ and two values of the offered load. First, for the same offered load, the packet loss probability increases, as expected, as the buffer size decreases. Second, for the same value of the buffer size, it increases with the offered load. Al-

Figure 4-25 The average waiting time in the output buffering scheme as a function of the offered load with the buffer size as a parameter [25]. © 1988 IEEE.

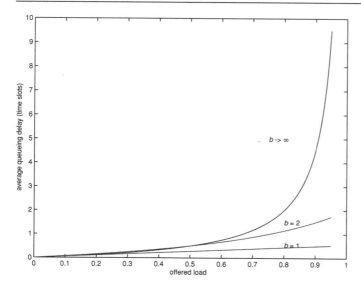

Figure 4-26 The packet loss probability in the output buffering scheme as a function of the buffer size for the limiting case of $N = \infty$. Two values of the offered load are used in the figure [25]. © 1988 IEEE.

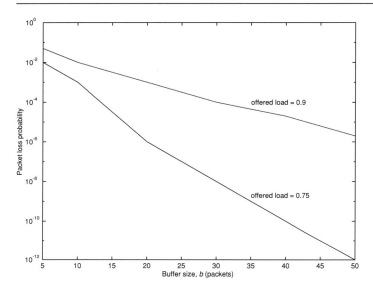

though it is not shown in this figure, the higher the value of N, the greater the packet loss probability.

Notice that the throughput and delay performance of output queuing are optimal because delays are encountered only when packets destined to the same output arrive simultaneously at two or more inputs. Since the switch is now assumed to be N times faster, the probability of this happening is much smaller. See Figure 4-27.

On the other hand, for bursty traffic, the input buffering scheme is inherently better for the following reason: If the incoming packets choose an output port randomly with probabil-

Figure 4-27 Congestion in the output queuing scheme. Since the switch is now N times faster, a packet takes only a fraction of a time slot to reach its destination. These fractions are shown as segment 1, 2, . . . , N of a time slot. There is congestion at the output only if two or more packets arrive at multiple inputs in the same segment.

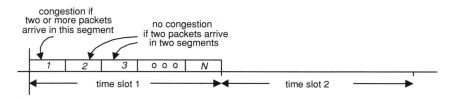

ity $1/N$, where N is the dimension of the switch, then the traffic at the output of the switch is no longer as bursty as at the input. Thus, if a switch has multiple stages, the traffic at the output becomes progressively smoother, and may eventually lead to improvement in congestion.

4.6.3 Completely Shared Buffering

This scheme, which is a variation of output queuing, uses a single buffer at the output instead of a separate buffer at each of the output ports of the switch as illustrated in Figure 4-28. This, in fact, represents the architecture of the Starlite Digital switch [21]. As shown in the figure, the switch fabric has now $N(1 + b)$ inputs and $N(1 + b)$ outputs, of which the first N inputs and outputs constitute a nominal $N \times N$ switch, while the remaining Nb inputs and Nb outputs form the shared buffer. Thus, in any given time slot, up to N new packet arrivals and up to Nb buffered packets contend for switch access. Suppose k of these packets are destined to the same output port. In this case, one of these k packets will pass through the switch to the desired port, and the remaining $k - 1$ packets will be routed to $k - 1$ of the Nb outputs of the shared buffer and wait there until the next time slot before they can re-enter the switch and contend for its resources with the new packet arrivals. Thus, if there are k packets in a given time slot with the same destination, they will be routed to the output port one packet per time slot, while the remaining packets recirculate through the switch until all are removed to their destination. With this scheme, the delay-throughput performance is optimal, as in the case of the output queuing scheme. The number of buffers required is reduced, but only at the expense of an increased switch size.

Figure 4-28 Shared buffering architecture.

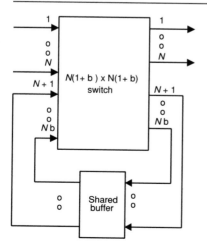

4.6.4 Input Bus and Output Buffering

In Section 4.6.2, we saw that for the output queuing scheme to work, it was necessary to increase the switching speed N times so that packets originating at N inputs with the same destination could be removed to the output in a single time slot. Reference [26] suggests a switching architecture where the same objective can be achieved without increasing the switch speed. The switch with this architecture is called a knockout switch for reasons that will be apparent shortly.

The basic switch architecture is shown in Figure 4-29(a). Here, as before, the switch has N inputs and N outputs. Each of the inputs can be viewed as a serial bus over which packets arriving in any time slot are broadcast to all outputs, which are connected to each bus over the specially designed bus interface circuit of Figure 4-29(b).

Each bus interface unit works in the following manner: Each input bus is connected through an address filter (AF) to an N-to-L concentrator, where $L < N$. The function of the address filter is to ensure that a packet arriving on an input link is applied to the input of the concentrator associated with an output port only if the destination address of the packet matches the port address of the output. In other words, any packet whose destination address is different from that of the given output port is filtered out and thus prevented from appearing at the

Figure 4-29   The knockout switch [26]. (a) The basic switch architecture. (b) The bus interface of Figure 4-18(a) for each output. © 1987 IEEE.

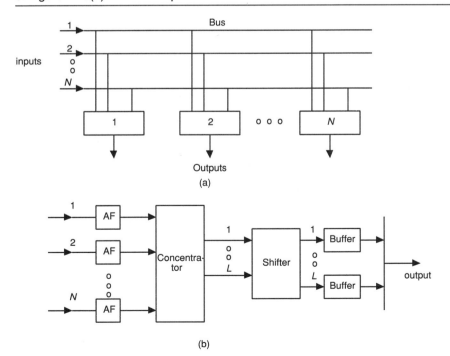

Figure 4-30   The packet loss probability of the knockout switch as a function of the number of the concentrator outputs L for two values of N, the switch size [26]. © 1987 IEEE.

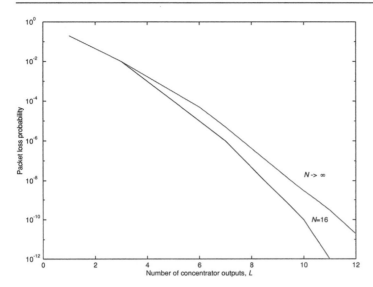

input of the concentrator. Any number of packets arriving at the inputs in a given time slot may be destined to the same output port. However, with $L < N$, only L of these packets are able to pass through the switch to the desired output, while the remaining $N - L$ packets fail to access the switch and are consequently dropped.[8]

The outputs of the concentrator pass through a shifter and then to L FIFOs that all connect to the output. Thus, in essence, the shifter and the L FIFOs constitute a shared buffer with L inputs and a single output, with packets leaving the shared buffer on a first-come, first-served basis.

Since the incoming packets are concentrated in a ratio of $N:L$, there is a non-zero probability that packets will be occasionally lost. This probability is shown in Figure 4-30 as a function of the concentrator outputs L for two values of N, which represents the switch size. Notice that since the probability of packet loss is very low for $L \geq 12$, for all practical purposes, a concentrator with $L = 12$ should be sufficient.

4.7 Summary

In the last few years, a large number of switching architectures suitable for VLSI technology have been proposed and investigated for high-speed packet switches. In this chapter, we pre-

---

8. In other words, $N - L$ packets are knocked out of the contention for network resources. Hence the name "knockout switch."

sented an overview of the architectures that appear to be more commonly used in currently available ATM switching systems. We showed that it is possible to design a high-speed, $N \times N$ packet switch around a space-division fabric with the necessary memories and control. However, since switch complexity grows as N^2, these square arrays are not very economical when N becomes large.

The majority of the ATM switch fabrics in present-day commercial and experimental systems are based on self-routing banyan networks. These networks, which are topologically equivalent to other networks of the so-called delta class, have the property that when packets with arbitrary destination addresses arrive randomly at their input ports, there is a high probability that they will experience internal blocking within the switch fabric. To overcome this problem, banyan networks are used with Batcher sorting networks. However, this sorting network is fairly complex. For example, a 1024×1024 switch requires a Batcher network with 55 stages.

Even though a Batcher-banyan network is free from internal blocking, it is still possible that there would be some output blocking at the switch. This type of blocking is caused when two or more packets arriving at an input port are destined to the same output address. We discussed how this problem could be overcome by providing buffers at the outputs and increasing switch speed appropriately. We also saw that buffers could be placed at the input, within the switching elements themselves, or at the output, and that the throughput, delay, and probability of packet loss depend not only on the buffer size and servicing strategy, but also on the location of the buffers. The output buffers provide a higher throughput than the input buffers. For example, for large values of N, the maximum throughput available with input buffering may be about 0.58, whereas with output buffers, it is possible to achieve a throughput that is close to unity. However, in a practical system, input buffers are more easily managed than output buffers.

A small switching fabric can be designed in a number of ways. For example, one could use the principles of asynchronous time-division multiplexing or even multiple processors to design a switch with a limited bandwidth and a small number of inputs and outputs without greatly affecting its performance. A large switch, on the other hand, is sensitive to internal architectures, and is almost always built around a space-division fabric with self-routing networks and memories at both the inputs and outputs.

4.8 References

[1] H. Ahmadi and W. Denzel, "A survey of modern high-performance switching techniques," *IEEE J. Selec. Areas Commun.*, Vol. SAC-7, No. 7, Sep. 1989, pp. 1091–1103.

[2] R. Y. Awdeh and H. T. Mouftah, "Survey of ATM switch architectures," *Computer Networks and ISDN Systems 27*, 1995, pp. 1567–1613.

[3] R. Rooholamini, V. Cherkassky, and M. Garver, "Finding the right ATM switch for the market," *IEEE Computer*, Vol. 27, No. 4, Apr. 1994, pp. 16–28.

[4] Y. Oie, T. Suda, M. Murata, and H. Hyashara, "Survey of switching techniques in high-

speed networks and their performance," *Int. J. Satellite Commun.*, Vol. 9, 1991, pp. 285–303.

[5]   X. Chen, "A survey of multistage interconnection networks for fast packet switches," *Int. J. of Digital and Analog Commun. Systems*, Vol. 4, 1991, pp. 33–59.

[6]   F. A. Tobagi, "Fast packet switching architectures for broadband integrated services digital networks," *Proc. IEEE*, Vol. 78, No. 1, Jan. 1990, pp. 133–166.

[7]   A. R. Jacob, "A survey of fast packet switches," *Computer Commun. Review*, Vol. 20, No. 1, Jan 1990, pp. 54–64.

[8]   M. Listani and A. Roveri, "Switching structures for ATM," *Computer Commun.*, Vol. 12, No. 6, Dec. 1989, pp. 349–358.

[9]   C. Clos, "A study of non-blocking switching networks," *Bell Sys. Tech. J.*, Vol. 32, Mar. 1953, pp. 406–424.

[10] L. R. Goke and G. J. Lipovski, "Banyan networks for partitioning multiprocessing systems," *Proc. 1st Annu. Comput. Architect. Conf.*, Dec. 1973, pp. 21–28.

[11] J. H. Patel, "Processor-memory interconnections for multiprocessors," *Proc. 6th Annu. Int. Symp. Comput. Architecture*, Apr. 1979, pp. 168–177.

[12] C. P. Kruska and M. Snir, "The performance of multi-stage interconnection networks for multiprocessors," *IEEE Trans. Computers*, Vol. 32, No. 12, Dec. 1989, pp. 1091–1098.

[13] D. M. Dias and J. R. Jump, "Analysis and simulation of buffered delta networks," *IEEE Trans. Computers*, Vol. C-30, Apr. 1981, pp. 273–282.

[14] J. S. Turner and L. F. Wyatt, "A packet network architecture for integrated circuits," *Proc. of Globecom '83*, Nov. 1983, pp. 45–50.

[15] J. S. Turner, "Design of an integrated services packet network," *Proc. 9th ACM Data Commun. Symp.*, Sept. 1985, pp. 124–133. Also in *IEEE J. Selec. Areas Commun.*, Vol. SAC-4, No. 8, pp. 1373–1379, Nov. 1986.

[16] M. Kumar and J. N. Jump, "Performance of unbuffered shuffle-exchange networks," *IEEE Trans. Computers*, Vol. 35, No. 6, June 1986, pp. 573–577.

[17] F. A. Tobagi, T. Kwok, and F. M. Chiussi, "Architecture, performance and implementation of the tandem-banyan fast packet switch," *IEEE J. Selec. Areas Commun.*, Vol. 9, No. 8, Oct. 1991, pp. 1173–1193.

[18] V. E. Benes, "Optimal rearrangeable multistage connecting networks," *Bell Sys. Tech. J.*, Vol. 43, July 1964, pp. 1641–1656.

[19] K. E. Batcher, "Sorting networks and their applications," *Proc. AFIPS Spring Joint Comp. Conf.*, Vol. 32, 1968, pp. 1641–1656.

[20] M. Narasimha, "The Batcher-Banyan self-routing network: universality and simplification," *IEEE Trans. Commun.*, Vol. 36, No. 10, Oct. 1988, pp. 1175–1178.

[21] A. Huang and S Knauer, "Starlite: a wideband digital switch," *Proc. of Globecom '84*, Nov. 1984.

[22] J. Hui and E. Arthurs, "A broadband packet switch for integrated transport," *IEEE J. Selec. Areas Commun.*, Vol. SAC-5, Oct. 1987, pp. 264–273.

[23] H. S. Stone, "Parallel processing with the perfect shuffle," *IEEE Trans. Comp.*, Vol. C-20, Feb. 1971, pp. 153–161.

[24] M. J. Karol, M. G. Hluchyj, and S. P. Morgan, "Input versus output queueing on a space-division packet switch," *IEEE Trans. Commun.*, Vol. COM-35, No. 12, Dec. 1987, pp. 1347–1356.

[25] M. G. Hluchyj, and M. J. Karol, "Queueing in high-performance packet switching," *IEEE J. Selec. Areas Commun.*, Vol. SAC-6, No. 9, Dec. 1988, pp. 1587–1597.

[26] Y. S. Yeh, M. G. Hluchyj, and A. S. Acampora, "The knockout switch: a simple, modular architecture for high-performance packet switching," *IEEE J. Selec. Areas Commun.*, Vol. SAC-5, No. 8, Oct. 1987, pp. 1274–1283.

[27] M. Dieudonne and M. Quinquis, "Switching techniques for asynchronous time division multiplexing (or fast packet switching)," *Proc. ISS '87*, Phoenix, AZ, Mar. 1987, pp. 367–371.

[28] J. P. Coudreuse and M. Servel, "Prelude: An asynchronous time division switched network," *Proc. ICC '87*, Seattle, WA, June 1987, pp. 769–773.

[29] C. D. Tsao, "A local area network architecture overview," *IEEE Comm. Mag.*, Vol. 22, No. 8, Aug. 1984, pp. 7–11.

[30] J. O. Limb, "Performance of local area networks at high speed," *IEEE Comm. Mag.*, Vol. 22, No. 8, Aug. 1984, pp. 41–45.

[31] H. J. Siegel and S. D. Smith, "Study of multistage SIMD interconnection networks," *Proc. 5th Annu. Symp. Comput. Architect.*, Apr. 1978, pp. 223–229.

Problems

4.1 Calls are arriving randomly at the input of a 16×16 ATM switch at a rate of 120 calls/hour. The average holding time for each call is 5 minutes. The total traffic, expressed in Erlangs, is given by the product of the call arrival rate per hour and the average holding time of each call. Thus, the traffic in this system is 10 Erlangs. Assuming Poisson distribution for the call arrival process, determine the probability that a call will be blocked. See the following references: D. Bear, *Principles of Telecommunication Traffic Engineering.* London: Peter Peregrinus, Ltd., 1976; R. D. Rosner, *Packet Switching.* Belmont, CA: Lifetime Learning Publications, 1982, pp. 52–102.

4.2. If the busy hour traffic is 24 Erlangs, what size switch would you recommend if the probability of blocking is not to exceed 0.1?

4.3 Refer to Figure 4-P.1. A non-blocking, space-division, $N \times N$ switch is connected to eight input lines through interface cards. Each line operates at a SONET OC-3 rate. ATM cells are synchronized with a common clock. Consequently, they can be assumed to arrive on all inputs synchronously. Each input line is connected to a separate FIFO. A controller selects each FIFO in a round-robin fashion, and when it finds that it contains a packet whose destination port at the output of the switch is idle, it reads that cell and writes it into the one-cell buffer at the switch input. If the destination port of the packet is busy, the packet is written into FIFO-9. At the beginning of a scan cycle, the controller first ser-

Figure 4-P.1   A switch with input buffers on each line and an overflow buffer on the input side.

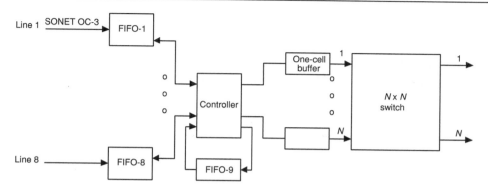

vices FIFO-9. If the FIFO is not empty, it reads the packet from the FIFO and writes it into an input port of the switch, provided its destination port is idle. Otherwise, as we said before, the packet is written back into FIFO-9 again. The controller then moves to other FIFOs sequentially, and services them as described above. Find the throughput of the switch as a function of buffer size and offered load.

4.4 Continuing Problem 4.3, find the delay as a function of the buffer size and offered load.

4.5 If the controller reads up to two cells from FIFO-9 at the beginning of each scan cycle, assuming that it is not empty, and writes them into input ports of the switch, how would the throughput and delay change?

4.6 If FIFO-9 were absent, the service algorithm would be slightly changed. In this case, if the destination of the packet at the output of a FIFO is busy, the controller bypasses that FIFO and proceeds to serve the next one. What are the throughput and delay now?

4.7 Refer to Figure 4-P.2, which illustrates an $N \times N$ switch with both input and output buffers. First, assume that the switch uses an output buffering scheme. In other words, it uses a buf-

Figure 4-P.2   A switch with input and output buffers.

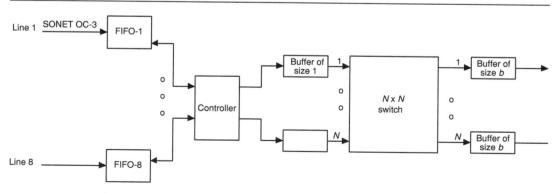

fer of size $b > 1$ at each output port, but no input FIFOs. Write a simulation program to determine throughput and delay as a function of b. The offered load varies from 0.25 to 2.0. Assume that $N = 16$. List all necessary assumptions in your simulation program.

4.8 Refer again to Figure 4-P.2. Assume that the switch now uses buffers of size 128 at each input port and buffers of size 4 at each output port. Show how the throughput and delay vary as a function of the offered load. As before, assume that $N = 16$. List all necessary assumptions.

4.9 In Problem 4.8, what is the maximum number of VCs that the switch can support if the throughput is to be at least 0.5 at an offered load of 1?

4.10 What qualitative conclusions can you derive from Problems 4.3–4.9?

Traffic Management in ATM Networks

5.1 Introduction

A public switched telephone network (PSTN) connects a large number of users. Because service requests from input sources follow a probabilistic pattern, one can take advantage of this statistical nature of the traffic to design a network that uses its resources efficiently to provide satisfactory service to a large number of customers. For example, circuit-switched public telephone networks provide a five-to-one concentration between lines and trunks. The randomness of the traffic pattern is also taken advantage of in existing packet-switched networks, where input sources are concentrated even more. Given the limited resources, it is likely that sometimes there would be congestion in the network resulting from too many sources being active at the same time.

In traditional packet-switched networks, flow control schemes are used to control the incoming traffic and thus prevent congestion. These schemes are implemented at different protocol layers. For example, an end-to-end flow control can be provided by the transport-layer protocol. Or, two adjacent nodes can be flow-controlled using the so-called sliding window mechanism at the link layer. Here, the link-layer protocol provides for sequenced and acknowledged data transfer, whereby each frame that the source originates has a sequence number and must be acknowledged by the receiving end.

The maximum number of frames that a source can originate before receiving acknowledgment is determined by the window size. For example, if the window size is 8, the sending end can send eight frames sequentially, one after another, without receiving acknowledgment. But, before sending the next frame, it must wait until the receiver acknowledges the receipt of one or more frames. Hence, if the receiver is congested, it can clear this condition by simply withholding the acknowledgment. There are other ways to avoid congestion. For example, one can over-design the network by providing more bandwidth than would ever be used in the system, or allow for alternate routing when fixed-path routing can no longer handle the outgoing traffic.

An ATM network, like any other packet-switched network, is designed with limited resources such as bandwidth and buffers. Hence, conditions that might eventually lead to congestion may also exist in these networks. The congestion control mechanisms that work so effectively in traditional packet-switched networks could work to a certain extent in an ATM network. However, there are differences here. First, the ATM protocol does not provide any acknowledged data transfer. Second, while a conventional packet-switched network only supports data services, the basic motivation behind the development of an ATM network is the need to use a single protocol to support different service types — not only the common variable-bit-rate data services that can tolerate delays, but also the new, emerging, high-bandwidth multi-media services that are sensitive to delays and thus must have a minimum guaranteed bandwidth at all times. In these cases, each user must be assured of a certain quality of service (QoS),[1] which may be either fixed at subscription time or negotiated with the network at call request time. If a particular user generates too much traffic at a given instant, it might still be possible to allocate a greater bandwidth to that user. However, it must be done in such a way that all other users continue to get their share of the network's resources.

The purpose of this chapter is to describe how congestion is controlled in ATM networks. We begin with the definition of a few terms. Since quality of service plays such an important role in the development and selection of congestion control algorithms, we present a brief description of this subject in Section 5.3. Based on the requirements for network resources, ATM services have been classified into a few categories. These are discussed in Section 5.4. Over the last few years, many researchers have worked in the areas of performance analysis, congestion control, and resource management in ATM networks. A brief summary of the early work in these areas is presented in Section 5.5. Also described in this section are different congestion control types and, in particular, the ATM Forum's congestion control scheme for available-bit-rate (ABR) services.

We have studied in some detail the delay, throughput, buffer utilization, and a few other characteristics of congestion control algorithms for unspecified-bit-rate (UBR) and ABR services. The approach we have taken here is based on computer simulation. The results of this study are presented in Section 5.6. An example is included that shows how the results of this study can be used to characterize the performance of an ATM switch. Resource management is intertwined with congestion control. As such, instead of devoting an exclusive section to this topic, we touch upon the subject wherever appropriate.

5.2 Some Definitions

Throughput — The ratio of the packets that are successfully transmitted by a switch output port to the total number of packets received. For a more elaborate discussion of this term, see Section 5.6.1.

Buffer utilization — Indicates what percentage of a buffer is being utilized at a given instant, and is measured by averaging over a period the fraction of a buffer at a port that is filled up by incoming or outgoing packets.

---

1. We shall define the term "QoS" more elaborately in Section 5.3.

Cell loss ratio (CLR), or cell loss probability — The ratio of the number of cells lost (caused, generally, by a shortage of buffers) to the total number of cells received.

Delays — A packet may encounter delays at a number of points as it travels from its source to its destination. As we shall see later, an important component of delay is due to buffering at an input or output port.

5.3 Quality of Service

Quality of service (QoS) is generally indicated in terms of parameters that are meaningful to the service. For example, to indicate the quality of plain old telephone service (POTS) provided by a PSTN, one may state that on subjective listening tests, 75% of the customers judged the network to be excellent and 90% of them judged the network as better than average [38]. So, a network that was considered excellent by 80% of its customers is better than one that was judged similarly by only 75% of them. A number of factors, for example, signal-to-noise ratio, delay variations, etc., affect the subjective quality of speech. Not all of those parameters, however, are necessarily relevant to services supported in an ATM framework.

Parameters that are used in an ATM network as QoS indicators are cell loss ratio (CLR), cell transfer delay (CTD), and cell delay variation (CDV) [29]. Acceptable error rates are not specified as a QoS parameter. The reasons are the following: Since data transfers (e.g., email, file transfer, etc.) are not error-tolerant, the transmission protocol must incorporate suitable forward error control (FEC) schemes for error recovery. Voice and video traffic, on the other hand, is much less sensitive to channel errors [38]–[41].[2] As such, the receiver may choose to ignore them for voice and video packets, except for their header portions, which provide addressing and controls.[3]

Delays and delay variations, on the other hand, are used as QoS indicators. Delays are important because they affect not only the response time, but also the subjective quality of voice and video, and in the case of the former, may even modify the conversational behavior patterns of users [42].[4] In circuit-switched networks, the delay is fixed. In packet-switched net-

---

2. This remark does not apply to perceptual audio coders, in which signal redundancies and speech components that do not contribute to the perceptual quality are first removed, and the resulting compressed signal packetized. Digital audio of these coders is sensitive to bit errors and must be encoded in error-correcting codes.

3. With some coding schemes, an acceptable speech quality is obtained even when the error rate is as high as 10^{-2} [38], [39]. As for video, bit error rates on the order 10^{-8} or less have negligible or no effect. However, error rates in the range of $10^{-3} - 10^{-8}$, if not corrected, will have a significant effect. If they are any higher, the system will probably not operate at all [43].

4. For example, even with echo cancellers, round-trip delays of 600ms or more (e.g., those associated with satellite links) may cause a statistically significant increase in the frequency of confusion on the part of the listener, and may even cause both parties to talk simultaneously. If the delays are in the range of only 100ms or so, such effects are not noticeable. Similarly, speech becomes unintelligible if packets of lengths, say, 100ms are subjected to variable delays in the range of 100–170ms [42].

Table 5-1   Different Services Together with the QoS Parameters that Characterize Them

Services	QoS Parameters
Voice—Sensitive to delays; can withstand random bit errors, but not many long error bursts; fixed bandwidth for constant-bit-rate-encoded audio, bandwidth can vary for variable-bit-rate coder outputs.	Low cell delay variations and low cell loss ratios
Interactive video as part of multimedia services—Sensitive to delays; can stand some random errors, but not long error bursts; bandwidth can be fixed or variable depending on the coding used.	Low cell delay variations and low cell loss ratios
Interactive data as part of multimedia services—Variable bandwidth; can stand delays or delay variations, but no errors at all.	A reasonable amount of delays or cell delay variations, but no cell loss
Variable data transfer (as in file transfers)—Can stand delays and cell delay variations, but no errors at all.	Delays and cell delay variations, but no errors at all

works, it is variable because at any node, the delay is the sum of the processing delays, the packetization delay, if any, and the transmission delay. In a LAN, this delay is generally small, but in a WAN, the end-to-end delays may be significantly longer and vary from one packet to another. Furthermore, an error control procedure may add substantial delays. Table 5-1 summarizes the QoS parameters that characterize different services.

5.4 Service Categories

The ATM Forum has defined a number of service categories based on their requirements for network resources [29]. Some of these categories require tightly constrained cell transfer delays (CTDs) and cell delay variations (CDVs), but reasonable amounts of cell loss ratios (CLRs), while others are not so sensitive to these delays or cell losses. The goal of any network is to provide the necessary resources so that the integrity of each service is maintained. The service categories are:

  • Constant-bit-rate (CBR) service — This category of service, as the name implies, requires a dedicated bandwidth that remains constant for the entire duration of a call. In this case, all cells are subjected to the same delay, if any. The delay variations across different cells are virtually zero. The required bandwidth is determined by the peak cell rate (PCR) specified by the user.[5] As long as the source conforms to the negotiated PCR, the QoS is guaranteed. Congestion control is achieved generally by means of the call admission control (CAC) at connection times. Thus, the network accepts a call

---

5. This is indicated by the user at call request time via the traffic descriptor IE of the SETUP message.

request only if it can provide the requested bandwidth. Included in this service are delay-sensitive, real-time applications such as voice, video, and circuit-emulated data.

- Real-time, variable-bit-rate (rt-VBR) service — This service category requires variable bandwidths, but being real-time in nature, is characterized by low CTD and CDV. In allocating the bandwidth for this service, the network takes into consideration such traffic descriptors as the PCR, sustainable cell rate (SCR), and maximum burst size (MBS). An end-point specifies these parameters to the network at call setup time. An example of this service category is packet mode transmission of multimedia services.

- Non-real-time, variable-bit-rate (nrt-VBR) service — Like rt-VBR, this service category also requires variable bandwidths. However, since it is non-real-time in nature, there are no maximum CTD or CDV requirements. The network determines its bandwidth requirement on the basis of the PCR, SCR, and MBS. It is not necessary to specify the cell loss ratio; however, it is expected that the network will keep it low. Services such as traditional file transfer, email, etc. are in this category.

- Unspecified-bit-rate (UBR) service — This is similar to the nrt-VBR service, except that sources do not specify the usual traffic descriptors. The same applications that are suitable for nrt-VBR services can also be handled by the UBR service. Since the user does not specify its cell rate, the network may, in the event of congestion, reduce its bandwidth allocation. The congestion control may be provided by a switch at the ATM layer, but it could also be provided at the upper layers of the protocol.

- Available-bit-rate (ABR), or "best effort" service — With this service category, an end-point indicates to the network the upper and lower limits of its bandwidth requirement by specifying both the PCR and minimum cell rate (MCR). Consequently, there is no straightforward way for the network to use CAC algorithms. A congestion control scheme based on the use of resource management (RM) cells has been standardized by the ATM Forum for this service category. With this scheme, the amount of bandwidth allocated to a user may vary during the life of a call depending on the congestion experienced by the network. As such, this service is not suitable for real-time applications. Table 5-2 is a summary of these service categories, along with their traffic descriptors and QoS parameters.

5.5 Congestion Control in ATM Networks

Performance management, congestion controls, and resource allocation schemes are inter-related topics. Congestion is created when input sources begin to exceed their negotiated rates. Normally, a network would be designed with some spare capacity. Thus, if a limited number of sources exceed their subscribed PCRs or SCRs for some limited length of time, it should not be much of a problem. The reason is that since the traffic arrival process from each source is random and perhaps independent, the probability that all sources will exceed their allocated bandwidth at the same time is low. It may, therefore, be possible, up to a certain point, to assign a higher bandwidth to the sources without exceeding the switch capacity. If, however, there is congestion in the network, there are ways to control it. One obvious way is

Table 5-2 Service Categories Defined by the ATM Forum

Service Category	Applications	Traffic Descriptors	QoS Parameters	Comments
CBR	Constant-bit-rate-encoded audio and video, and circuit-emulated data	Peak cell rate	No need to define cell transfer delays or cell delay variations. All cells are subjected to the same delay. There are no delay variations.	Congestion control through call admission control based on the peak cell rate
rt-VBR	Variable-bit-rate-encoded audio and video (e.g. multimedia services)	Peak cell rate, sustainable cell rate, and maximum burst size	Limits on cell transfer delays and cell delay variations.	Call admission control based on real-time traffic analysis and dynamic bandwidth allocation
nrt-VBR	File transfer, email, etc.	Peak cell rate, sustainable cell rate, and maximum burst size	Only cell loss ratio is specified. The network guarantees a low cell loss ratio. There may be significant cell transfer delays and cell delay variations, which are not specified.	
UBR	File transfer, email, etc.	Cell rates not specified by sources	The network does not guarantee any maximum cell loss ratio or cell delay variations.	Congestion control at the ATM layer of a switch or at higher layers
"Best Effort," or ABR	Non-real-time applications	The end-point specifies peak cell rate and minimum cell rate	The network makes no commitment with respect to cell transfer delays or cell delay variations.	Congestion control through resource management cells leading to variable bandwidths

to adopt some policing mechanism — if a VC is emitting at a higher rate than permitted, it can be asked to slow down or its rate can forcibly be reduced until congestion has cleared from the network. In this way, the network, in essence, reallocates the bandwidth to the offending VC.

As for bandwidth allocation, it can be either static or dynamic. Static allocation is fixed for the entire duration of a call and does not change as the volume of incoming traffic changes.

In dynamic allocation, on the other hand, the network monitors incoming traffic in real time and assigns or re-assigns bandwidth accordingly to different connections. For instance, it can reduce the allowed cell rate to one or more connections when there is congestion in the network, or increase it when there is unused bandwidth. Thus, the dynamic allocation scheme is adaptive in nature, and is inherently capable of utilizing network resources more efficiently.

Broadly speaking, there are two types of congestion controls used in ATM networks: preventive controls and reactive controls. With preventive controls, the network limits the number of connections based on its available resources using a call admission control (CAC) scheme and the usage parameter control (UPC). With reactive controls, the network monitors traffic indicators (e.g., the average buffer utilization, average link utilization, packet retransmission rate, and the average length of a queue on outgoing trunks) and then provides feedback to the source so that it can adjust its cell emission rate. However, once congestion has set in, packets may be lost and throughput may diminish. In a situation like this, these control procedures hold congestion to a minimum and eventually eliminate it.

Over the years, these and many other algorithms for congestion control and bandwidth management have been proposed, and their performance in terms of delays, throughput, and buffer utilization have been analyzed both mathematically and by computer simulation. In this section, we will first summarize the work done in this area and then describe a few congestion control schemes, focusing mostly on those which have been adopted as standards by the ATM Forum and implemented in ATM switches.

5.5.1 Early Work

Performance analysis includes the determination of throughput, delay, buffer utilization, and cell loss probabilities using different congestion control mechanisms. Network resources include input ports, input and output buffers, output link capacity, the number of paths permitted through the switch fabric, virtual circuits, etc. However, the term "resource management" in the ATM literature is used in a restricted sense and is concerned with allocating bandwidth and buffers to multiple connections in a manner that would maximize their utilization and yet maintain the QoS for each user. These topics are dealt with in great detail in many books and research papers. See, for instance, References [1]—[6] and [45]. Reference [6] is a collection of papers on various aspects of ATM switching and transmission, many of which provide excellent references at the end.

Reference [7] mathematically derives the bounds on both end-to-end session delays and backlogs for a class of fair-queuing algorithms, where each session is serviced according to its allocated share, and concludes that the self-clocked, fair-queuing scheme in this class performs adequately for the delay-sensitive traffic in ATM networks. The suggested algorithms use the so-called "leaky bucket" characterization of traffic [8], [9]. Kawahara, et al. [10] provide an analytical model and approximate analysis of the delay and cell loss probability of an ATM network using reactive congestion control algorithms. The model consists of a two-stage queuing network as shown in Figure 5-1. Two congestion control schemes are used. The first

Figure 5-1   The two-stage queueing model of Reference [10].

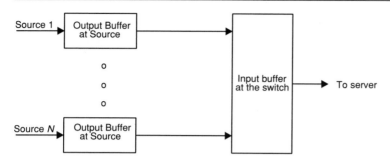

one is based on Forward Explicit Congestion Notification (FECN). When a source finds that the FECN bit of a received cell is set, it stops sending any further cells to the network. In the second scheme, each input source monitors its buffer length to estimate the congestion in the network, and adjusts its cell emission rate accordingly. In this model, bursty traffic is generated using a Markov-modulated Bernoulli process.

Fang, Chen and Hutchins [11] and Romanow and Floyd [12] have studied the performance of TCP traffic over an ATM network using computer simulation. They have concluded that if an ATM switch is intelligent enough to remove from the buffer all cells of a TCP packet of which even a single cell has been dropped because of congestion in the network, the throughput achieved for a reasonable buffer size is almost the same as for TCP over conventional packet networks.

To provide QoS to each user, it is necessary for the ATM switch to determine the traffic pattern generated by each source. One can model the input traffic statistically and then measure the cell loss ratio, average cell delay, and cell delay variance. These parameters are called QoS parameters. Since there is always some inaccuracy in modeling bursty traffic, Duffield, et al estimate the QoS parameters using the concept of thermodynamic entropy at an input port, and claim that their algorithms are simple enough to be implemented in real time at the input ports of an ATM switch [13].

A congestion control scheme based on cell spacing has been proposed and analyzed using both mathematical and simulation models [14]. In this scheme, at the customer premises equipment, a functional entity called a shaper is used to demultiplex all VCs coming from each input source, increase the spacing of ATM cells of a burst to some minimum time interval, and then multiplex all VCs back again before transmitting the cells to the network [15], [16]. Elwalid, et al. [17] have derived theoretical bounds on the performance of ATM multiplexers with many heterogeneous sources as inputs, computed their capacity for a given buffer size, link bandwidth, and CLP, and checked the accuracy of their analyses using variable-bit-rate video teleconferencing traffic. Since the proposed analytic technique is efficient enough to be implemented in real time at a switch port, one can use it to design an effective CAC algorithm for statistical allocation of bandwidth in an ATM network. An excellent review of similar CACs, the difficulties associated with the statistical allocation of bandwidth, and a description of the research done in the area of preventive controls has been given by Perros and Elsayed [18]. See also the references quoted in this paper for more detailed analysis of the suggested algorithms. The broad topics of bandwidth allocation and CACs have also been studied by Gelenbe, et al [19], Gaiti, et al. [31], and Sriram [44]. Bolla, et al [20] have analyzed the statistical multiplexing operation in an ATM network and shown how one can allocate bandwidths on an outgoing link based on categorization of services. Liu, et al. [21] consider a network-wide bandwidth management framework and propose a resource-sharing strategy that guarantees the QoS for each connection.

Golestani [23] and Faber, et al. [24] have proposed simple congestion control schemes whereby each virtual connection is allowed to transmit only a given number of cells over a certain time period. This period, or time window, as it is called, is the same for all VCs. With a properly designed window, it is possible for the network to operate congestion-free. A similar flow control mechanism suitable for a node-to-node connection is presented in Reference [25]. A node is allowed to transmit only a certain number of cells — specified as allocated credits — over each fixed time period. The receiving node indicates how many credits the source has. A source can transmit a cell only if its credit is greater than zero. If it runs out of credit before the period elapses, it cannot transmit any more cells.

Two other areas of active research are reactive congestion controls and the related field of dynamic allocation of network resources. In reactive controls, each source, when informed by the network (or destination end-point) of an impending congestion, dynamically adjusts its cell emission rate [22], [26]–[30]. Control schemes based on this concept have been recently standardized by the ATM Forum for available-bit-rate services (ABR) [29], [46]. In dynamic allocation of resources, the network analyzes the traffic behavior of existing connections to obtain an estimate of, say, the CLP and then decides whether or not to admit a new user into the network. Similarly, the network can use it to dynamically adjust the bandwidth of a VP and thus maximize the utilization of its resources. This subject has been widely studied in the literature [32]–[34]. Recently, a number of authors have applied fuzzy logic and artificial neural networks to congestion controls and traffic management of ATM systems. Their work is described in [35]–[37], and references are quoted in these papers.

5.5.2 Preventive Controls

The idea behind preventive control schemes is as follows: When a user originates a call to the network requesting a desired QoS, the network must do two things before accepting the call request. First, it must make sure that it has sufficient bandwidth to allocate for that user. Second, it must determine if, after admitting the user, it can continue to provide the same QoS for all existing connections. One QoS objective may be a desired CLP. Thus, before the network admits the new user, it should determine whether it can meet its CLP goal for all connections, the old as well as the new.

A network can proceed to do this in two ways. The simplest way is to set aside a portion of its available bandwidth that is equal to (or perhaps slightly greater than) the requested PCR of the incoming call, and reserve that bandwidth for the entire duration of the call. This is possible only if the sum of the bandwidth requirements of the existing and new connections does not exceed the total bandwidth. Or, considering a more complex situation, assume that each user provides the network with information about its traffic characteristics during call establishment, e.g., its PCRs and SCRs. The network can now analyze the traffic using a fixed reference model that is known *a priori*, determine the mean cell rate, cell rate variance, and CLP, and then, based on some criteria, decide whether or not to admit the requesting user. Once admitted, it is allocated a fixed bandwidth. This is called non-statistical, or fixed allocation. This control scheme is suitable for CBR services.

The above allocation has some inaccuracies. For one thing, a source may not be able to describe its traffic accurately. For another, the real-time traffic from an ATM source is generally quite complex in nature (e.g., the VBR-encoded audio or video), and very often cannot be represented by a fixed reference model. To correct these inaccuracies, the network may set the CLP objective slightly lower than the desired value. In this case, the QoS can be maintained with a higher probability, but only at the expense of lowering the throughput.

An alternative approach would be for the network to actually analyze the packet arrival processes from all existing connections, estimate the desired QoS parameter assuming that the requesting source is admitted into the network, and then determine if it can meet the CLP objective for all users. If it cannot, it rejects the incoming call. Otherwise, it connects the user to the network. This allocation scheme is called statistical allocation. An advantage of this scheme is that the network can now serve more users than would be possible with the fixed allocation scheme. However, since the traffic analysis must now be done by the network in real time, these schemes are generally very difficult to implement. The problem becomes even more complex when the network consists of many switches over geographically dispersed areas.

We will illustrate these concepts using a dynamic CAC algorithm that was first proposed and analyzed by Saito [32]. Suppose that a VP consisting of a number of VCs specifies its traffic in terms of the PCR. When a VC requests admission, the network can determine its admissibility in the following way: Cells arriving at the output buffer of the desired VC are monitored over N equal measurement periods. The number of cells during each of these periods is then used to evaluate the following expression:

$$q(k) = \frac{1}{N} \sum_{i=1}^{N} a_{ik}$$

where $a_{ik} = 1$ if k cells arrive in the i-th measurement period, and 0 otherwise. Here $k = 0$, 1, . . . Based on the sequence $\{q(k)\}$, the probability distribution of the number of cells that arrive in the measurement period is estimated as

$$\{\hat{p}(k), \quad k = 0, 1, \ldots\}$$

Now let

$$\{p(k), \quad k = 0, 1, \ldots\}$$

be the true probability distribution. Suppose that there are L buffers in the system. Clearly, when the number of cells arriving at the output buffer exceeds L, some cells will be lost. Hence, the CLP, p_{CLR}, can be obtained using the following relation:

$$p_{CLR} = \sum_{k=L}^{\infty} (k - L) p(k)/A$$

Here, A is the total number of cells arriving during the observation period. After every measurement period, a new estimate is made using the old estimate and the just-computed value of $q(k)$ as follows:

$$\hat{p}(k)_{new} = \alpha q(k) + (1 - \alpha) \hat{p}(k)_{old}$$

where a parameter, $\alpha < 1$, is introduced to account for possible measurement errors.

When a VC requests admission, the number of cells, R, that it can emit during the observation period is estimated from the traffic descriptor parameters — PCR, cell delay variation (CDV), and cell delay variation tolerance (CDVT) — that the source provides to the network. Procedures to estimate are discussed in References [22], [32], and [45]. In the simplest case,

$$R = PCR \times \text{observation period}$$

Assuming that this new VC is admitted, the new value of the CLP is computed using the following relation:

$$p_{CLR} = \sum_{k=L}^{\infty} (k - L) \hat{p}(k - R)/(A + R)$$

If this p_{CLR} is higher than the cell loss ratio objective, the VC is denied admission into the network. Otherwise, it is admitted. Saito [1] has implemented this algorithm and has concluded from his field results that, in some cases, dynamic allocation is more effective than static allocation by an order of magnitude.

5.5.3 Reactive Controls

In most reactive control schemes, the network measures the fraction of its resources that are being used at any instant. When a threshold is reached, it declares congestion and sends an indication to the source that encounters this congestion. On receiving the indication, the source may either stop emitting cells or reduce its cell emission rate in steps. Once congestion clears from the network, the source can increase its cell emission rate in steps until it reaches its allowed PCR. If all sources follow these rules, there is a high probability that congestion in the network will be held to a minimum and fairness will be preserved for all users.

The following reactive control schemes are used in ABR services:

- Forward Explicit Congestion Notification (FECN) scheme — In this scheme, when a switch experiences congestion, it constructs a forward resource management (RM) cell with the congestion indication (CI) bit set to 1 and sends it downstream toward the destination. The destination end-point, after receiving the cell, sends it back to the source to indicate congestion. The source may either reduce the rate at which it is emitting cells or stop emitting any more cells.
- Backward Explicit Congestion Notification (BECN) scheme — This congestion control mechanism is similar to the FECN scheme, except that the switch experiencing congestion generates a backward RM cell with the CI bit set to 1 and sends it upstream toward the source end-point.
- Rate-based control scheme — The switch, at a point of congestion, sends a cell with the explicit forward congestion indication (EFCI) bit set. When the destination detects that this bit is set, it generates an RM cell and sends it toward the source end-point, which then decreases the rate according to some algorithm. With the initial design of the scheme, the source rate could only be decreased. Later, however, it was modified to allow for a rate increase through the RM cells as well, and provide for an explicit rate (ER) specification.

  A combination of the above three schemes is used to provide congestion control in ABR services, as we shall describe shortly.
- Credit-based flow control scheme — This scheme works on a per-VC, per-link basis. Before sending a cell on a given VC, a node[6] determines if the adjacent downstream switch to which it wants to send the cell has an empty buffer for the VC. This is done in the following way: Each sending node keeps a count of the number of buffers that are available at any time for a VC. This is called the credit; it is initially set to the number of input buffers that the VC is assigned based on its bandwidth requirement and the round-trip propagation delay. If the credit balance is greater than zero, the source node sends a cell and subtracts one from the credit. When the receiving node has been able to forward the cell toward its destination, it sends a credit to the sender, whereupon the latter increments its credit by one. Credits may be sent either over a null cell or by piggybacking over a data cell. Some schemes use the VPI field and the high-order four bits of the VCI field of the ATM cell header to send credit information [11].

5.5.4 The ATM Forum's Congestion Control Scheme for ABR Services

In a number of instances, sources in an ATM network cannot characterize their traffic adequately. To address this situation, the ATM Forum has defined a traffic management model

---

6. This node is either an upstream switch or a source end-point.

for ABR services that has been studied rather extensively in the literature. We will describe this model in this section and present its performance quantitatively.

Suppose an ATM end-point is connected to its destination through a series of switches, and is using a known VC for transmitting ATM cells. We will assume this source to be an ABR source. The source does not, generally, transmit its data at a uniform or constant rate; in fact, as long as it can transmit its ATM cells at a reasonable rate, it would find the service perfectly acceptable. It may, however, indicate to the switch the maximum rate at which it ever intends to transmit its ATM cells, and also a minimum rate below which it considers the service unacceptable. The first is the PCR and the second the minimum cell rate (MCR). As for the switch, since a basic requirement in ATM is to maintain the QoS for all users, it may at times find it necessary to restrict the rate at which a particular source is emitting its cells at a given instant. Thus, each source has an allowed cell rate (ACR), where MCR < ACR < PCR.

To help provide feedback, a special ATM cell, called the RM cell, has been defined in ATM. An ABR source generates these RM cells periodically at a fixed rate, say, one out of every 32 cells, and sends them in the forward direction. An RM cell may indicate, among other things, the rate at which it wishes to transmit. When it reaches its destination, the end-point examines the rate at which the source is transmitting. If it cannot support that rate, it modifies the relevant fields of the RM cell, indicating whatever rate it can support, and then sends it upstream toward the source.

5.5.4.1 RM Cell Format

The format of an RM cell is shown in Figure 5-2(a). Here, the ATM header is the same as the standard 5-octet ATM cell header. Following the ATM header is the protocol identifier field that indicates which service is using the given RM cell. In the ATM Forum standard, the protocol ID has been assigned the value 1 for the ABR service.

Next is the 1 octet message type field. Figure 5-2(b) shows the assignment of each bit of this field. Its five active bit fields are:

DIR   Direction bit — 0 for a forward RM cell, 1 otherwise.

BN   BECN — 0 if the RM cell is an FECN cell, and 1 if it is a BECN cell.

CI   Congestion indication — This bit is set to 1 if there is congestion in the network, and 0 otherwise.

NI   No increase — When a network element senses an onset of congestion, it may set this bit to 1 to indicate that it does not want a source to increase its ACR.

RA   Request/Acknowledge bit — Not used by ATM Forum.

The purpose of the ER field is to allow a switch (or destination end-point) to explicitly indicate to a source the data rate that it can support. Similarly, a source may use this field to request a desired rate; the network may initially agree to that rate but later reduce it by specifying a lower rate over the ER field.

Figure 5-2   The RM cell. (a) The structure of an RM cell. (b) The message type field of an RM cell. (c) The format of the 2-octet rate field. (d) Flow of RM cells in an ATM network.

ATM Header 5 octets	Protocol Identifier 1	Message Type 1	Explicitly Rate (ER) 2	Current Cell Rate (CCR) 2	Minimum Cell Rate (MCR) 2	Queue Length 4	Sequence Number 4	Reserved – 3 octets and 6 bits of the next octet	CRC 10 bits

(a)

DIR 1 bit	BN 1 bit	CI 1 bit	NI 1 bit	RA 1 bit	Reserved 3 bits

(b)

Reserved 1 bit	nz 1 bit	e 5 bits	m 9 bits

(c)

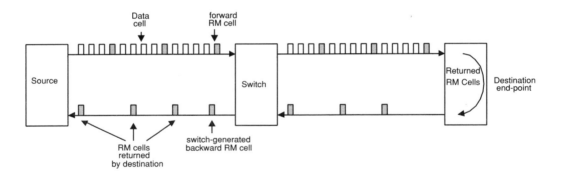

The current cell rate (CCR) field, as the term implies, indicates the current cell rate of a source. Its value is equal to the allowed cell rate of the source. Both the CCR and MCR are zero for a BECN cell. The generic format of the ER, CCR, and MCR rate fields is shown in Figure 5-2(c). It may be recalled from Chapter 3 that cell rates are expressed as 14-bit, floating point, binary numbers with a 9-bit mantissa and 5-bit exponent using the following formula [1]:

$$R = [2^e(1 + m/512)] * nz$$

where $0 \leq e \leq 31$ is the above-mentioned exponent and $[0 \leq m \leq 511$ the mantissa. nz is 1 if the rate is non-zero, and zero otherwise.

5.5.4.2 The Congestion Control Scheme

The congestion control mechanism in the ABR service has the following specific details (refer to Figure 5-2(d)):

1. Before transmitting the first data cell, the ABR source sends an RM cell to the adjacent switch indicating (i) the cell rate at which it is currently allowed to transmit, and (ii) the rate at which it wishes to transmit. The cell rate at which the source can initially transmit, i.e., the initial cell rate (ICR), may be as high as its PCR. Consequently, the source sets the CCR field of the RM cell to its ACR and its ER field to its PCR value. This RM cell is then followed by $N_{rm} - 1$ data cells. Thereafter, the RM cells are emitted periodically such that one out of every N_{rm} cells is an RM cell.

2. The first-generation ATM switches that were built prior to the ATM Forum specification of RM cells cannot generate an RM cell or distinguish it from data cells. To indicate congestion, these switches use the payload type indicator (PTI) field of the ATM header cell. In this case, the congestion bit, called the EFCI bit of the PTI field, is set before the cell is forwarded to the destination.[7] However, the ATM Forum's traffic management model is such that these switches would interwork correctly with new-generation switches since they treat RM cells as data cells and pass them on without any modification. By contrast, the new switches explicitly indicate the rates that they can support at a given instant by setting the ER field of the RM cell to the desired value.[8]

3. When a destination end-point receives an RM cell, it examines its CCR and ER fields and determines if it can sustain the source rate. If it cannot support the rate that the source wants, it modifies the ER field. Similarly, to be backwards-compatible with EFCI-marking switches, if the EFCI bit of a data cell is set, the end-point sets the CI bit to indicate congestion, changes the direction bit to indicate a backward RM cell, and then sends the RM cell, back to the source.

4. As the cell passes in the backward direction, each ER-marking switch examines the ER field and determines if it can support that rate. If it cannot, it reduces the value of the ER field in the RM cell to whatever value it can support. Otherwise, it keeps that field unchanged and then sends the cell to the next switch upstream. Notice that as the RM cell travels toward the source, a switch must never increase the setting of its ER field since a higher rate may be beyond the capacity of a downstream switch.

5. Sometimes, it may be necessary for a switch to react more promptly in the event of congestion, and not wait for an RM cell to be returned by the destination. In these cases, the switch itself can generate an RM cell toward the source, setting its BN field to 1 to indicate that it is a backward RM cell, and either its CI or NI bit to 1 to indicate congestion.

---

7. These switches are called EFCI-marking switches.
8. As such, these second-generation switches are called ER-marking switches.

6. When a source receives an RM cell, it examines its various fields. If the CI bit is 1 and the source ACR is greater than the rate indicated by the ER field of the RM cell, the source must decrease its ACR by the rate decrease factor (RDF).[9] If the new ACR is still higher, it must set its ACR to the larger of the ER value or its MCR, which is the minimum rate for satisfactory operation of this source. If the NI bit is set, the source must not increase its ACR even though it may not be operating at its PCR. If both NI and CI bits are O_2, the ER field was not modified at all by any switch or the receiving end-point. In this case, the source may increase its ACR by a rate increase factor (RIF). However, the new rate must never be more than its PCR. Values of the RIF and RDF are negotiated at connection setup time.

Notice that as soon as a destination detects congestion, it immediately signals the source what cell rate it can support. If the source adjusts its rate accordingly, there is some probability that the cells will not be dropped, thus leading to a better cell loss ratio; however, the cell may have to wait in a buffer a little longer. The same procedures can also be used for VBR services.

5.6 Delay/Throughput Characteristics

5.6.1 The Simulation Model

The approach we have taken here to analyze the performance of an ATM network is based on computer simulation. The simulation model used in our study is shown in Figure 5-3. It consists of a rather small, 16×16 switch with 16 input ports and 16 output ports. A switch may be buffered at the inputs only, at the outputs only, or at both the inputs and outputs. In our simulation, we are assuming that (i) the switch is only input-buffered, and (ii) each input port has a single buffer. Assumption (i) simply means that if there are buffers at the outputs, there are no buffering delays there. In other words, an ATM cell coming out of the switch fabric always finds a buffer available at an output. Assumption (ii) implies that cells from multiple links and VCs at any input port are stored in the same buffer in the order in which they arrived. They are then taken out from the head of the queue and switched through the fabric according to their destination VC. It is assumed that a cell that is ready to be switched can immediately find a path to the destination port. Thus, the only delay encountered here is the delay in configuring the path through the switch.

To accommodate various data rates with different physical layer interfaces, the switch uses the appropriate line interface modules outside of the switch fabric. Since each path through the switch fabric has an OC-3c capacity, a number of lower-speed input sources are multiplexed[10] and then connected to the input buffer of a switch port as shown in Figure 5-3.

---

9. In other words, its ACR must now be reduced to ACR*RDF.

10. Depending on the actual implementation, this multiplexing block may not exist as a separate physical entity. However, the idea is that the same input buffer might be shared by a number of slow-speed input sources.

Figure 5-3 The simulated network used for performance studies.

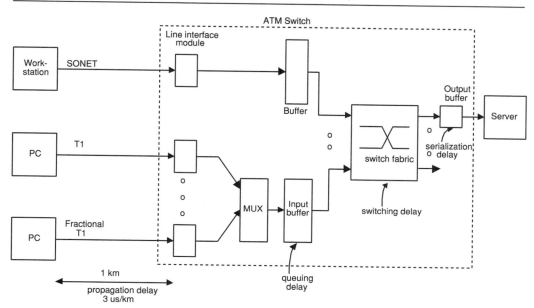

If, on the other hand, an input port operates at an OC-3c rate, it is directly connected to the input buffer and not multiplexed with other inputs.

It is customary to specify a buffer size in terms of ATM cells. For a small switch, an input buffer may be 1024–4096 ATM cells wide. In other words, the buffer size may be 50–200KB. However, we have considered sizes in the range of 1024–8192 ATM cells.

The protocol stack used in this model to transfer packets from the application layer to the ATM layer is shown in Figure 5-4. We are assuming that packets are arriving from the TCP layer to the ATM convergence layer below randomly such that the inter-arrival times are exponentially distributed with a mean that is proportional to the offered load in the system. Furthermore, the TCP is assumed to be sending fixed-length packets, each with 9180 octets. We use this packet size because it is the suggested default for transmitting TCP/IP packets over ATM [11], [12], [44].

As each packet comes into this sublayer, a common-part convergence sublayer protocol data unit (CPCS PDU) is formed, adding the required CPCS-PDU trailer and pad octets such that the resulting packet becomes an integral multiple of 48 octets. This new packet is then passed on to the SAR sublayer. Because it is already in multiples of 48 octets, there is nothing for the SAR sublayer to do. And so, it simply passes the packet, 48 octets at a time, to

Figure 5-4   Transmission of fixed-length TCP packets over ATM. (a) The protocol stack. (b) TCP packets, each 9180 octets long, are reformatted in the AAL and ATM layers so that they can be transmitted as ATM cells. (c) Packets are shown arriving at the convergence sublayer at random instants. Notice that on detecting congestion in the network, the source reduces its cell transmission rate.

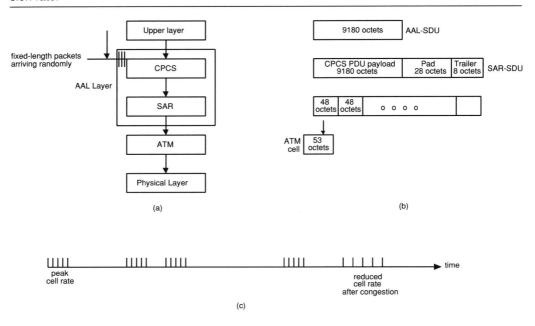

(a)   (b)

(c)

the ATM layer. Since the overhead added in the CPCS is much smaller than the overhead due to the ATM headers, we ignore the CPCS overhead. Each TCP packet then translates to (9180 + 28 + 8)/48 = 192 ATM cells (Figure 5-4(b)).

As an ATM cell travels from its source to its destination, it encounters delays at different points along the route. First, there is the propagation delay. In Figure 5-3, this is the delay that an ATM cell undergoes as it travels from the source to the switch, or from the switch, to the destination end-point. This is the electromagnetic propagation delay and is about $3\mu s/km$. The second component is the buffering delay. As we will show, for a LAN, this is the most significant delay because depending on the buffer size and offered load, this delay can be as high as a few milliseconds. When an ATM cell is put on the output buffer, it takes about 2.73 μs to clock it out at the 155.52 Mb/s STS-3c rate, or 524.16 μs to clock out 192 ATM cells that constitute a TCP packet. The other delay is the switching delay, which is the time taken by the controller to set up the path plus the time taken by the ATM cell to propagate through the switch. We have assumed this delay to be negligibly small. Thus, if TCP packets arrived at a rate of one packet every 524.16 μs, and if there were no congestion in the network, the throughput achieved would be equal to 100% of the link capacity.

If a switch or the destination terminal is congested, an RM cell is generated with the CI bit set (or alternatively, the EFCI bit of a data cell is set). The source receives this cell after a delay of

$$D_{prop} + D_{queuing} + D_{serialization} + D_{switching}$$

and then adjusts its cell rate. If the switch is congested, and as a consequence, generates a forward RM cell with the CI bit set, the cell would take longer to reach the source, and accordingly, a longer delay would have to be incorporated in the simulation model so that the source end-point could adjust its cell rate correctly.

In our simulation, we used the term "throughput" to indicate the fraction of all packets originating at a source that were successfully transmitted by the switch. It was, therefore, a measure of how efficiently the link was being utilized.

A feature of the TCP protocol is that when the source does not receive an acknowledgment from the destination within a certain time-out period, it retransmits the packet. Consequently, one could compute the number of higher-layer packets that reach the destination end-point and use it to indicate an effective throughput. In our simulation, a packet or cell was occasionally dropped, which in turn triggered TCP retransmission. In our analysis, these retransmitted packets are included in the packets that were successfully transmitted.

Finally, as a word of caution to the reader, the simulation results presented below are only approximate. With a different set of assumptions — for example, packet arrivals with the distribution of a Markov-modulated Poisson process or its discrete, time-equivalent, Markov-modulated Bernoulli process, or arrivals from a so-called "greedy" source that always has some packets ready to be transmitted, or exponentially distributed packet sizes — the results would be slightly different. However, the general conclusions would remain the same.

5.6.2 Unspecified-Bit-Rate (UBR) Services

In UBR services, since the user does not specify the bit rate at which it wants to transmit, when there is congestion, the network simply drops the ATM cells without providing any feedback to the end-points. Thus, there is no way for the source to adjust its cell rate. When an ATM cell is dropped, the entire packet of that cell is useless. In this situation, the packet can be treated by the ATM switch in one of three ways: (i) Even though one or more cells of the packet have been dropped already, the ATM switch can continue to buffer its subsequent cells when congestion clears, and service them when their turn comes (i.e., forward them to their destination). (ii) The switch can ignore all subsequent ATM cells of the corrupted packet and not buffer them in a queue, even when congestion clears. However, cells received prior to the congestion are preserved in the queue and serviced according to the scheduling algorithm. (iii) The switch can discard all subsequent cells, and, furthermore, remove from the buffer all earlier cells of that packet. Option (i), which is referred to as plain ATM over TCP [12], is not satisfactory because the buffer continues to be used for the errored packet. Even though some of the cells of the original packet are missing, the switch forwards them to their destination anyway. Since the TCP procedures will eventually cause the source to retransmit the packet,

Figure 5-5 Throughput vs. the offered load for UBR services with TCP over ATM using early packet discard (EPD).

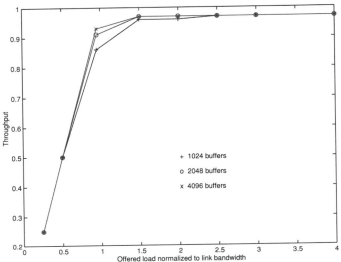

the network is further congested. Consequently, the achievable throughput with this option is much less than with traditional TCP. Option (ii) is known as partial packet discard. The throughput improves somewhat, but is still significantly less than what can be achieved with packet TCP. The third option (iii), called early packet discard (EPD), provides the best throughput. It is this option that is used in our simulation.

Figures 5-5–5-9 give a few performance parameters for UBR services assuming early packet discard. Here, a single VC, operating at OC-3 rate, has been used. Congestion is declared and cells are dropped whenever more than 50% of the buffer is filled.[11] The throughput has been normalized to the capacity of the OC-3 link. Figures 5-5 and 5-6 show how it varies with the offered load. As the offered load increases, so does the throughput, reaching an asymptotic value of about 0.95 for an offered load of 2.5. For larger values of the offered load, the throughput remains virtually constant for buffer sizes of 2000 cells or more. For smaller values of the offered load, say in the range of 0.25–1.25, the throughput increases somewhat with the buffer size, but as Figure 5-6 shows, not very significantly with buffers beyond 2000 cells. Thus it is reasonable to design a small ATM switch of the type discussed in our simulation with a buffer size of about 2048 cells (per switch port).

Figure 5-7 shows the average buffer utilization as a function of buffer size for two values of the offered load (normal and heavy load conditions). The average buffer utilized is expressed

---

11. In other words, the congestion detection threshold is set at 0.5.

Figure 5-6   Throughput vs. buffer size for UBR services with TCP over ATM using EPD.

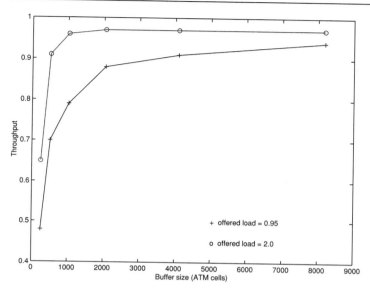

Figure 5-7   Average buffer utilized as a function of the buffer size for two values of the offered load for UBR services with TCP over ATM using EPD.

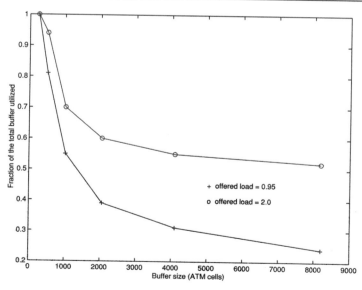

Figure 5-8   Average delay vs. offered load for UBR services for TCP using EPD.

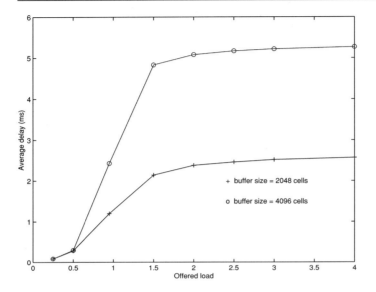

as a fraction of the total buffer size. Notice that if a system is designed with a buffer size of 2000 cells and the offered load increases to 2.0, the average buffer utilized is 1200 cells long and we still achieve a high throughput (about 0.85 from Figure 5-6). Notice also that if the congestion detection threshold is set at a higher value, that is, the network is considered congested when the buffer is, say, 75% full, the throughput, as well as the average buffer utilization, will increase.

Figure 5-8 shows how the average buffering delay varies with buffer size. For offered loads up to about 1.5, the average delay is almost linearly proportional. Also, the greater the buffer size, the longer the delay. It can be concluded from Figures 5-6 and 5-8 that a larger throughput can be achieved with a larger buffer at the expense of increased delays.

Figure 5-9 is a plot of the CLP as a function of the buffer size for two values of the offered load. When the offered load is 1, the CLP depends on the buffer size used, decreasing as the buffer size increases. (Compare this with Figure 5-6.) When the offered load exceeds the link capacity, most of the excess packets generated by the source are dropped regardless of the size of the buffer, thereby holding the CLP constant.

5.6.3 Available- and Variable-Bit-Rate Services

The performance of ABR services using the EFCI bit to alleviate congestion in the network for a single VC is shown in Figures 5-10–5-13. The ICR was set to the PCR. As the network became congested, sources cut their cell rate to one-fourth their peak rate. In other words, the

Figure 5-9   Cell loss probability for UBR services over TCP as a function of the buffer size for two values of the offered load.

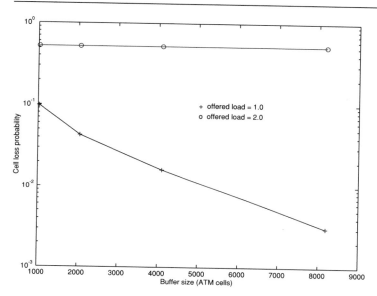

Figure 5-10   Throughput vs. the offered load for ABR services using the EFCI bit. Here, MCR = PCR/4.

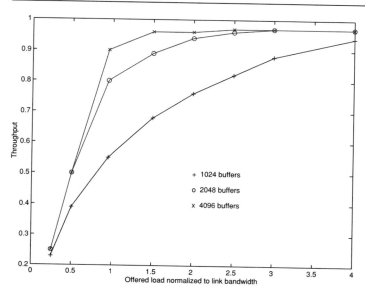

Figure 5-11 Average buffer utilized vs. the buffer size for ABR services using the EFCI bit. Here, MCR = PCR/4.

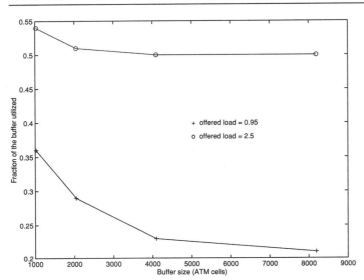

RDF was 4. The simulation was repeated with an RDF of 8. The model takes into consideration the delay between the time congestion is first detected and the instant the source receives the RM cell with the EFCI bit set. This delay was chosen to be 1ms. Notice that this is about the average queuing delay for moderate values of the offered load. When congestion cleared from the network, each connection resumed transmitting at the PCR.

Comparing Figures 5-5 and 5-10, one should notice that for buffer sizes of 2000–4000 cells, the throughputs are almost the same for the two cases. However, there are differences. First of all, with these buffer sizes, the average buffer utilization is less for ABR services (compare Figures 5-7 and 5-11). Second, for moderate offered loads (i.e., up to about 1.5), the average delay is also less for ABR services (compare Figures 5-8 and 5-12), indicating that with ABR-over-EFCI, the network is less congested. This is to be expected since sources reduce their cell emission rates when the buffers reach their congestion threshold. Because cell delay variations play a role in the fairness of congestion control schemes, we plotted the delay distribution in Figure 5-12(b). Notice that for normal loads (i.e., offered load = 0.95) and a buffer size of 2048 cells, about 60% of the cells have a delay of 1ms or less and more than 90% have a delay of 2ms or less. Under heavy load conditions (i.e., offered load = 2) and with the same buffer size, 53% of the cells have a delay of 2ms or less and about 94% have a delay of 3ms or less.

Similarly, as shown in Figures 5-9 and 5-13, the cell loss probabilities for ABR services

Figure 5-12 Delay vs. the offered load for ABR-over-EFCI for a single VC. Here, MCR = (PCR)/4. (a) Average delay as a function of the offered load. (b) Delay distribution.

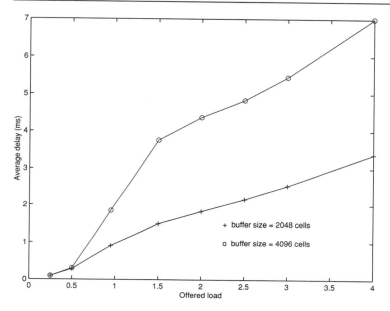

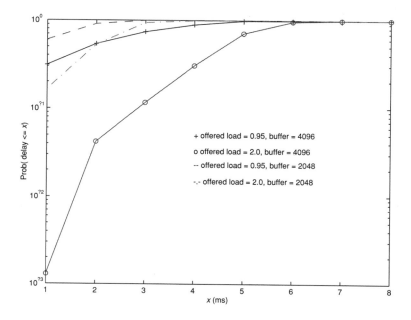

Figure 5-13   CLP vs. buffer size for ABR services using the EFCI bit. Here, MCR = PCR/4.

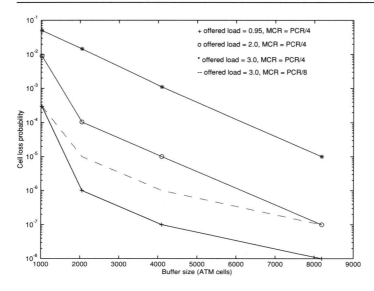

Figure 5-14   Throughput vs. number of VCs for ABR services over EFCI for two offered loads. For each VC, PCR = 155 Mb/s, MCR = PCR/8, and buffer size = 8192 (cells).

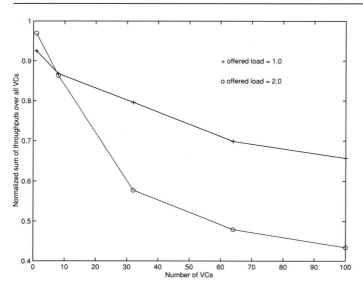

are better. In fact, as may be seen from the corresponding cell loss probability curve of Figure 5-13, the system performs even better when the rate decrease factor is increased to 8.

The performance of ABR-over- EFCI was also studied with multiple VCs on a link. The results are shown in Figure 5-14, where the sum of the throughputs from all VCs is plotted against the number of VCs for two values of the offered load. For all VCs, the PCR was set to 155 Mb/s and the MCR to PCR/8. The simulation revealed that for the system to provide a reasonable throughput with multiple VCs, it was necessary to have a buffer size larger than 4096 (cells). So, a buffer size of 8192 was chosen. Congestion was declared when the buffer was half-full. Cells were dropped when the available buffer fell below 256. The simulation was designed such that all connections were treated fairly. "*Fairness*," in this case, was defined in terms of the maximum difference in the throughputs and average delays for all VCs. It was found that for the two values of the offered load, the maximum variation in the throughput was about 5% and the maximum variation in the delay was about 20%. As Figure 5-14 shows throughput decreases as the number of VCs increases. However, even under the extreme conditions of our simulation, where all VCs emit at the PCR of 155 Mb/s, the throughput is at least 43% of the maximum. The decline in throughput is larger under heavier load conditions (i.e., an offered load of 2 or more). It was found that if all VCs have a high PCR, the performance under heavy loads improves with a larger buffer. For example, if the buffer size is increased to 16384, the throughput with 100 VCs increases from 43% to 52%.

System performance, particularly CLP, further improves if the switch explicitly specifies the correct rate at which sources should emit their cells in the event of congestion in the ER field of an RM cell.

From this study, we can make some general conclusions. For example, ABR-over-EFCI performs much better than UBR with EPD. Larger RDFs lead to better CLP. With multiple VCs, the throughput decreases as the number of VCs increases, but can be increased with a larger buffer size.

Using the results of this study, let us characterize the performance of an ATM switch. Consider the network of Figure 5-15, where a number of Ethernet LAN segments are connected to an ATM backbone switch over 155-Mb/s ATM user-to-network interfaces (UNIs).

The switch is a 16×16 non-blocking switch with a full-duplex bandwidth of 2.48 Gb/s. If it is to handle a reasonable number of VCs, say, about 128 per port, the buffer size should be at least 8192 cells, or 424 KB. In this case, with ABR services, a throughput of 43% of the maximum (i.e., about 67 Mb/s per port) is achievable under heavy load conditions. This assumes that all VCs emit at a PCR of 155 Mb/s and reduce their emission rate by an RDF of 8 (see Figure 5-14).

If there were only a single VC, the CLR under normal loads would be below 10^{-8} (see Figure 5-13). With multiple VCs, the CLP (not shown in the figures) under normal load conditions will be somewhat higher. However, if the offered load increases (say, from 1 to 2), the CLP increases by orders of magnitude (about 10%).

Since the switch may at times experience increased offered loads, and since the CLP can

Figure 5-15   An ATM backbone switch connecting a number of LAN segments and servers.

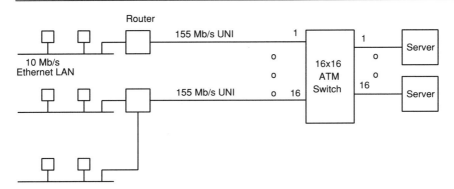

be improved by increasing the buffer size, larger buffers, say, 848 KB or more, should be used. In this case, the throughput increases to 52%, or 81 Mb/s. Thus, if there were 100 VCs, then with the above assumptions, each VC would have a throughput of 810 kb/s. Similarly, with 8000 VCs, each would have a throughput of 10.1 kb/s.

5.7 Summary

In this chapter, we described how congestion is controlled in an ATM network. QoS plays an important role in the selection of congestion control algorithms. QoS indicators are different for different services, and include cell loss ratios, cell transfer delays, and cell delay variations. We discussed these parameters for multimedia services, and categorized ATM services based on the network resources they require.

Over the last few years, a large number of congestion control and resource management schemes for ATM networks have been studied. We presented a brief summary of this work. Congestion control schemes can be broadly classified into preventive controls and reactive controls. With preventive controls, a new user is admitted only if the network is sure that it can provide the bandwidth requested by that user and at the same time guarantee the QoS of all connections, old as well as new. A number of reactive control schemes are used in ABR services. These were briefly described. The ATM Forum has specified a reactive congestion control scheme for ABR services, which is based upon the use of resource management cells. We provided a detailed description of this scheme.

We studied in some detail the delay and throughput characteristics of congestion control schemes for UBR and ABR services. The study was based on computer simulations. In UBR services, since the user does not specify the bit rate at which it wants to transmit, when there is congestion, the network simply drops the ATM cells without providing any feedback to the source. Thus, there is no way for the source to know when to adjust its cell rate. When an ATM cell is dropped, the entire packet of the cell is useless. In this situation, the network has a number of options by which it can treat the packet. We showed that the early packet discard option provides the best throughput.

The congestion control scheme for ABR is based on forward explicit congestion notification using RM cells. We provided the throughput, buffer utilization, delay, delay distribution, and cell loss probability for various values of minimum and peak cell rates. Also shown was the variation of throughput with the number of VCs for different values of the offered load. Finally, an example was included to illustrate how the results of this study can be used to characterize the performance of an ATM switch for a typical application.

5.8 References

[1] J. Roberts, U. Mocci, and J. Virtamo (eds.), *Broadband Network Teletraffic*. Berlin: Springer, 1996.

[2] O. Onvural, *Asynchronous Transfer Mode Networks: Performance Issues*. Boston: Artech House, 1993.

[3] D. E. McDysan and D. L. Spohn, *ATM — Theory and Application*. New York: McGraw Hill, 1994.

[4] U. Black, *ATM: Foundation for Broadband Networks*. Englewood Cliffs, New Jersey: Prentice Hall, 1995.

[5] R. Handel, M. N. Huber, and S. Schroder, *ATM Networks — Concepts, Protocols and Applications*. Reading, Massachusetts: Addison-Wesley, 1994.

[6] M. Toy (Ed.), *Development and Applications of ATM — Selected Readings*. Institute of Electrical and Electronic Engineers, Inc., 1996.

[7] S. J. Golestani, "Network Delay Analysis of a Class of Fair Queueing Algorithms," *IEEE J. Select. Areas Commun.*, Vol. 13, No. 6, Aug. 1995, pp. 1057–1070.

[8] J. S. Turner, "New Directions in Communications (or Which Way to the Information Age?)," *IEEE Commun. Mag.*, Vol. 24, Jan. 1986, pp. 8–15.

[9] N. Yamanaka, et al, "Performance Limitation of the Leaky Bucket Algorithm for ATM Networks," *IEEE Trans. Comm.*, Vol. 43, No. 8, Aug. 1995, pp. 2298–2300.

[10] K. Kawahara, et al., "Performance Analysis of Reactive Congestion Control for ATM Networks," *IEEE J. Select. Areas Commun.*, Vol. 13, No. 4, May 1995, pp. 651–661.

[11] C. Fang, H. Chen, and J. Hutchins, "A Simulation Study of TCP Performance in ATM Networks," *Proc. IEEE GLOBECOM*, 1994, pp. 1217–1223.

[12] A. Romanow and S. Floyd, "Dynamics of TCP Traffic over ATM Networks," *IEEE J. Select. Areas Commun.*, Vol. 13, No. 4, May 1995, pp. 633–641.

[13] N. G. Duffield, et al, "Entropy of ATM Traffic Streams: A Tool for Estimating QoS Parameters," *IEEE J. Select. Areas Commun.*, Vol. 13, No. 6, Aug. 1995, pp. 981–990.

[14] F. Hubner and P. Tran-Gia, "Discrete Time Analysis of Cell Spacing in ATM Networks," *Telecommunication Systems*, 3, 1995, pp. 379–395.

[15] F. M. Brochin, "A Cell Spacing Device for Congestion Control in ATM Networks," *Performance Evaluation*, 16, 1992, pp. 107–127.

[16] P. Boyer, et al, "Spacing Cells Protects and Enhances Utilization of ATM Network Links," *IEEE Network*, 6(5), 1992.

[17] A. Elwalid, et al., "Fundamental Bounds and Approximations for ATM Multiplexers with Applications to Video Teleconferencing," *IEEE J. Select. Areas Commun.*, Vol. 13, No. 6, Aug. 1995, pp. 1004–1016.

[18] H. G. Perrros and K. M. Elsayed, "Call Admission Control Schemes: A Review," *IEEE Commun. Mag.*, Nov. 1996, pp. 82–91.

[19] E. Gelenbe, et al., "Bandwidth Allocation and Call Admission Control in High-Speed Networks," *IEEE Commun. Mag.*, May 1997, pp. 122–129.

[20] R. Bolla, et al., "Bandwidth Allocation and Admission Control in ATM Networks with Service Separation," *IEEE Commun. Mag.*, May 1997, pp. 130–137.

[21] K. Liu, et al., "Design and Analysis of a Bandwidth Management Framework for ATM-Based Broadband ISDN," *IEEE Commun. Mag.*, May 1997, pp. 1138–145.

[22] H. Saito, "Dynamic Resource Allocation in ATM Networks," *IEEE Commun. Mag.*, May 1997, pp. 146–153.

[23] S. J. Golestani, "Congestion-free Communication in Broadband Packet Networks," *IEEE Trans. Comm.*, Vol. COM-39, 1991, pp. 1802–1812.

[24] T. Faber and L. Landweber, "Dynamic Time Windows: Packet Admission Control with Feedback," *Proc. SIGCOM*, 1992, pp. 124–135.

[25] F. Vakil and R. P. Singh, "Shutter: A Flow Control Scheme for ATM Networks," *Proc. 7th ITC Spec. Sem.*, Morristown, NJ, Oct. 1990.

[26] H. Saito, et al. "Performance issues in public ABR service," *IEEE Commun. Mag.*, Vol. 34, No. 11, Nov. 1996, pp. 40–49.

[27] K. W. Fendick, "Evolution of Control for the Available Bit Rate Service," *IEEE Commun. Mag.*, Nov. 1996, pp. 35–39.

[28] R. Jain, et al., "Source Behavior for ATM ABR Traffic Management: An Explanation," *IEEE Commun. Mag.*, Nov. 1996, pp. 50–55.

[29] The ATM Forum Technical Committee, "Traffic Management Specification," Version 4.0, af-tm-0056.000, April 1996.

[30] A. Arulambalan, et al., "Allocating Fair Rates for Available Bit Rate Service in ATM Networks," *IEEE Commun. Mag.*, Nov. 1996, pp. 92–100.

[31] D. Gaiti and N. Boukhatem, "Cooperative Congestion Control Schemes in ATM Networks," *IEEE Commun. Mag.*, Nov. 1996, pp. 102–110.

[32] H. Saito and K. Shiomoto, "Dynamic Call Admission Control in ATM Networks," *IEEE J. Select. Areas Commun.*, Vol. 9, No. 7, 1991, pp. 982–989.

[33] H. Saito, "Simplified Dynamic Connection Admission Control in ATM Networks," *Proc. ICCCN*, San Francisco, CA, 1995.

[34] R. Griffiths and P. Key, "Adaptive Call Admission Control in ATM Networks," *Proc. ITC14: The Fundamental Role of Teletraffic in the Evolution of Telecom. Networks*, 1994, pp. 1089–98.

[35] V. Catania, et al., "Using Fuzzy Logic in ATM Source Traffic Control: Lesson and Perspectives," *IEEE Commun. Mag.*, Nov. 1996, pp. 70–81.

[36] C. Douligeris, et al., "Neuro-Fuzzy Control in ATM Networks," *IEEE Commun. Mag.*, May 1997, pp. 154–162.

[37] A. Hiramatsu, "Integration of ATM Call Admission Control and Link Capacity Control by Distributed Neural Networks," *IEEE J. Select. Areas Commun.*, Vol. 9, No. 7, 1991, pp. 1131–38.

[38] N. S. Jayant, "High quality coding of telephone speech and wide-band audio," *IEEE Commun. Mag.*, Jan. 1990, pp. 10–20.

[39] N. S. Jayant, "Effects of packet losses in waveform coded speech and improvements due to an odd-even sample-interpolation procedure," *IEEE Trans. Comm.*, Vol. COM-29, Feb. 1981, pp. 101–109.

[40] M. R. Karim, "Packetizing voice for mobile radio," *IEEE Trans. Commun.*, Vol. 42, No. 2/3/4, Feb./Mar./Apr., 1994, pp. 377–385.

[41] M. R. Karim, "Packet Communication on a Mobile Radio Channel," *AT&T Tech. J.*, Vol. 65, May/June 1986, pp. 12–20.

[42] J. G. Gruber, "Delay related issues in integrated voice and data networks," *IEEE Trans. Comm.*, Vol. COM-29, No. 6, June 1981, pp. 786–800.

[43] R. Schaphorst, *Video Conferencing and Video Telephony*. Boston: Artech House, 1996, p. 24.

[44] K. Sriram, "Methodologies for Bandwidth Allocation, Transmission, Scheduling, and Congestion Avoidance in Broadband ATM Networks," *Comput. Networks and ISDN Syst.*, Vol. 26, 1993, pp. 43–59.

[45] H. Saito, *Teletraffic Technologies in ATM Networks*. Boston: Artech House, 1994.

[46] K. W. Fendick, "Evolution of Controls for the Available Bit Rate Service," *IEEE Commun. Mag.*, Nov. 1996, pp. 35–39.

Problems

5.1 Consider an $N \times N$ switch that uses an input buffering scheme, that is, each of its input ports has a buffer of appropriate size while the output ports have no buffers other than the minimum required to interface to the output serial link (see Figure 5-P.1). Suppose that

Figure 5-P.1 The network model used in Problem 5.1.

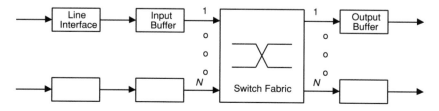

a network has been designed for nrt-VBR services, where each user requests a QoS based on the following traffic descriptors: the SCR, the PCR, and the MBS. Recall that the SCR is the average number of cells per second generated by the source during the life of a call. The PCR is defined as the maximum of all cell rates determined by observing the number of cells emitted over an interval, say, t, where t is much smaller than the duration of the call. Assume that for each user,

SCR = 3600 cells/s averaged over 1 min

PCR = 14,400 cells/s averaged over 250 ms

MBS = 8000 cells

The average duration of a call is 5 min. The protocol used is IP over ATM with TCP at the transport layer. Packets are arriving from the TCP layer to the ATM convergence layer randomly, such that the inter-arrival times are exponentially distributed with a mean that is proportional to the offered load.

Write a simulation program to determine the throughput as a function of the buffer size as the offered load varies from 0.75 to 2.5. Use the EPD algorithm.

5.2 For the switch described in Problem 5.1, find the bounds on the average CLR.

5.3 Refer to Problem 5.1. Choose the buffer size such that the throughput is 90% when the offered load is unity. Determine how the switch will perform when RM cells are used to control congestion in the network. Does the offered load ever exceed 1.0 in this case?

5.4 As in Problem 5.1, assume that a 1.25-Gb/s, non-blocking, full-duplex switch is being used for UBR services. The protocol used is TCP/IP with LAN emulation. Packets are arriving at the convergence layer randomly with exponential distribution. The switch uses the input buffering scheme, and the buffer size at each port is 16,384 (cells). Assume that the offered load varies from 1.0–2.0. If the desired throughput is to be at least 0.5, determine, by simulation or otherwise, the maximum number of VCs that the switch can support. List any assumptions that you make.

CHAPTER   6

ATM Network Management

6.1 Introduction

The purpose of this chapter is to describe the network management functions required of an ATM network, and indicate how those functions are performed. The Simple Network Management Protocol (SNMP) is the most commonly used protocol — it is used to manage intranets (i.e., TCP/IP-based networks), private networks, and most networking devices currently available in the market [1], [2]. SNMP is also used to manage ATM devices and networks. Here, however, there are some alternatives. For example, if an ATM device is managed from an SNMP management station over a legacy LAN, the device must be part of the emulated LAN. In this case, the standard SNMP protocol stack is used. If the network management station is directly connected to a managed ATM device over an ATM interface, we can use the ATM Forum-specified Integrated Local Management Interface (ILMI) [11].

This chapter is organized as follows: The general network management functions are described in Section 6.2. The next section describes how a network management station (NMS) is connected to the network or end-devices being managed. Section 6.4 is devoted to SNMP. Here we provide an overview of the protocol, and describe, among other things, the managed objects and the way the management information base (MIB) is organized. The next section presents a brief discussion of exactly how an ATM network is managed. More specifically, ILMI and the ATM interface MIB are described.

6.2 General Network Management Functions

Broadly speaking, the following functions are addressed by a network management system [1]:

- *Security management* — It allows only selected persons the capability of accessing the network via the network manager. Each user has a login ID, a password, and a certain privilege level. This function might indicate whether or not a user is allowed to make any configuration changes or access the network using SNMP or other protocols such as telnet.

- *Configuration management* — It involves configuring the network and viewing the configuration. Some parameters that need to be configured are:

  - ATM system parameters — These parameters include the IP address of the ATM switch, the version of the UNI that is currently in use, and whether signaling is enabled or disabled.
  - ATM ports — The user must enable or disable a port, enable or disable signaling at the port, enable or disable ILMI, set the maximum number of VCCs for each port, and configure each port to operate either in the network mode or in the user mode.
  - ATM routing table — The database on the managed node maintains the routing information used in forwarding ATM cells. Configurable parameters associated with a route include the output port number, the ATM address of the route, the priority of the route, etc.
  - PVC, virtual paths (VPs), maximum number of SVCs, etc.

From the network manager, the user should be able to configure the device being managed in any desired way, store the configuration information in a file on the network manager, archive it, download the file to the managed device, make profile changes, and upload the profile from the device when needed.

In addition, the network manager may have the capability of automatically generating a graphical view of the network configuration. When the power is first turned on, each node on the network and each port on a node sends a sign-on message to the NMS. Using this information as a basis, the network manager may automatically generate a graphical representation showing each node with its associated ports, and may indicate if a port is terminated properly. The network manager may continually monitor and discover the network, update the network view, and show changes to the network configuration as they take place. It may have other capabilities as well. For example, from the NMS, one should be able to configure the network or a sub-network even if the station is not connected to the network.

The user should be able to view desired parameters such as the system version number, port status, cabling type, physical interface type (DS1/DS3/SONET), interface state, signaling state, signaling version number (UNI 3.0/3.1), VCCs in use, maximum number of VCCs configured for each port, the IP address of an ATM switch, the ATM address of a port, etc.

- *Fault management* — Normally, the NMS is informed about faults in the system by means of alarms that the network generates as SNMP traps. There are various types of alarms. For example, they may indicate if the physical layer at a port has failed, or if the upper layers are not functioning. One might use this feature to trouble-shoot and diagnose a faulty link or node. In some systems, a maintenance feature that gives the user the capability of resetting the network or some components of the network is added to this function.

- *Performance management* — This function allows the network administrator to see how well the network is performing. To do this, it is necessary to monitor the traffic on each virtual circuit and each port. The information presented may include, among other things, the number of point-to-point or point-to-multipoint connections, the number of ATM cells that a VC or a port transmits or receives in either direction, average and peak cell rates on desired VCs, the number of cells received in error, the number of calls successfully completed, the number of calls rejected because of network congestion, the number of misdirected calls, etc. In some instances, it may be desirable to view all of this information only when some user-specified criteria are satisfied. For example, the user may be interested in the instantaneous traffic at any time or the so-called historical traffic that is averaged over a given interval only when it exceeds a certain level.

Other additional features of network management allow the user to

- Set up a call.
- View Q.2931 call control messages exchanged at an interface between a managed entity (e.g., a switch) and an external unit (e.g., a user device), as well as software functions invoked as a call is processed by the node.
- Execute utility commands (e.g., reset a board, set a protocol timer to a desired value, etc.).
- Upgrade the software by downloading new software into, say, the flash PROM of a system, etc.

The NMS may be a single PC, a single workstation, or a number of workstations connected in an hierarchical manner with management modules running concurrently under a shared interface. A management station can run on the following operating systems: Windows 95, Windows NT 3.5 and NT 4.x, and UNIX (e.g., HP-UNIX, IBM Netview, AIX, and Solaris). Both MIB II and ATM MIBs must be supported as part of the SNMP management agent suite.

6.3 The Interface between the Network and Network Manager

The interface between a management station and the network to be managed may consist of one or more RS-232 ports, Ethernet or IBM token ring ports, ATM ports, or any combination of these ports. A management station can be connected to a network or network element to be managed either locally over any of these ports or remotely over a modem via a PSTN or over an Ethernet interface across the Internet.

More than one NMS can access a given network or network element at any time and simultaneously view or monitor the alarms, the exchange of call control messages, and the traffic flows. For example, multiple network managers can access a switch over an Ethernet port and view the desired data. However, at any time, only one of them is allowed to change the

Figure 6-1   The connection between the NMS and the network equipment being managed.

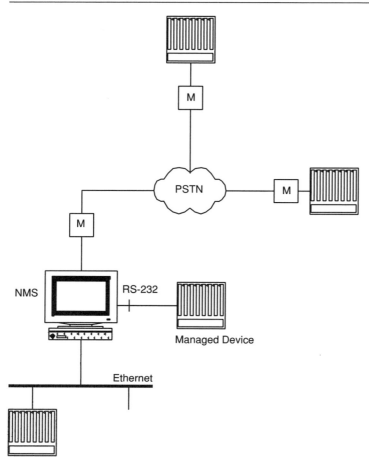

network configuration. In this case, certain rules may be used in assigning priorities to the network managers. For example, when a remote management station is connected via a modem, configuration change requests from other management stations may be denied. Or, a management station connected to the managed network over an ATM interface using ILMI may take precedence over other stations connected to the network over Ethernet ports.

Figure 6-1 shows how an NMS can be used to manage multiple devices. Notice that an NMS can be connected to a managed device either locally or remotely with a modem (M) over a PSTN. At the same, it can be connected over a LAN to other equipment. The user can monitor any equipment item at any time. Alternatively, the NMS can automatically poll each device either regularly or at a prescribed time of the day, and collect all the desired information. Yet

Figure 6-2 Network management stations connected in an hierarchical manner to manage a number of network devices.

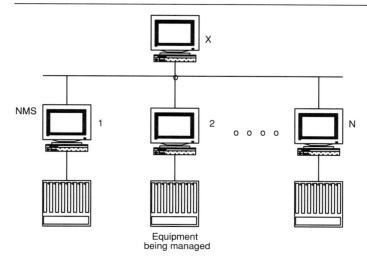

NMS

1

2

o o o o

N

X

Equipment
being managed

another possibility is for each device to automatically report alarm conditions (or performance parameters) based on some criteria.

When the network being managed is large, it may be necessary to use a number of NMSs connected in some hierarchical order. One such configuration is shown in Figure 6-2. Here, each NMS in the bottom hierarchy collects management information from the element of the network to which it is assigned, and reports the data to an NMS, labeled X in the figure, in the upper hierarchy. Similarly, the user can configure any network element from NMS X by sending an SNMP request to the appropriate NMS associated with the desired network element.

6.4 The Simple Network Management Protocol (SNMP)

6.4.1 An Overview

The Simple Network Management Protocol evolved under the auspices of the Internet Activities Board (IAB) [1]. To understand the protocol, consider the following: Suppose that an equipment vendor manufactures a number of different products, one of which is an ATM switch type. There may be many different models of the ATM switch depending on the number of user ports, the type of interfaces on the ports, and the maximum capacity of the switch. At a given instant, the status of the ports may be different — some ports may be enabled, others may be disabled; some of those that are enabled may be active, while the rest may be inactive. In SNMP, each of these parameters of the switch — the number of interfaces, the interface description, the interface type, and the operational status of the interface — is called an object.

There are, of course, many other objects that are of interest when managing an ATM switch. Some of these objects are alterable, but there are many that cannot be changed. For example, an object called *sysDescr*, which provides a textual description of the system being managed, cannot be changed.

A software application, called an agent, runs on the switch that interacts with each object. An application on the NMS can query an object or configure it, if possible, through the agent. In this way, one can assume that the agent has an MIB [1], [3], [4]. It is important to mention here that the MIB is not a database in the ordinary sense of the term — the switch does not maintain a physical database, although when queried, the agent can collect information from the switch and report it to the management station. If necessary, the agent application on a managed node may automatically send the status to the network manager.

Some objects may have values, and in these cases, the particular value of an object is called an instance of the object. For example, an ATM switch may have many interfaces, and the user may like to know the operational status of, say, interface 3. This is referred to as instance 3 of the object called *ifOperStatus*.

The SNMP is an application-layer protocol, and in the case of TCP/IP-based networks, it uses the services of the transport and network layers to transfer messages to its peer. The physical- and link-layer protocols depend upon the medium used. The transport-layer protocol is chosen, generally, on the basis of the desired transport efficiency, and may depend upon the specific network management functions to be performed. For the basic network management functions, the protocol stack is shown in Figure 6-3(a), where the five operators of the SNMP protocol are explicitly indicated. They are:

- *get request.*
- *get-next.*
- *set.*
- *get response.*
- *trap.*

To understand how an NMS and its managed elements exchange management information in the SNMP protocol, refer to Figure 6-3(b). While the details may vary, the model of Figure 6-3(b) remains conceptually valid. Here, a managed entity (e.g., a switch) is represented as a collection of processes running on a hardware platform under a real-time operating system. Now, suppose that the user wants to know the system description of a vendor's particular ATM product. To this end, the NMS sends a *get request* message to the switch with the following operand:[1]

system.sysDescr

---

1. The meaning of this will be clearer later.

Figure 6-3   The SNMP protocol. (a) The protocol stack. (b) A functional model of the SNMP protocol implementation on the managed entity. This entity could be, for example, an ATM switch.

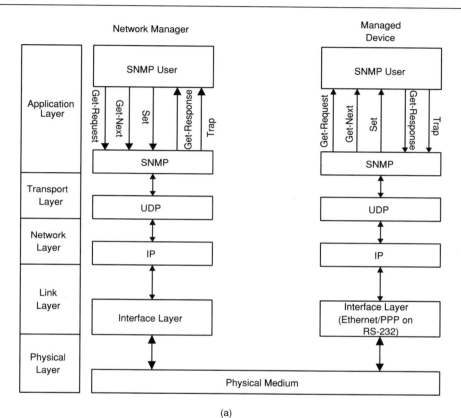

(a)

(b)

The encoded message is retrieved and decoded at various layers of the protocol (e.g., the link layer, IP layer, UDP layer, and SNMP layer), and is finally delivered to the agent process on the switch. Depending upon the product implementation, the agent process may or may not have the information. If it does not, it requests the information from the configuration management process, whereupon the latter collects the requested information and passes it to the agent process, which then sends it to the NMS.

If a vendor's product uses a proprietary management protocol instead of the SNMP standard and Internet Protocol suite, its agent process is required to perform additional functions — it must convert SNMP messages into its native protocol messages that it understands before it can exchange information with the management station. In a case like this, the agent is called a proxy agent.

get request

The purpose of this operator is to obtain the desired instance of an object. It is generally used when an object has a single instance. If the named instance exists, the agent returns a *get response* with the value of the variable properly set. Otherwise, it returns a *get response* with the *noSuchName* error. More than one object can be named in the operator.

get-next

The *get-next* operator is generally used when an object has multiple instances that are arranged in an array or table. When called with an appropriate operand, it obtains the instance of the object that is next to the named instance in the table. However, if it is used on an object that has a single instance, it returns an instance of an object that appears next to the named object in the MIB tree (see below). For example, suppose that we make the following call:

get-next(sysDescr.0)

Here, the NMS will receive *sysObjectID.0*, which is an instance of the next object in the tree after the *sysDescr* object. The suffix 0 in the operand *sysDescr.0* indicates the instance of the object. If we did not include this suffix, but simply made the call *get-next(sysDescr)*, the agent would have returned *sysDescr.0*, which is the name and value of the first instance of *sysDescr* in the tree. Thus, it is possible to see if a particular object is being managed in a device by simply naming that object as the operand of the *get-next* operator without including its instance.

The most common use of the *get-next* operator is in table traversal, i.e., obtaining the array of values assigned to an object. Suppose, for example, that a network element has a routing table. Each row of the table may contain a destination, the next hop, and a metric. By sending the *get-next* operator with known OBJECT IDENTIFIER values of the three objects — *ipRouteDest, ipRouteNextHop*, and *ipRouteMetric1* — as operands, the NMS can obtain the next entry of the table. The entire routing table can be read by repeating this command. If the command is repeated one more time after the table has been fully traversed, the agent will send the value of another object that is adjacent to the routing table in the MIB tree, and not the three objects covered in the table traversal.

An SNMP message contains exactly one operator. However, as we indicated in connection with the *get request* operator, more than one object can be included in the same message. In this case, each object name is a variable.

set

The purpose of the *set* operator is to set the named instance of an object to a desired value. On receiving this message, the agent checks to see if there is indeed any object by that name, if the named instance permits writing, or if the value is not too large or poorly constructed. If any of these errors is detected, a *get response* is returned with the appropriate error code. If there are no errors, each instance in the message is set to the indicated value, and a *get response* message is returned with the same value.

get response

The NMS, after receiving a *get response* message, checks to see if indeed a request was initiated that triggered this response. If it was, the NMS takes the appropriate action. Otherwise, it discards the response.

trap

A network manager should have the capability of capturing alarm conditions and displaying them to the user. There are two ways of doing this. One of them is polling, whereby a network manager can dial a list of managed nodes (e.g., remote ATM switches) and upload the alarm information, if any, from each of them. In fact, many networking devices provide the following two options for alarm polling: automatic and manual. In automatic polling, the user can set the day and time a polling sequence is to commence, the time interval between two consecutive polling sequences, the maximum number of call attempts to be made to each ATM switch in the event of unsuccessful calls, etc. In manual polling, the user can initiate a polling sequence at any time.

The other way of collecting alarm conditions is through an SNMP trap, which is somewhat similar to an interrupt in a processor environment. In this approach, when an extraordinary event occurs at a node, for example, if the ATM layer in a switch stops working, the agent could send a message immediately to the network manager rather than wait for its turn to be polled. This is called a trap. Normally, an option is provided in the managed node whereby the agent would only generate a trap if alarms have reached a certain threshold.

For a description of the UDP, TCP, IP, and interface-layer point-to-point protocol (PPP), see References [1], [12]–[14].

6.4.2 The Way an MIB is Organized

When sending a query to an agent about any object, it is first necessary to uniquely identify the object. To do this, all objects are arranged in a tree (see Figure 6-4). The tree consists of a number of nodes, connected by means of an edge (or a branch), and the associated "leaves." Each of the nodes has a label, and all, with the exception of *root*, have been assigned a number.

A node is called a group — for example, *system* below *mib-2* is a group, *interface* is another group, and so on. A leaf is an object. For example, the *system* group has seven leaves, or objects, one of which is *sysDescr*. A subtree corresponding to a node refers to all the nodes, branches, and leaves below the node. For instance, the *mib-2* subtree is composed of the nodes labeled *system, interfaces, snmp*, etc., and all the leaves associated with each of those nodes.

The first version of the MIB was defined in 1988 and was called MIB-1. Initially, it contained 114 objects arranged into 8 groups: *system, interfaces, address translation, IP, ICMP, TCP, UDP*, and *EGP*. An expanded version of this MIB was published in 1992 and was called MIB-2 [5]. It contained an extra 57 objects and 3 more groups.

Figure 6-4   MIB organization in the form of a tree.

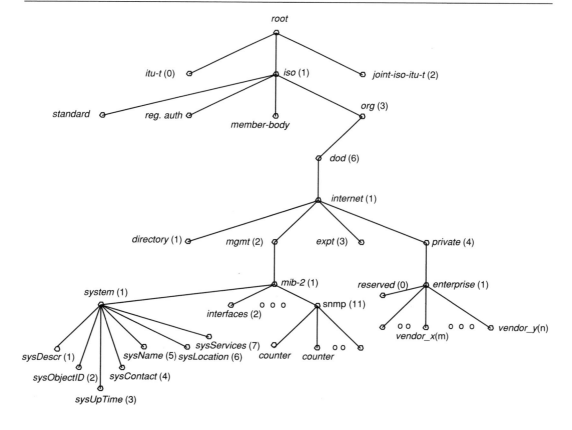

Figure 6-5   The interface subtree in the Internet MIB-II standard.

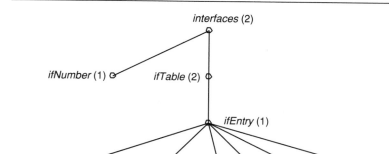

To specify an object in SNMP operation, an OBJECT IDENTIFIER is used. It is obtained by noting the nodes that one encounters while traversing from the root to the leaf representing the desired object, and is constructed by separating the label (or number) of each node by a dot. Thus, the OBJECT IDENTIFIER of the object called *sysDescr* in the *system* group under the *mib-2* subtree is

iso.org.dod.internet.mgmt.mib-2.system.sysDescr

when labels are used. Equivalently, the numerical identifier is 1.3.6.1.2.1.1.1.

The object *sysObjectID* is somewhat different from other objects. Its purpose is to find out what type of agent software is running on a vendor's product. If there is more than one instance of an object, it must be indicated in the object identifier. For example, suppose that a system has multiple interfaces of a given type. For clarity, the interface subtree is shown separately in Figure 6-5. If we want to query the object *ifOperStatus* of interface 3 in the system, then we must append 3 to the OBJECT IDENTIFIER of the object. Thus, the full OBJECT IDENTIFIER to be used in the query is

iso.org.dod.internet.mgmt.mib-
2.interfaces.ifTable.ifEntry.ifOperStatus.3

or numerically,

1.3.6.1.2.1.2.2.1.8.3

If all vendors are to use the SNMP standard to manage their equipment, it is necessary to avoid any duplication of object identifiers. To help accomplish this objective, the Internet Activities Board (IAB)[2] assigns each vendor a unique subtree. For example, a vendor could be assigned the following subtree:

1.3.6.1.4.1.2000

---

2. The Internet Activities Board is an administrative body that has authority over the *internet* and *enterprises* subtree, and assigns each equipment vendor that registers with it a unique subtree.

Each vendor then registers, under its assigned subtree, its own enterprise-specific MIBs for each of its different products. For example, suppose that the above vendor has registered one of its ATM switch products under the following subtree:

1.3.6.1.4.1.2000.2.1

If we now query the *sysObjectID* (i.e., send a *get request* with 1.3.6.1.2.1.1.2) using the MIB browser on this equipment, the agent will respond with, say,

1.3.6.1.4.1.2000.2.1.2

indicating that version 2 of the agent software is running on this product.

A standard format is used to define objects of the Internet standard. This format is known as the structure of management information (SMI). There are two versions of SMI: SNMPv1 and SNMPv2. In either case, each object is defined in Abstract Syntax Notation 1 (ASN.1). According to this notation, each object type has a name or an OBJECT IDENTI-FIER, a syntax, and an encoding. For example, consider the group called *system* in Figure 6-4. In ASN.1, we could identify *system* as

system OBJECT IDENTFIER ::= {mib-2 1}

which is the same thing as

1.3.6.1.2.1.1

In ASN.1 the object *sysUpTime* under the *system* group is

sysUpTime OBJECT-TYPE
SYNTAX INTEGER
ACCESS read-only
STATUS mandatory
::= {system 3}

As mentioned previously, the OBJECT IDENTIFIER is unique for each object type. The syntax for the object is its data type; for example, it may be an integer or an octet string. The encoding indicates how an instance of the object is to be represented as a data sequence so that it can be sent across the network.

6.5 ATM Network Management

An NMS can be connected to an ATM device either over a legacy LAN or directly over an ATM interface. In the first case, the managed device must be part of an emulated LAN. SNMP messages from the LAN emulation client, at the MAC layer, are converted into ATM cells using AAL Type 5 (see Chapter 8), using a pre-assigned VC. The ATM cells associated

Figure 6-6 A functional representation of NMS and managed ATM device based on ILMI.

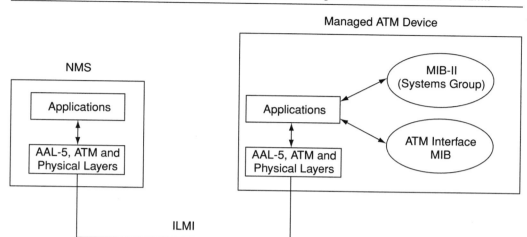

with that VC are forwarded to the client on the managed device which then decodes the various protocol layers — MAC, IP, UDP and SNMP — and sends an appropriate response.

The ATM Forum has specified a protocol called Integrated Local Management Interface (ILMI) that allows an NMS to be connected to a managed ATM device directly over an ATM interface [11].[3] This protocol defines an ATM interface MIB in terms of objects that describe ATM links, addresses registered, and LAN emulation services available, if any. As we shall see later, the managed objects applicable to an ATM interface may include the address of that interface, the transmission type, the media type, the number of VCs and VPs defined on each VC, etc. The ILMI protocol is simpler since it does not use the UDP/IP protocol. A functional representation of ILMI is shown in Figure 6-6. The application layer encodes SNMP messages directly into AAL-5, and then sends them via ATM cells in the usual way. An ATM device should implement the ATM interface MIB as defined by the ATM Forum. In addition, it should also implement the system group of the *mib-2* subtree that we described earlier.

When a private network is connected to a public network, there are many alternative ways of accessing a desired ATM device from an NMS. These are discussed in References [7]—[9]. In this section, we will present a brief description of ILMI. For details, the reader is referred to Reference [11].

---

3. To completely define an interface, one must, of course, specify not only the physical layer, but all upper layers as well.

6.5.1 The ATM Interface MIB

6.5.1.1 The Link Management MIB

The ILMI procedures are applicable whether the ATM device to be managed is connected to a public or private ATM network. The managed device could be an ATM workstation, an ATM switch, or even a traditional LAN router connecting to an ATM switch in an emulated LAN. Additionally, it may have one or more ATM interfaces, each with a number of VPCs and VCCs. Normally, for an ILMI, there should be one ATM interface MIB for each physical interface. However, if a managed entity has multiple interfaces (e.g., an ATM switch), it is possible to define a single MIB that is indexed for all interfaces.

In ASN.1 notation, the ATM interface MIB and its associated objects may be described as follows [11], [6]:

```
IMPORTS
        enterprises                     FROM RFC1155-SMI;
— a subtree for defining ATM Forum MIB object types
atmForum                                OBJECT IDENTIFIER ::= {enterprises 353}
— a subtree for defining ATM Interface MIB object types
atmForumUni                             OBJECT IDENTIFIER ::= {atmForum 2}
atmfPhysicalGroup                       OBJECT IDENTIFIER ::= {atmForumUni 1}
atmfAtmLayerGroup                       OBJECT IDENTIFIER ::= {atmForumUni 2}
atmfAtmStatsGroup                       OBJECT IDENTIFIER ::= {atmForumUni 3}
atmfVpcGroup                            OBJECT IDENTIFIER ::= {atmForumUni 4}
atmfVccGroup                            OBJECT IDENTIFIER ::= {atmForumUni 5}
atmfAddressGroup                        OBJECT IDENTIFIER ::= {atmForumUni 6}
atmfNetPrefixGroup                      OBJECT IDENTIFIER ::= {atmForumUni 7}
atmfSrvcRegistryGroup                   OBJECT IDENTIFIER ::= {atmForumUni 8}
atmfVpcAbrGroup                         OBJECT IDENTIFIER ::= {atmForumUni 9}
atmfVccAbrGroup                         OBJECT IDENTIFIER ::= {atmForumUni 10}
atmfAddressRegistrationAdminGroup       OBJECT IDENTIFIER ::= {atmForumUni 11}
```

In ILMI specifications, the term "link" indicates a physical interface, the attributes of the ATM layer, and the VCCs and VPCs defined on the interface. Table 6-1 lists objects included in the link management MIB.

The adjacency information object in the Physical Interface group indicates what other devices or nodes are adjacent to this particular entity, and is used by an NMS in auto-discovery and auto-configuration. The objects that provide this information include *atmfPortMyIfName, atmfPortMyIfidentifier, atmfMyIpNmAddress, atmfMyOsiNmNsapAddress* and *atmfMySystemIdentifier.*

The ATM Layer object ILMI version should be the latest ILMI version implemented on the interface. Similarly, the ATM Layer objects UNI signaling version and NNI signaling version should indicate their latest versions.

Table 6-1 Objects in the ILMI Link Management MIB

Group	Objects
Physical Interface	Interface index, interface address, transmission type, media type, physical layer operational status, port-specific information, adjacency information
ATM Layer	Interface index, maximum number of active VPI bits, maximum number of active VCI bits, maximum number of VPCs, maximum number of VCCs, number of configured VPCs, number of configured VCCs, maximum SVPC VPI, ATM interface type (public/private), ILMI version, UNI signaling version, NNI signaling version
Virtual Path	Interface index, VPI value, operational status, transmit traffic descriptor, receive traffic descriptor, best effort indicator, transmit QoS class, receive QoS class, service category
Virtual Path ABR	Interface index, VPI value, ABR operational parameters
Virtual Channel	Interface index, VPI/VCI value, operational status, transmit traffic descriptor, receive traffic descriptor, best effort indicator, transmit QoS class, receive QoS class, transmit frame discard indication, receive frame discard indication, service category
Virtual Channel ABR	Interface index, VPI/VCR value, ABR operational parameters
Traps	VPC change, VCC change

An ATM device should implement not only the above MIB, but also the *system* group under the *mib-2* subtree [7], [10]. As shown in Figure 6-4, there are seven objects in the *system* group. The meanings of these objects are self-explanatory. For example, the *sysServices* object indicates what kinds of services this entity provides. For instance, it could provide just the layer 1 function (e.g., a repeater), or layer 1 and layer 2 functions (e.g., an ATM switch), or layer 3 functions (e.g., an IP router), etc.

6.5.1.2 The Address Registration MIB

To set up a connection between a user device and a network over a UNI, it is necessary to know the ATM address of the called party. A UNI may be assigned one or more ATM addresses. The term "address registration" refers to procedures by which a user device and a network can exchange their ATM addresses.

In most cases, an ATM address consists of a user part and a network part. The user part has two components: the end system identifier (ESI) and the selector (SEL). The network part, known as the network prefix, is provided by the network itself. This is shown in Figure 6-7.

Figure 6-7 The ATM address at a UNI. It consists of 20 octets.

User Part		Network Part
ESI	SEL	Network Prefix

Table 6-2   The ATM Address Registration MIB. Copyright 1995 the ATM Forum.

Group	Objects
NetPrefix	Interface index, network prefix, network prefix status
Address	Interface index, ATM address status, ATM address organizational scope indication
Address Registration Admin	Interface index, address registration admin status

(See also Section 6, Chapter 3.) The address registration procedures allow for more than one user part and more than one network prefix at any UNI. In other cases, an ATM address consists entirely of the network part and is based on the numbering plans described in Recommendations E.164. An ATM device, whether on a public or private UNI, must support address registration.

The address registration MIB has three groups: NetPrefix, Address, and Address Registration Admin. Their objects are shown in Table 6-2.

The *atmfAddressStatus* object indicates whether or not the ATM address on an interface is valid, and can be set by sending a *set* message for the object. The *atmfAddressRegistrationAdminStatus* object indicates if the NetPrefix and Address groups are supported. Clearly, to be supported, the object must be supported on both sides of the interface. A network-side interface management entity (IME) can register its network prefixes with the user-side IME by issuing a series of *sets* and *get requests* (or *get-nexts*) and checking the *get responses* from the user-side IME. If it does not receive a *get response* message within a certain interval, it should retransmit its *set* message. The user-side IME may follow a similar procedure when it wishes to register its ATM address with the network.

6.5.1.3 The Service Registry MIB

If an ATM network emulates a LAN, the associated LAN Emulation Configuration Server (LECS) and ATM Name Server (ANS) can be located by means of the ATM service registry MIB. This MIB is an extension of the ATM interface MIB, and consists of two groups: *atmfServiceRegTypes* and *atmfServiceRegistryGroup*. The associated objects are shown in Table 6-3.

Table 6-3   The ATM Service Registry MIB

Group	Objects
atmfServiceRegTypes	*atmfSrvcRegLecs*—This object is the LECS *atmfSrvcRegAns*—This object is the ANS
atmfServiceRegistryGroup	*atmfSrvcRegTable*—This object is a list of all services available to the user-side IME, and is maintained by the network-side IME.

Actually, the object *atmfSrvcRegTable* itself is a group and contains one object type called *atmfSrvcRegEntry*, which in turn contains the following objects: *atmfSrvcRegPort, atmfSrvcRegServiceID, atmfSrvcRegATMAddress, atmfSrvcRegAddressIndex*, and *atmfSrvcRegParm1*.

6.5.2 The Protocol Stack in ILMI

Each ATM interface has an ATM IME that supports the ILMI functions. When two devices are connected across an interface, the two adjacent IMEs communicate with each other to exchange SNMP messages. Since the device on either side can originate an SNMP message, each IME contains an agent application and a management application. SNMP messages are encapsulated in AAL5 and sent out over ATM cells using VCI = 16 and VPI = 0. In this communication, UDP and IP protocols are not used. This is shown in Figure 6-8.

ILMI uses MIB-2, and as of now, it is based on SNMP version 1. The community name used in SNMP messages is "ILMI," or in terms of the OCTET STRING,

49 4c 4d 49 (hex)

In ILMI, only *coldStart* and *enterpriseSpecific* traps are supported. Other traps should not be used, and if they are used, they will be ignored at the receiving end. The maximum size of an SNMP message is 484 octets. Larger sizes can be used only via out-of-band negotiation.

ILMI uses the message mode service and assured operation of AAL5 with null SSCS. The CPCS-PDU, which contains the SNMP message sequence in its payload portion, has the

Figure 6-8   The protocol stack on two adjacent IMEs.

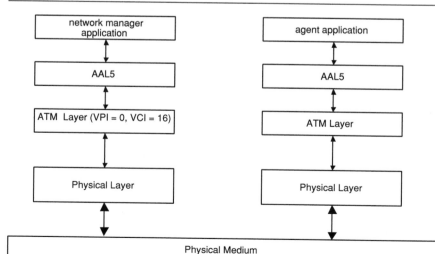

Figure 6-9 The CPCS-PDU format for AAL5.

CPCS-PDU Payload (CPCS-SDU)	PAD	CPCS-PDU Trailer			
Variable-length	0–47 octets	CPCS-UU 1 octet	CPI 1 octet	Length 2 octets	CRC 4 octets

format of Figure 6-9. The CPCS-UU field allows user-to-user information to be transported across the network transparently. Currently, it is only used to align the CPCS-PDU trailer to 64-bit boundaries. The length field indicates the number of octets contained in the CPCS-PDU payload. When set to zero, the receiver should interpret this as a request to abort. The 32-bit CRC is computed using the rest of the CPCS-PDU as the message polynomial.

The SAR sublayer performs straightforward segmentation without adding any header or trailer. As such, the 3-bit payload type (PT) field of the cell header is used to indicate the segment type. When a CPCS-PDU contains multiple segments, the ATM layer user-to-user (AUU) bit of the PT field is set to 0 for the first or any middle segment, and set to 1 for the last segment. If, on the other hand, a CPCS-PDU contains just one segment, that bit is set to 1. Additionally, the CLP bit is set to 0, the CI bit is set to 0, and the CPCS-UU octet of the CPCS-PDU is set to 0.

6.5.3 Auto-Discovery

Auto-discovery is a process whereby an ATM device such as a switch can determine what other devices it is connected to either directly or indirectly and use that information to generate a graphical view of the network containing those devices. The ILMI provides procedures that make auto-discovery possible. For example, recall that the ATM link management MIB contains objects that can be queried to build a table of adjacent systems. Furthermore, there are simple procedures for detecting the establishment and loss of a physical or logical connection.

Assuming that initially there is no connection, the IME will periodically[4] send a single *get request* or *get-next* for the following objects: *atmfPortMyIfidentifier, atmfMySystemIdentifier* and *sysUpTime*. If it receives a valid response from its peer IME, the link is assumed to be connected. At this point, the auto-configuration, and subsequently, the address registration process can begin.

Once a connection is established, the IME will periodically[5] check to see if the connection is still up by sending a single *get request* or *get-next* message. If there is no valid response, the IME will repeat the process four times. At the end, connectivity will be assumed to be lost.

---

4. The suggested period is 1s. The user might use a different value.
5. This period is 5s.

Similar procedures can be used to determine if an ATM device has been moved from one port to another. After a connection has been established across an interface, the IME on the desired end of this interface saves, in its memory, values of the above objects from its peer entity. It then periodically queries those objects and compares the returned values with the saved ones. If they do not match or if the received *sysUpTime* is less than the local copy, it will assume the old ILMI connection to be lost, release all SVCs that it controls, restart the interface, send a *coldStart* trap to its peer, assume that a new connection (to a different port or device) was established, and perform address registration if necessary.[6]

6.5.4 System Requirements

The ILMI specifications set some limits on the effective bandwidth used for management purposes and provide some performance guidelines. For example, the sustained and peak cell rates of the management traffic should be no more than 1% and 5% of the physical line rate, respectively. The agent should be able to respond to an SNMP operator (e.g., a *get request* operation requesting the value of a single object) within 1s about 95% of the time. When a management station queries an object, the value that the agent returns should be the latest value. In no case, however, should it be any older than 30s.

6.6 Summary

In this chapter, we showed how an ATM device can be managed. First, we described functions that a network management system is required to perform. Since SNMP is used to manage not only TCP/IP-based networks, but also ATM devices, we provided a comprehensive description of that protocol. SNMP is an application-layer protocol that runs on both the managed system and network manager. The managed device interacts with the network manager via a so-called agent process. The various parameters of a system to be managed are called objects. An NMS can query the status of an object using the SNMP operators—GET, GET NEXT, and SET. Similarly, the device being managed can report the status of an object by means of the GET RESPONSE and TRAP operators. We described these operators in detail. Managed objects are arranged in the form of a tree so that each of them can be uniquely identified in a query. We showed how these objects are arranged in an MIB.

An ATM network can be managed from an NMS over a legacy LAN. In this case, the managed device should be part of an emulated LAN. SNMP messages from a LAN emulation client at the MAC layer are converted into ATM cells using AAL-5 on a pre-assigned VC. Alternatively, the NMS can be connected to the managed ATM device over an ATM interface. In this case, procedures defined by the ATM Forum in ILMI can be used. We described the salient features of ILMI. More specifically, the ATM interface MIB, the protocol stack in ILMI, and auto discovery were described.

---

6. A private user or private node may automatically configure its ATM interface as a public UNI or private UNI.

6.7 References

[1] M. T. Rose, *The Simple Book*. Englewood Cliffs, NJ: Prentice Hall, 1991.

[2] J. Case, M. Fedor, M. Schoffstall, and J. Davin, "A Simple Network Management Protocol," RFC 1157, Network Working Group, May 1990.

[3] M. Rose and K. McCloghrie, "Structure and Identification of Management Information for TCP/IP-based Internets," RFC 1155, Network Working Group, May 1990.

[4] K. McCloghrie and M. Rose, "Management Information Base for Network Management of TCP/IP-based Internets: MIB-II," RFC 1213, Mar. 1991.

[5] K. McCloghrie and F. Kastenholz, "Evolution of the Interface Group of MIB-II," RFC 1573, Jan. 1994.

[6] M. Ahmed and K. Tesink, "Definitions of Managed Objects for ATM Management, Version 8.0 Using SMIv2," RFC 1695, Aug. 1994.

[7] The ATM Forum Technical Committee, "Customer Network Management (CNM) for ATM Public Network Service (M3 Specification)," af-nm-0019.000, Oct. 1994.

[8] The ATM Forum Technical Committee, "M4 Interface Requirements and Logical MIB," af-nm-0020.000, Oct. 1994.

[9] The ATM Forum Technical Committee, "CMIP Specification for the M4 Interface," af-nm-0027.000, Sept. 1995.

[10] The ATM Forum Technical Committee, "ATM Remote Monitoring SNMP MIB," af-nm-test-0080.000, July 1997.

[11] The ATM Forum Technical Committee, "Integrated Local Management Interface (ILMI) Specification," Version 4.0, af-ilmi-0065.000, Sept. 1996.

[12] M. Naugle, *Network Protocol Handbook*. New York: McGraw Hill, 1994.

[13] W. Simpson, "The Point-to-Point Protocol (PPP)," RFC 1661, July 1994.

[14] D. Rand, "The PPP Compression Control Protocol (CCP)," RFC 1962, June 1996.

Problems

6.1 A non-blocking ATM switch with a capacity of 650 Mb/s consists of four full-duplex, OC-3c, 155-Mb/s ATM ports, four DS-3 ATM, ports and four dedicated Ethernet ports as shown in Figure 6-P.1. Each input port is connected to a 16384-cell buffer. The switch supports a maximum of 2000 PVCs and SVCs, and provides ABR and UBR services. For congestion control, RM cells are used. An NMS is connected to the switch at an ATM interface port to (i) configure the system, (ii) detect faults, and (iii) monitor its performance on a per-port and per-VC basis using ILMI procedures.

Generate a list of the objects to be managed and indicate how they should be grouped so that they can be conveniently controlled. Assume that currently, Ethernet ports are not being used and that only the ATM ports are configured. See B. Boutaba and S. Znaty, "Integrated Network Management: From Concept to Application to ATM-Based Networks," *Globecom*, 1994, pp. 1409–1413.

Figure 6-P.1 An ATM switch being managed from an NMS connected at an Ethernet port.

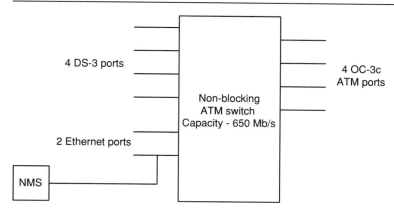

6.2 Construct messages corresponding to the five SNMP operators so that they can be transmitted over ILMI.

6.3 Repeat Problem 6.1 assuming that the switch only supports nrt-VBR and uses the EPD algorithm for congestion control.

6.4 Suppose that the switch in Problem 6.1 above is managed from an NMS over an Ethernet port as shown in Figure 6-P.1. Construct messages corresponding to the SNMP operators.

Circuit Emulation over ATM

7.1 Introduction

Many customer premises equipment (CPE) connect to a network over one or more DS1 or PRI interfaces. These networks are circuit-switched, and the information they carry consists of voice, data, image, and video. In many applications involving wide-area networking of geographically dispersed, private ATM networks, it is necessary to provide an interface between ATM and these circuit-switched telephone networks. Recall that ATM is a packet-switching protocol, and as such, causes variable delays. Circuit-switched information, on the other hand, is characterized by a constant bit rate (CBR) and generally cannot tolerate excessive variable delays or, for that matter, excessively long constant delays. However, the ATM protocol can be adapted to carry such delay-sensitive information. The procedure by which circuit-switched information can be transported across an ATM network without any of the significant variable delays that are inherent in a packet-switched protocol is called circuit emulation. In other words, circuit emulation provides transparent transport of circuit-switched information across an ATM network, ensuring that the delay introduced in this transport, if any, is constant. Circuit emulation procedures have been standardized by the ATM Forum [1]. The purpose of this chapter is to describe these procedures.

A common interface between a private network and a circuit-switched public telephone network is either a DS1 interface or a structured or unstructured E1 interface. The DS1 interface is a digital signal at 1.544 Mb/s with 24 time slots. It uses either D4 or ESF framing. In some cases, the interface can be a PRI, where time slot 24 is used for common channel signaling for the remaining time slots or for all 24 channels of one or more PRI interfaces. A structured E1 interface, on the other hand, operates at 2.048 Mb/s, each frame of the signal containing 32 time slots of which the first is used for framing and the sixteenth for signaling. Generally, an end-user device uses multiple channels of these interfaces. Bearer capabilities such as speech, 56-kb/s data, 64-kb/s unrestricted data, and $N \times 56$-kb/s or $N \times 64$-kb/s data are supported on a PRI interface.

Until recently, these interfaces have been primarily used for 64-kb/s PCM speech. Nowadays, however, they carry various types of user data which is generally embedded in some higher-layer protocols. For example, in video conferencing units, the information streams consisting of voice, video, and data are multiplexed onto one physical connection according to the ITU-T standard H.320. Here, all three information streams, depending on the applications, may use some compression algorithms that are also part of the standard. In any case, whether the information carried on the T1 channels is speech or digital data, the ATM network should emulate those channels such that the higher-layer protocols, if any, are preserved at the destination end-points.

For DS1 and E1 interfaces, it may be necessary for the emulation process to provide source clocking or timing information to the remote end-user equipment across the ATM network. Consider, for instance, Figure 7-1. For video conferencing, codec 1 must be connected to codec 2 across an ATM network. Interfaces IW-1 and IW-2 provide the interworking functions between the T1-based networks and the ATM network. If the two networks were directly connected via T1 facilities, and if there were no ATM network in between, one of them would be providing the system clock while the other would derive its clock from the incoming data stream. In the presence of the ATM network, suppose that the clock for IW-1 were derived from the T1 interface from Network 1. In that case, the ATM network would be synchronized with the latter. If the T1 timing on IW-2 were derived from the incoming ATM stream, the timing in all three entities — Network 1, the ATM network, and Network 2 — would all be phase-locked, and so in this case, there would be no need to send timing information via the ATM cells. But, if the clocks were not derived that way and as a result the T1 interface clock in Network 2 was not synchronized to the T1 clock in Network 1, the two networks could not stay in synch for long. In this case, the timing information would have to be sent from one network to the other. The circuit emulation procedure provides for the transfer of timing information across the ATM network.

Figure 7-1 Circuit emulation of a T1/PRI interface. IW-1 and IW-2 provide the interworking between a T1/ PRI and an ATM interface. The hubs perform switching and concentration. CPE may connect to the hub over a number of interface types. In this figure, only two interface types are shown—T1/PRI and RS-449. On the ATM network side, however, the interface is only T1/PRI. IW-1 and IW-2 perform circuit emulation.

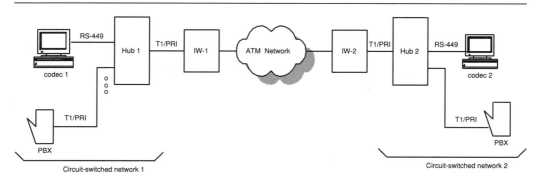

Similarly, the signaling bits and facility data link of the DS1 or E1 interface should be transported transparently across an ATM network so that the remote end-user equipment can continue to monitor the DS1/E1 link's quality and isolate faults.

Since DSI is a common interface, we shall describe circuit emulation procedures with reference to that interface. Other interfaces such as E1, J2, DS3, etc. or interfaces with non-standard framing are not specifically discussed, but can be emulated in a similar way.

7.2 Functions to Emulate

Suppose that an ATM network interconnects two traditional networks as shown in Figure 7-1. There are two interworking entities, IW-1 and IW-2, that provide the interface between a DS1 link and an ATM network. It follows from the previous discussion that for correct circuit emulation, it is necessary that the ATM cells be assembled at the source — say, IW-1 — and delivered to their destination in such a way that the signal quality of the DS1 facility is not affected or altered in any way by the spanning ATM network. For example, in Network 1, all frames on a DS1 link have a constant delay. Similarly, it is possible that the signal in Network 1 might have some framing or burst errors, or there could be a momentary loss of signal. The objective of ATM circuit emulation is to ensure that the DS1 signal at the output of IW-2 is exactly the same as the input to IW-1.

In what follows, we shall only consider point-to-point, fractional DS1 interfaces. We will also assume that the end-user equipment in the DS1 network uses standard framing.

The following parameters associated with a T1/PRI circuit are to be considered in circuit emulation over an ATM network.

- *Channels to be emulated* — $N \times 64$-kb/s bandwidth, where N can be any number between 1 and 24, inclusive. There may be a number of users that share the same physical DS1 interface, each assigned one or more channels. Referring to Figure 7-2, User 1 and User 2 might use Channels 1–6, whereas User 3 and User 4 might use only one channel, say, 13. In this case, the ATM network shall assign one VCI for Channels 1–6 and another for Channel 13.
- *Framing* — Both D4 and ESF framing are supported.
- *Signaling* — There are two service types: basic service and non-basic service. In basic service, only common channel signaling, as opposed to channel-associated signaling

Figure 7-2 Circuit emulation of two channel groups on the same T1/PRI interface—one used by User 1 and User 2 and the other by User 3 and User 4. For emulation, the interworking functions must use two separate VCIs.

(CAS), is used. In other words, signaling is done for all bearer channels over a separate channel that is dedicated for this purpose. An example is D channel signaling in an ISDN. In non-basic service, the CAS, or so-called robbed bit signaling, is used. In this case, the ATM network must be able to transport the signaling bits via the ATM cells without any modification.

- *Clocking* — The ATM network must be capable of providing the timing information so that the two DS1 networks connected by the ATM network are synchronized to each other, unless they are synchronized by some other means (e.g., timing information is obtained from a public network).

- *Facility Data Link (FDL)* — A two- or four-kHz facility data link can be created in a DS1 interface with ESF framing. The ATM network transports the FDL from one circuit-switched network to another. For this purpose, only DS1 links with ESF framing are supported. An FDL can also be created in a facility with D4 framing (e.g., SLC96). However, an FDL with D4 framing is not supported in this circuit emulation.

- *Alarms* — In a DS1 facility, the receiving end continually monitors the received signal for errors such as loss of framing, bipolar violations, the unframed all 1's condition, and loss of carrier. If any of these problems are detected, the DS1 facility informs the other end of the link. Consider Figure 7-3. Here, A, B, and C are three DS1 devices. Assume that in the received DS1 stream, B has detected an out-of-frame condition. This is called a red alarm condition. B continues to transmit normal operational frames to A. However, in these frames, it sets the yellow alarm to indicate to A that it has detected a loss of frame in the signal that it is receiving from A. In the SF mode, the yellow alarm is sent by setting bit 2 equal to 0 in all channels. In the ESF mode, it is sent by setting 16 repetitions of the 8 1's and 8 0's pattern on the data link. At the same time, B informs downstream device C of the loss of framing on the link from A by sending an unframed all 1's pattern. This is called a blue alarm condition. The same thing happens if the transmit link from A has developed a fault at point X in the figure, resulting in a loss of the received signal at B.

The interworking function must be able to transport these alarm conditions across the ATM network to the other DS1 circuit. In this case, the upstream IWF continues to

Figure 7-3 Emulating alarm conditions in a T1/PRI interface.

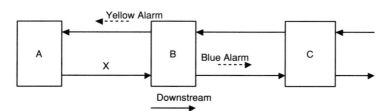

emit cells at the nominal rate, but sets the DS1 payload to an appropriate code to indicate an out-of-service condition. Furthermore, if signaling bits are being carried by the upstream IWF, it will insert the appropriate signaling code before AAL1 segmentation takes place.

- *Bit-oriented messages* — In the ESF mode, a separate channel (i.e., time slot 24) may sometimes be used to send the bit-oriented signaling messages for the remaining 23 bearer channels (e.g., Digital Multiplexed Interface). In this case, the IWF must terminate the bit-oriented messages for yellow alarms and loop back following the procedures of T1.403.

The goal is to do circuit emulation in such a way that both the end-to-end delay [1] from one DS1 interface through the ATM network to the other DS1 interface and the overall performance in terms of bit error rates, errored seconds, severely errored seconds, etc. are within the limits as specified by the application [2].

7.3 Emulation Procedure

In this emulation, procedure AAL1, as specified in ITU-T Recommendations I.363, is used. This procedure delineates repetitive, fixed-size "blocks" of data, each block being an integral number of octets in size. It is also used in the $N \times 64$-kb/s service to carry N DS0 time slots, organized into blocks.

7.3.1 64-kb/s Service

To emulate a single DS0 channel, the block size is clearly one octet. In this case, AAL1 provides block delineation merely by aligning each user octet with an ATM cell payload octet.

7.3.2 $N \times 64$ kb/s Structured without CAS

This circuit emulation is performed in the following way:

First, consider the emulation of an $N \times 64$-kb/s service of a structured interface (T1, PRI, E1, J2) without channel-associated signaling (CAS) bits. This is basic service. Here, the AAL depends on the application type. The circuit emulation that we are trying to perform involves constant bit rates. For this application, AAL1 is used.

For $N > 1$, a CS protocol that uses the concept of the structured data transfer (SDT) method has been defined for AAL1. This CS protocol for SDT uses a pointer to delineate structure boundaries. It will support any fixed, byte-oriented structure, and particularly an 8-kHz frame structure that is used in all DS1 or E1 interfaces. The procedure is best explained by an example.

Consider the case where we must emulate six contiguous time slots, say slots 1–6, of a DS1 interface that uses ESF framing without CAS signaling (i.e., A, B, C, and D signaling bits

Figure 7-4   The data block used to emulate a 6 × 64-kb/s circuit-switched channel of a DS1 interface with ESF framing. The block has 144 octets of data. This is the AAL-SDU.

Time slots 1–6 of Frame 1 of this ESF	Time Slots 1–6 of Frame 2 of this ESF	o o o	Time Slots 1–6 of Frame 24 of this ESF

are not used). Suppose further that in our emulation, we will preserve the ESF framing across the ATM network. First, in the user (or application) layer, a block of data is constructed by taking the first 6 octets corresponding to time slots 1–6 of Frame 1 of the ESF and placing them in byte positions 1–6 of the block. Next, from Frame 2 of the ESF, the first 6 octets are placed in byte positions 7–12, and so on until the first 6 octets from Frame 24 of the ESF have been inserted in byte positions 139–144. This is shown in Figure 7-4.

So, this block of data consists of 144 octets. It is passed on to the AAL as the AAL-SDU. The AAL consists of the CS and SAR sublayers. There are a number of functions that the CS performs in circuit emulation. Some of them are:

- It provides a means for tracking lost and misinserted cells.
- It provides a means for transferring the timing information so that the AAL-SDU can be delivered to the user at a constant bit rate, which is an essential feature in DS1 equipment.

The function of the SAR sublayer for this application is to take this rather large block of data (called the AAL-SDU), segment it into a number of smaller blocks, and then send the blocks out in a sequence. These smaller blocks are called SAR-PDUs, each of which has a total length of 48 octets.

At the transmitting end, the CS delivers a CS-PDU of 47 octets to the SAR sublayer, which adds one octet of header to it. The header is actually a sequence number (SN), which consists of a one-bit convergence sublayer indication (CSI), a three-bit sequence count (SC), a three-bit CRC, and one bit of parity (see Figures 7-5 and 7-6). The SC is modulo 8, starts with 0, and increments by 1 for each sequence. Normally, the 47-octet SAR-PDU payload, along with this header, would be passed on to the ATM layer as an ATM-SDU. However, the SDT method that is used here employs a slight variation of this normal procedure.

In this method, the first octet is still the SAR-PDU header, and every even-numbered SC (i.e., SC = 0, 2, 4, 6) uses a pointer in byte position 2 to indicate the start of the structure block. In the standards document [3], this is known as the P format, and it is shown in Figure 7-5. Every odd-numbered SC (i.e., SC = 1, 3, 5, 7), on the other hand, contains a 47-octet payload. The format of this SAR-PDU is called the non-P format, and it is shown in Figure 7-6.

Figure 7-5 The format of an SAR-PDU with an even-numbered SC in AAL1 for circuit emulation. This is called the *P* format.

Bit 8	7	6	5	4	3	2	1
CSI		SC			CRC		P
0		Pointer to First Octet, say *M*					
Fill Data - Octet 1							
Fill Data - Octet 2							
o							
o							
Fill Data - Octet *M*							
First Octet							

Figure 7-6 The format of an SAR-PDU with an odd-numbered SC in AAL1 for circuit emulation. This is called the non-*P* format.

Bit 8	7	6	5	4	3	2	1
CSI		SC			CRC		P
Payload Octet 1							
o							
o							
Payload Octet 47							

As shown in Figure 7-5, the pointer value M indicates an offset in bytes between the pointer field and the first octet of the structured block. Normally, M ranges from 0 to 92, inclusive. Clearly, the first octet of the user information (of this or the next SAR-PDU) will be positioned in this SAR-PDU if $M < 46$, and in the next SAR-PDU payload (i.e., in the next odd-numbered SC) if $M > 46$. Figure 7-7 shows the SAR-PDUs for CS = 0, . . . , 7, which are used to transmit the 144 octets of the ESF.

The CSI bit in the non-P format of Figure 7-6 over the four sequence counts (i.e., SC = 1, 3, 5, 7) can be used to carry the residual timestamp (RTS) to convey the information about the frequency difference between a common reference clock derived from the network and a service clock to the remote end.

The CSI bit of the P format in every even-numbered cell (i.e., CS = 0, 2, 4, and 6) is set to 1. Bit 8 of the pointer field octet is reserved for future use and is set to 0. Following the CS specifications of AAL1, a Structure Data Transfer (SDT) pointer is inserted at the first opportunity in a cell with an even SC value. The fill octet is generally all 1's.

The CSI bit in odd-numbered cells (i.e., CS = 1, 3, 5, and 7) may be used to transfer in-

Figure 7-7   The format of the SAR-PDUs used to transmit the 144 octets of user information of an ESF.

Bit 8	7	6	5	4	3	2	1
CSI	SC = 0, 2, 4, 6			CRC			P
0	Pointer Value M = 57 (decimal)						
46 'Fill' Octets							

CSI	SC = 1, 3, 5, 7			CRC			P
11 'Fill' Octets							
36 Octets of User Information							

formation about the data structure or timing information. In the latter case, the synchronous residual timestamp (SRTS) is used to indicate the frequency difference between a common reference clock derived from the network clock and a service clock.

The SC value in the header field allows lost or misinserted cells to be detected at the receiving end. However, since the maximum value of this field is 7, if 8 or more contiguous cells are lost, they will not be detected. The three-bit CRC is computed on the CSI and SC bits. Its generator polynomial is

$$G(x) = x^3 + x + 1$$

The P bit is the even parity bit on the SAR-PDU header.

7.3.3 $N \times 64$ kb/s with CAS

For $N \times 64$-kb/s channels with CAS, the necessary signaling bits are embedded in the superframe. Thus, the payload part of the structure in the CAS mode is one superframe in length. And, with ESF framing, the payload part of the AAL1 structure is $N \times 24$ octets in length. For D4 framing, it is $N \times 12$ octets in length.

As an example, consider the case where we must emulate six contiguous time slots, say slots 1–6, of a DS1 interface with ESF framing with A, B, C, and D bit signaling. Since a signaling bit for any time slot appears in every sixth frame of a superframe, one must wait for an entire ESF to assemble the necessary four signaling bits of any time slot. In this case, the data block has two parts. The first part, called the payload substructure, contains the octets of the bearer channels. The second part contains the signaling bits. For the first part, the first 6 octets of Frame 1 of an ESF are placed in byte positions 1–6 of the block. Next, from Frame 2 of the

Figure 7-8 The data block for emulating six contiguous channels in a PRI interface (with CAS signaling).

Time Slot 1 of Frame 1	
Time Slot 2 of Frame 1	
Time Slot 3 of Frame 1	
Time Slot 4 of Frame 1	
Time Slot 5 of Frame 1	
Time Slot 6 of Frame 1	
Time Slot 1 of Frame 2	
Time Slot 2 of Frame 2	
Time Slot 3 of Frame 2	
Time Slot 4 of Frame 2	
Time Slot 5 of Frame 2	
Time Slot 6 of Frame 2	
o	
o	
o	
Time Slot 1 of Frame 24	
Time Slot 2 of Frame 24	
Time Slot 3 of Frame 24	
Time Slot 4 of Frame 24	
Time Slot 5 of Frame 24	
Time Slot 6 of Frame 24	
ABCD Bits of Time Slot 1	ABCD Bits of Time Slot 2
ABCD Bits of Time Slot 3	ABCD Bits of Time Slot 4
ABCD Bits of Time Slot 5	ABCD Bits of Time Slot 6

ESF, the first 6 octets are placed in byte positions 7–12, and so on until the first 6 octets from Frame 24 of the ESF have been inserted in byte positions 139–144.

The second part, called the signaling substructure, contains the signaling bits — in this example, the A, B, C, and D signaling bits — of the multiframe. As shown in Figure 7-8, an octet is formed with the signaling bits of time slots 1 and 2, and is placed in byte position 145. Two other octets are similarly formed for time slots 3–6 and placed in the last two byte positions, 146 and 147.

The format of the SAR-PDU for this application is the same as in Figure 7-7 for CS = $0, \ldots, 5$. For CS = 6 and 7, the format is shown in Figure 7-9.

If the number of time slots to be emulated, N, is odd, bits 4–1 of the last octet of the signaling substructure are unused and set to 0.

In D4 framing, a superframe consists of 12 frames. Here, only the A and B bits are used for signaling. Hence, in this case, the payload substructure is $n \times 12$ octets in length, but is otherwise constructed in the same way. Depending on the number of time slots to be emu-

Figure 7-9 The format of the SAR-PDUs used to transmit the last 39 octets of the data block of Figure 7-8.

Bit 8	7	6	5	4	3	2	1
CSI	SC = 6			CRC			P
0	Pointer Value M = 54 (decimal)						
46 'Fill' Octets							

CSI	SC = 7			CRC			P
8 'Fill' Octets							
39 Octets of User Information							

lated, the signaling substructure may contain one or more octets, and it may be necessary to pad them with zeros at the least-significant-bit positions.

For $N \times 64$ kb/s on an E1 interface with G.704 framing, the data block is constructed in the same way except that the payload substructure is $N \times 16$ octets long. The signaling substructure is built the same way.

7.4 An Example of Circuit Emulation— Voice and Telephony Over ATM (VTOA)

An example of circuit emulation is voice and telephony over ATM (VTOA). Recently, the ATM Forum has adopted a standard [5] that defines how two end-points of an N-ISDN or traditional PSTN can be connected together over an ATM network for 64-kb/s voice and telephony services. To provide interoperability between an ATM and a non-ATM network for voice services, the Forum makes use of an IWF. This is shown in Figure 7-10. Here, the entity

Figure 7-10 Voice and telephony over ATM. Here, two N-ISDN end-points connect over an ATM network.

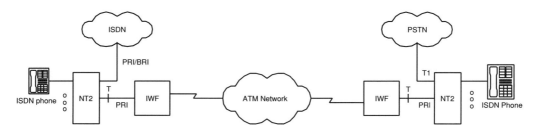

Figure 7-11   Protocol stacks showing the functionalities of the IWF used in VTOA.

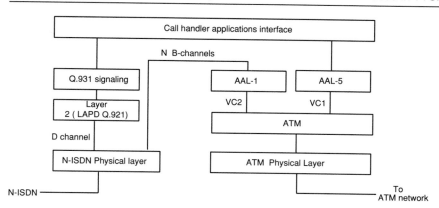

marked NT2 would normally be connected to an N-ISDN over a PRI interface using the so-called 64-kb/s D channel for out-of-band signaling according to specifications Q.931 and one or more bearer channels for voice (i.e., the B channels). An example of an NT2 is a PBX. The IWF may be implemented as part of NT2, as a line interface module of an ATM switch, or as a stand-alone device.

The IWF must perform two things. First, it must convert the Q.931 or CAS of the narrow-band circuit-switched network into ATM signaling, and vice versa. The AAL protocol for signaling is AAL5. Second, it must convert the circuit mode voice into ATM cells, and vice versa. The format used for this purpose is the one specified for AAL1 for circuit emulation.

The above conversion functions performed by the IWF for an N-ISDN are based on the protocol stack of Figure 7-11, where the signaling procedures are represented by the outer stacks and the bearer channel functions by the middle. The ATM signaling messages from one IWF to the other are transported over one VCC and the B channel voice over another. The two VCCs are carried over the same physical channel to the ATM network. For a more detailed description of the signaling procedures required in VTOA, refer to Chapter 3.

7.5 Generating Source Clock Information

When a customer's network consists of two or more T1-based subnetworks, it is necessary to have a single, coherent clock so that events in different parts of the network can be synchronized. Normally, it is not difficult to achieve this goal since one subnetwork could act as the master and drive the timing in the rest of the network. Suppose, however, that two T1-based networks are connected over ATM interfaces and that the ATM clock is not driven by either. In this case, to maintain a single clock in the two T1-based networks, the ATM network must measure the source clock frequency and convey it to the destination. The AAL protocol provides the means for doing this [3].

Clearly, one could continuously measure the source clock and transmit its value (in Hertz) to the receiving end. Since this value would be generally large,[1] and since this information must be regularly transmitted, it would take up a significant portion of the ATM cell's payload. Moreover, it is not really necessary if there is a network-derived clock at the source and destination. In this case, it would be sufficient to monitor only a certain number of the service clock cycles, measure the variation, and send that information to the remote end over the ATM cells. This procedure is known as the SRTS method.

Assume that we monitor only N cycles of the service clock at the sending end and measure their fluctuations. At the nominal service clock, f_{snom}, this would be contained in a period $T = N/f_{snom}$. The frequency variations are measured using a network-derived signal of frequency, say, f_r. Hence, the number of cycles M at frequency f_r contained in period T is given by

$$M = N\frac{f_r}{f_{snom}}$$

This is depicted in Figure 7-12. Suppose now that the service clock frequency, f_s, has decreased by a fraction, x. In other words, this frequency is now $f_{snom}(1 - x)$. If we continue to monitor exactly N cycles of the service clock as before, clearly they will occupy a period longer than T, and hence the service clock frequency variation will be given by y cycles of f_r, where y is

$$y = Nx\frac{f_r}{f_{snom}}$$

The above parameter, y, can be measured using the circuit of Figure 7-13. The p-bit counter should be selected so as to measure the largest expected variation in the service clock. Hence, the following relation should hold:

$$2^p - 1 > y$$

If y is not a whole number, it is rounded off to the next highest integer. As an example, assume that $N = 4096$. Also, suppose that the maximum value of x is 200×10^{-6} (i.e., 200 parts per million) and $f_r/f_{snom} = 16$. In this case, $y = 13.1$ and hence, $p = 4$. In other words, we should use a 4-bit counter. If the service clock does not fluctuate, then the output of the p-bit counter will be zero and the receiving end should make no adjustment to its clock. If the clock has decreased by, say, 100 parts per million, the 4-bit counter will count modulo 16 exactly 4096 times

---

1. For example, if the service clock is 64 kb/s, it would be 16 bits long.

Figure 7-12 Computing the variation in the service clock frequency. Only N cycles of the service clock are monitored. If the frequency changes by a fraction, x, there will be a change of Nx cycles in the number of service clock cycles, N.

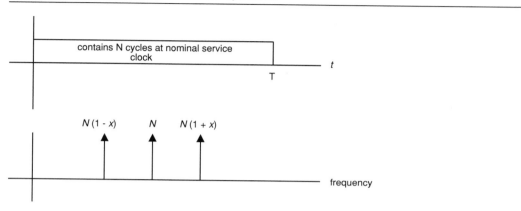

Figure 7-13 The circuit used to measure the variation in the service clock.

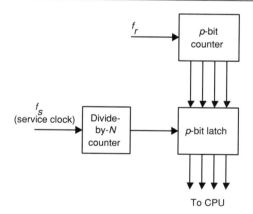

and then 6. In other words, its output will be 6. This output is called the RTS, and it should be transmitted to the receiving end for adjusting its clock.

As mentioned in Section 7.3.2, the RTS value is transmitted to the remote end using the CSI bits of the odd-numbered SAR-PDUs. In other words, the CSI bit of the SAR-PDU with SC = 1 will be set to bit 1 (i.e., the most significant bit) of the RTS. Similarly, bit 2 of the RTS is sent via the CSI bit of the SAR-PDU with SC = 3, and so on.

Figure 7-14   Recovery of the source clock at the receiving end using the RTS.

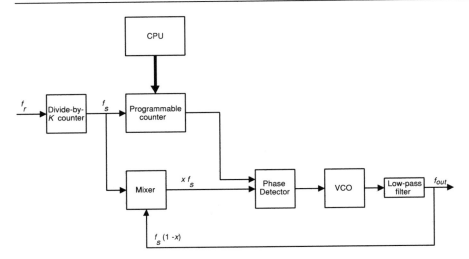

7.6 Clock Recovery at the Receiving End

Figure 7-14 is a block diagram of the clock recovery system that uses the RTS obtained from the source [4] at the receiving end. It is assumed that the network-derived clock, f_r, available at both ends, is Kf_s. Thus, f_s is obtained by dividing f_r by K. The programmable counter is used to derive the desired frequency offset of the clock at the receiving end. The CPU programs this counter based on the received value of the RTS.

The frequency, f_s, is mixed with the output, $f_s(1 - x)$, of the phase-locked loop. The output of the mixer, xf_s, and the output of the programmable counter are applied to the input of the phase detector whose output signal then feeds into the VCO. Since the output of the mixer may have harmonics, it may be necessary to use a higher-order low-pass filter. This may result in a smaller loop bandwidth. Hence, if the frequency offset is too large, the loop might take too long to lock, or, in an extreme case, might even be outside the pull-in range [4].

Another alternative method described in Recommendations I.363 is known as the adaptive clock method, whereby the receiver writes the received data into a buffer and clocks it out using a local clock. It measures the fill level of the buffer with respect to its median value and uses that value to adjust the VCO input.

7.7 Summary

The process by which circuit-switched information can be transported across an ATM network without any of the significant variable delays that are inherent in a packet protocol is called circuit emulation over ATM. For correct circuit emulation, it is necessary that the ATM cells be assembled at the source and delivered to the destination such that the information content and signal quality of the channels being emulated are not affected or altered in any way.

Circuit emulation procedures described in this chapter are based on the ATM Forum standard. Since DS1 is a common interface, emulation procedures are described with reference to that interface. Other interfaces such as E1, J2, DS3, E3, and so on are not discussed. However, they can be emulated in a similar way.

Parameters that should be considered when emulating multiple DS0 channels of a DS1 interface include framing, common channel and channel-associated signaling, facility data link, alarms, and bit-oriented messages. We presented the emulation procedures in some detail, and in particular, discussed how voice and telephony can be transported over ATM using circuit emulation. If two T1 networks are connected across an ATM network, the timing information from the source should be provided to the destination so that the two T1 networks remain synchronized to each other. Procedures to generate the clock information at the source and recover it at the receiving end were described.

7.8 References

[1] The ATM Forum, "Circuit Emulation Service Version 2.0," af-vtoa-0078.000, Jan. 1996.

[2] ANSI T1.510, "Network Performance Parameters for Dedicated Digital Services — Specifications," 1994.

[3] ITU-T Recommendation I.363, "Broadband ISDN ATM Adaptation Layer (AAL) Specification," Mar. 1993.

[4] F. M. Gardner, *Phaselock Techniques*. New York: John Wiley & Sons, pp. 40–46 and 104–106, 1966.

[5] The ATM Forum, "Voice and Telephony Over ATM — ATM Trunking for Narrowband Services," BTD-VTOA-LLT-01.11, Feb. 1997.

Problems

7.1 Figure 7-P.1(a) shows how a campus network could be connected to an ATM backbone. It consists of a PBX that provides circuit-switched voice and data connections, an Ethernet, and an IBM token ring LAN. The router performs interworking and routing functions, and also provides concentration of the various inputs. In a modular design, the router/concentrator may consist of a number of interface cards, say one for the PRI interface, a second one for an Ethernet port, a third one for a token ring, another for a DS3 interface of an ATM link, and so on. A functional block diagram of the router/concentrator for a PRI interface is shown in Figure 7-P.1(b). Suppose that this card is to provide circuit emulation for the 23 B-channels of the PRI interface. However, it must convert the signaling information of the D-channel into Q.2931 procedures for the ATM interface. Write a requirements document for this interface card so that it can be used by designers in the subsequent design process.

Figure 7-P.1 A campus network connected to an ATM backbone. (a) A PBX and LANs connected to an ATM network through an ATM router and concentrator. (b) A functional block diagram of an ATM router/concentrator for a PRI interface.

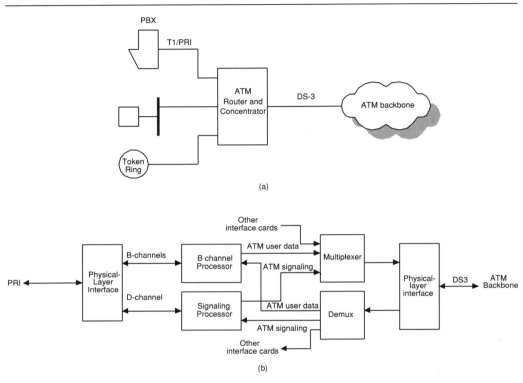

(a)

(b)

7.2 For the interface card of Problem 7.1, provide a detailed specification of the B-channel processing functions so that it can be used in the implementation phase of the design.

7.3 Repeat Problem 7.2 for the signaling function, assuming that the B-channels of the PRI interface are being used for VTOA.

7.4 Suppose that the interface between the PBX and ATM router/concentrator is a DS1 link where A and B bit signaling is used for all 24 channels of the interface. The DS1 interface must be circuit-emulated. Provide a detailed specification of this interface card.

LAN Emulation over ATM

8.1 Introduction

Currently, most networking equipment in the market allows various types of networks with different applications to be interconnected rather seamlessly. The protocol stack used in to-day's networks is depicted in Figure 8-1, which also shows how its different layers correspond to the OSI protocol model. At the core of these protocols are the Internet's transport-layer protocol, TCP, and the network-layer protocol, IP.

The typical applications on an end-user device on a traditional LAN[1] generally use such protocols as FTP, SMTP, SNMP, etc. Other common application-layer protocols include APPN, NetBIOS, IPX, and AppleTalk. Since there is a huge investment in the existing networks and software for these protocols, it makes sense to continue to use them as long as possible and move to ATM networks only when and where needed. For example, an enterprise network may use ATM as the backbone, while the local networks continue to be Ethernet 802.3 or IBM token rings. Similarly, ATM workstations can replace the slower workstations in a workgroup. In all of these cases, it is desirable to use the same applications and networking protocols on the ATM end-points because the end-points would then be able to communicate not only with similar equipment across the ATM network, but also with devices running the same applications and protocols behind traditional LANs. LAN emulation helps us achieve that goal.

LAN emulation is an ATM service that emulates a traditional LAN. The entity that provides this service is generally implemented in software, and may be incorporated in an ATM switch. To understand how LAN emulation works, consider Figure 8-2. Figure 8-2(a) shows a legacy LAN connected to an ATM host through an Ethernet-ATM bridge. The host may be just a stand-alone ATM host, or it may be part of a larger ATM backbone network. Figure 8-2(b) describes the functional entities that are required in the bridge and the ATM host, in addition to their usual functions. Suppose that the bridge gets an IP packet that has to be forwarded to the ATM host from an Ethernet end-point. On receipt of the packet, the

---

1. Also referred to as a legacy LAN.

Figure 8-1 The commonly used protocol stack. See how its different layers correspond to the OSI model.

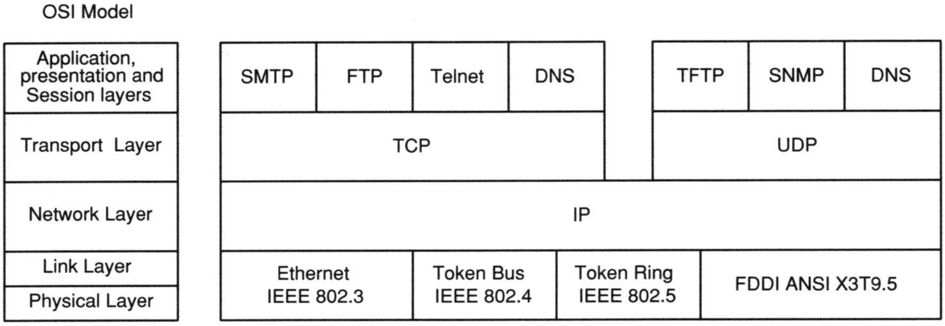

OSI Model

Application, presentation and Session layers	SMTP	FTP	Telnet	DNS		TFTP	SNMP	DNS
Transport Layer	TCP					UDP		
Network Layer	IP							
Link Layer / Physical Layer	Ethernet IEEE 802.3		Token Bus IEEE 802.4		Token Ring IEEE 802.5		FDDI ANSI X3T9.5	

SMTP - Simple Mail Transfer Protocol
FTP - File Transfer Protocol
DNS - Domain Name Server
TFTP - Trivial File Transfer Protocol
SNMP - Simple Network Management Protocol
TCP - Transmission Control Protocol
UDP - User Datagram Protocol
IP - Internet Protocol

bridge passes it to the LAN emulation client (LEC), whereupon the LEC requests services from the LAN emulation service entity of the ATM host, which then tries to forward the packet to the destination. For this to be possible, both the LEC and emulation service entity must run a set of LAN emulation protocols so that an ATM end-point can interwork with devices on traditional LANs. In this case, we say that the ATM network is emulating a LAN.

We have used the term "emulation service entity" rather loosely here to include all functions that are needed on the host to provide the emulation service to the client. Later on, we shall be more precise and describe its different functions. Also, notice that, in this figure, the emulation service entity has been shown as part of the ATM host. It does not have be implemented that way; in fact, it can be provided as a stand-alone entity. The same applies to the LEC.

Figure 8-3 gives an example of a very general network configuration that includes more than one Ethernet LAN segment connected by IEEE 802.1D transparent bridges.

The LAN emulation (LANE) protocol was developed by the LAN Emulation Sub Working Group (SWG) of the ATM Forum. The SWG began its work in the fall of 1993, and published the LAN Emulation Specification Version 1.0 in February 1995 [1]. The group has continued its work on the next generation of the specification [2], [3].

The LAN emulation protocol has been designed such that the inherent high-speed and low-latency features of an ATM network are not compromised. Also, it allows ATM end-

Figure 8-2 LAN emulation of an Ethernet segment. (a) An Ethernet-ATM bridge is connected to an ATM host, which is part of an ATM network. (b) The functional entities of the bridge and the ATM host. To invoke LAN emulation, the bridge must have an additional functionality called the LEC that requests the emulation service. There is a corresponding functionality—the LAN emulation server—in the ATM host that responds to the client request. The LEC and the emulation server on the host run a set of LAN emulation protocols to ensure that any station attached to the Ethernet can communicate to the ATM host as if the host were directly connected on the Ethernet segment.

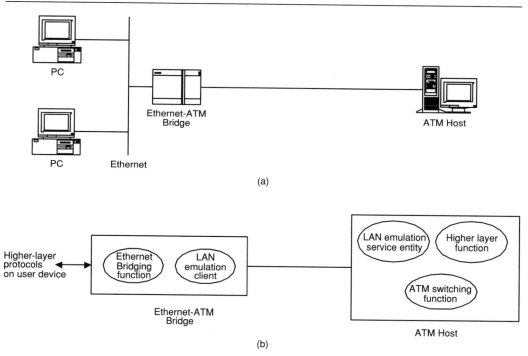

points such as high-end workstations, ATM hosts, etc. to be connected to multiple LAN segments, and provides support for a wide range of upper-layer protocols. As we shall show later, this protocol transparency is achieved by interfacing the emulation protocol to the MAC layer. In other words, it is the MAC layer frame that is passed to the emulation protocol for eventual transmission on an ATM link.

LAN emulation does not perform protocol conversion. In other words, an ATM cell in an emulated Ethernet LAN cannot be exchanged with an ATM cell in an emulated token ring LAN. Consider Figure 8-4, where ATM Network 1 emulates an Ethernet LAN and ATM Network 2 emulates a token ring LAN. ATM Host 1 can communicate across ATM Network 1 with an end-user behind the Ethernet. However, it cannot communicate with an end-user

Figure 8-3   LAN emulation of multiple Ethernet segments.

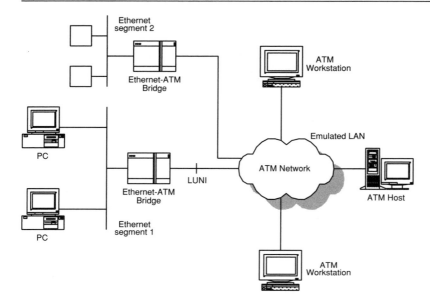

behind the token ring or with ATM Host 2, because, for this to be possible, it would be necessary to provide a protocol conversion. Such conversion must take place in an Ethernet-token ring router before MAC frames are passed to the emulation layer of the protocol stack described in Section 8.4.

Version 1.0 of the LAN emulation specification is designed to support both Versions 3.0 and 3.1 of the ATM Forum's UNI, and provides for both PVCs and SVCs. This specification identifies

- Protocols governing physical and upper-layer ATM interfaces.
- Signaling between ATM end systems (e.g., the ATM-Ethernet bridge, the ATM host, and the PC in Figure 8-2) and public and private ATM networks.
- ATM-layer management.

Applications or protocols that are media-dependent, such as SMT/Token Management and CSMA/CD, are not supported. ATM has its own protocol for media access, and thus LAN media access methodologies such as ring arbitration or collision detection in a carrier-sense multiple access scheme do not apply.

The purpose of this chapter is to present a comprehensive description of the LAN emulation procedures as specified in [1]. An attempt has been made to provide details that would be useful to designers.

Figure 8-4 This diagram shows that two ATM networks, one emulating an Ethernet LAN and the other a token ring LAN, cannot be connected together.

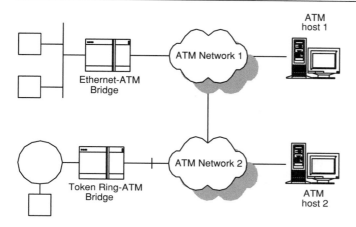

8.2 Emulated LAN Types

LAN emulation over ATM supports the two most widely used MAC layer types : Ethernet/ IEEE 802.3 and Token Ring/IEEE 802.5.

8.2.1 Ethernet LAN

An Ethernet LAN segment is connected to an ATM network through an Ethernet bridge. It is called a learning bridge because it constantly monitors all frames that appear on the LAN segment to which it is attached and "learns" the MAC addresses of all stations that are attached to the LAN. It saves that information in its database, uses it to filter packets received on the LAN, and also provides the same information to remote bridges across the ATM network. In the event of any changes, it will update its own database and also update the remote bridges. The Ethernet bridge is transparent because it does not get involved in specifying the route that a forwarded packet is to take. The topology of these bridges should be that of a spanning tree. In other words, there should be one and only one route between any two LAN stations. The IEEE 802.3 frame format is shown in Figure 8-5. Figure 8-6 gives an Ethernet frame format.

Figure 8-5 IEEE 802.3 MAC frame format.

Preamble (1010..) 7 octets	Start Frame Delimiter 1 octet	Destination Address 2 or 6 octets	Source Address 2 or 6 octets	Length 2 octets	LLC Data	Pad, if any	FCS 4 octets

Figure 8-6   Ethernet frame format.

Preamble (1010..) 62 bits	SYNC 2 bits (11)	Destination Address 6 octets	Source Address 6 octets	Type 2 octets	Data 46 – 1500 octets	FCS 4 octets

8.2.2 Token Ring LAN

A token ring bridge, on the other hand, may be either a transparent bridge or the more common type, a **source routing bridge**. A source routing bridge routes a frame on the basis of routing information included in the frame that it receives. Thus, it is not a transparent bridge. Since source routing bridges are an important part of an emulated LAN over the ATM, it is worthwhile to digress here and provide a brief introduction to them.

The IEEE 802.5 token ring frame format is shown in Figure 8-7. The address field may consist of either two or six octets, but all stations in a LAN segment must have the same length. The generic structure of a 6-octet address field is shown in Figure 8-8. If it is a source address, the first bit, namely the I/G bit of the figure, is unused and set to 0, except when providing the routing information in source routing (see below). If it is a destination address, the I/G bit, when set to 0, indicates an individual address of a station. When this bit is set to 1, it indicates a group address of a number of stations. The U/L bit indicates how the addresses are administered — if 0, they are administered universally by an agency such as IEEE, and if 1, they are administered locally.

In source routing, the routing information (RI) must be included in a MAC frame. Since this information is not present in situations that do not involve routing, it is necessary

Figure 8-7   IEEE 802.5 token ring frame format. The starting delimiter and access control constitute the start-of-frame sequence. The end-of-frame sequence is the ending delimiter and frame status.

Starting Delimiter 1 octet	Access Control 1	Frame Control 1	Destination Address 2/6	Source Address 2/6	Information Field	FCS 4	Ending Delimiter 1	Frame Status 1

Figure 8-8   The 6-octet MAC address field.

I/G 1 bit	U/L 1 bit	Remaining Address Field 46 bits

to indicate when this information is or is not included in the frame. This is done by means of the I/G bit in the source address. Thus, if the frame contains the routing information, this bit is set to 1; otherwise, it is set to 0.

The RI field, when included, is an additional field inserted between the source address and the information field. For IBM token rings, it consists of up to 18 octets, of which the first two constitute the routing control (RC). The remaining 16 octets form a string of eight routing descriptors (RDs), and provide the addresses of ring-bridge pairs that a frame originating from its source must pass through to reach its destination. The RI field is shown in Figure 8-9.

When a device attached to a ring segment wants to send a frame to another device that is attached to a different ring via bridges, it includes the 18-octet routing information field. When a bridge receives a frame, it checks to see if a bridge address included in the routing information field matches its own number. If it does, it routes the frame to the next ring associated with the bridge-ring pair.

Figure 8-9 The routing information field in a source routing frame. (a) Details of the 2-octet control field. (b) The routing descriptor.

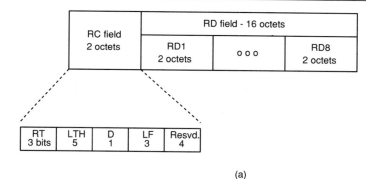

(a)

RT (routing type) - Indicates the type of route.
0xx - Specific route through the network.
10x - Frame to be routed along every unique route from source to destination. Route descriptors are added as the frame traverses.
11x - Spanning tree explorer frame. Frame appears only once on a ring. Route descriptors are added as frame traverses.

LTH (length) - Number of octets in the RD field.

D (direction) bit - Indicates if the frame traverses the network in the forward or reverse direction as specified by the route descriptors.

LF (largest frame) - Indicates the maximum size of a supported frame.

LAN ID - 12 bits	Bridge number - 4 bits

(b)

For LAN emulation, the formats have been modified to support larger frame sizes. According to the specification, frames longer than 0×800 bytes may be encoded with a length of 0 because the true length may be extracted from the AAL5 length indicator. With this change, it is now possible to run ATM-emulated LANs at very large frame sizes — up to 18K in length. Note however, that if an emulated LAN is running with a "non-standard" frame size, bridges must be replaced by routers because segmentation and reassembly may be needed as part of the protocol requirements.[2]

8.3 Functions Performed in Emulation

To provide for LAN emulation over ATM, it is necessary to have additional functionalities in the ATM network, as well as at the ATM end-points. To understand these requirements, refer to Figure 8-10. Here, ATM devices and Ethernet end-points communicate with each other via LAN emulation service entities of the emulated LAN.[3] On the LAN side, the bridge must continually monitor all LAN traffic. If a packet is received in error or if the received frame exceeds the permissible size, it is discarded. Similarly, the frame is thrown away if the bridge has run out of its internal buffers. In all other cases, it will accept the received frames and learn the MAC addresses of the devices attached to the LAN. These addresses are stored in the local database of the bridge, and are also "registered" with the emulated LAN, which then saves them in its database. These databases must be continually updated whenever a station is added to the LAN or removed from the LAN so that data packets can be correctly forwarded to their destination across the emulated LAN. When a bridge receives a unicast frame from the LAN side with a known destination address, it sends the frame to that address. If, on the other hand, it is a broadcast or multicast frame, the frame is sent to the emulated LAN, which then transmits it to either all end-points or a group of end-points. Similarly, if a frame originates from an ATM end-point, it may have to be sent to another end-point on the ATM side or flooded on one or more LAN segments, depending on its destination.

An LEC and an emulated LAN interact with each other over a LAN emulation UNI (LUNI) using multiple VCCs on the interface. As we will show shortly, some of these VCCs are used for control purposes and the rest for data transport. The functions of the LAN emulation service, which are depicted as a single block in Figure 8-2(b), consist of three distinct entities: the LAN Emulation Configuration Server (LECS), the LAN Emulation Server (LES), and the Broadcast and Unknown Server (BUS). Each LEC interacts with these entities over the interface. These entities are shown in Figure 8-11. The functions they perform are the following:

---

2. The difference between a bridge and a router is the following: Bridging takes place at the MAC layer, whereas routing involves layer 3 of the protocol stack.

3. We have used the term "LAN emulation service entities" for convenience to denote all functions that are needed in the ATM network to support LAN emulation.

Figure 8-10 An example of an emulated LAN. ATM switching is implicit in LAN emulation.

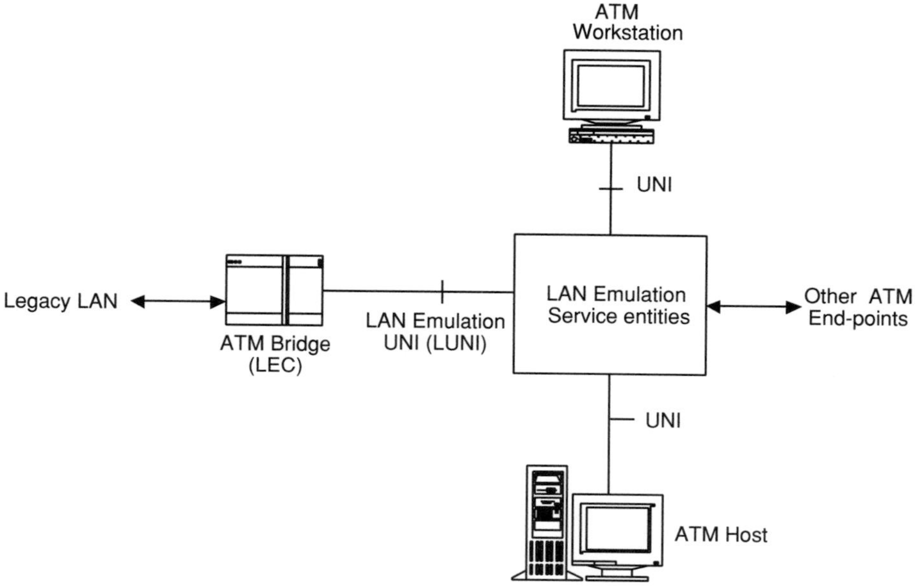

1. LECS — Before data packets can be forwarded over an emulated LAN, each LEC and emulated LAN must go through an initialization procedure and exchange configuration parameters that are subsequently used in emulation. On the emulated LAN side, this function is performed by the LECS. Parameters exchanged include the LAN type to be emulated, the maximum frame size, etc.

2. LES — After the configuration parameters have been successfully exchanged, an LEC must indicate its intention of "joining" an emulated LAN by sending, among other things, its MAC and ATM addresses. The emulated LAN responds by assigning a LAN emulation client identifier (LECID) to the client. When this happens, the LEC has successfully registered with the emulated LAN. The logical entity that performs this registration function for the emulated LAN is called the LES. If an LEC has other unicast MAC addresses or route descriptors, it may now register them with the LES.

    There is another function performed by the LES. When an LEC gets a frame with a destination unicast MAC address or next route descriptor for which it does not know the ATM address, it tries to resolve that address by sending an address resolution protocol (ARP) request frame to the LES.

3. BUS — This functional entity of the emulated LAN is responsible for forwarding all broadcast or multicast frames from an LEC to their proper destination. When an LEC

Figure 8-11   The functional entities of an emulated LAN.

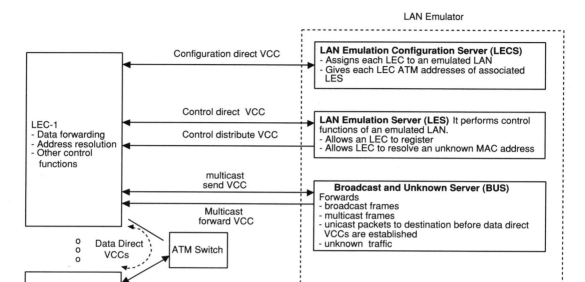

gets a unicast frame with a known destination ATM address, it encapsulates the LAN emulation service data unit (LE-SDU) in an AAL5 frame, and forwards it to the destination LEC. If, on the other hand, it is a multicast or broadcast frame, the LEC forwards it to the BUS, which in turn sends it to one or more LECs, depending on whether it is a unicast or multicast frame.

There is no hard and fast rule about where these functionalities should reside. The LEC function is generally implemented in the bridge or router, or in an ATM workstation. The three LAN emulation service entities may be implemented as one entity from the system's point of view, or each may be implemented as a separate entity. Furthermore, they may all be integrated into the ATM network itself, or they may be implemented as separate, stand-alone devices. Assuming the former to be the case, Figure 8-12 gives a functional block diagram of an emulated LAN. The ATM and AAL blocks are included in the figure to emphasize the fact that the emulated LAN must be able to encode and decode these protocols at appropriate points in the system.

Figure 8-12 A functional block diagram of an emulated LAN.

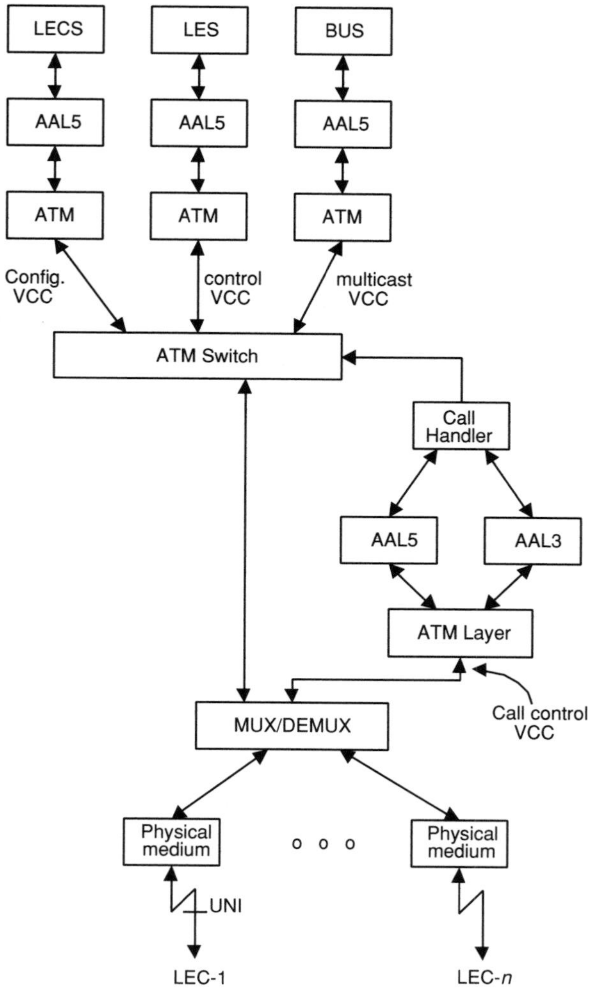

8.4 Protocol Stack

The protocol stack for user data frames and LAN emulation control frames at different interface points of an emulated LAN is shown in Figure 8-13. The user data frames may originate from, or terminate on, higher layers such as LLC or its equivalent, or a bridging function. When the LEC receives these frames from the higher layers, it adds its two-octet LECID, which it received during the registration phase, and passes the resulting packet to AAL5. As explained in Chapter 2, AAL5 adds a one-octet trailer and necessary padding octets so that

Figure 8-13   The protocol stack at different interface points in an emulated LAN.

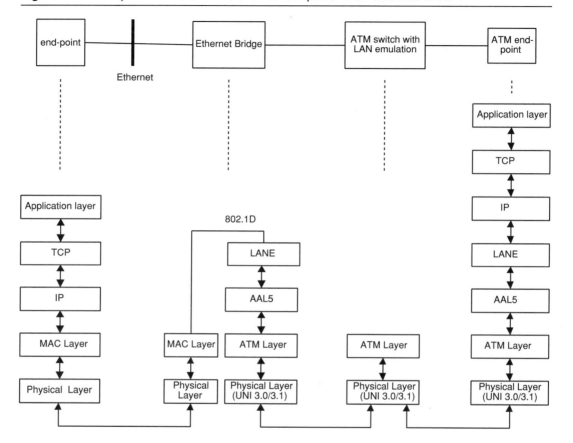

the frame becomes an integral multiple of 48 octets, and then sends it to the ATM layer below. In the other direction, when the LAN emulation entity receives a frame from AAL5, it
removes the LECID and presents the rest of the frame to the higher layers.

The control frames are exchanged between an LEC and the LAN emulation service components as an LEC leaves or joins an emulated LAN, or resolves an unknown address. These
frames are treated by the LAN emulation layer in the same way as the data frames.

8.5 Emulation Procedure

8.5.1 Overview

The emulation procedures from the perspective of the LEC are summarized in the flowchart
of Figure 8-14. Initially, each LEC, LECS, LES, and BUS must know, among other things,

Figure 8-14   The sequence of operations that an LEC goes through to participate in LAN emulation.

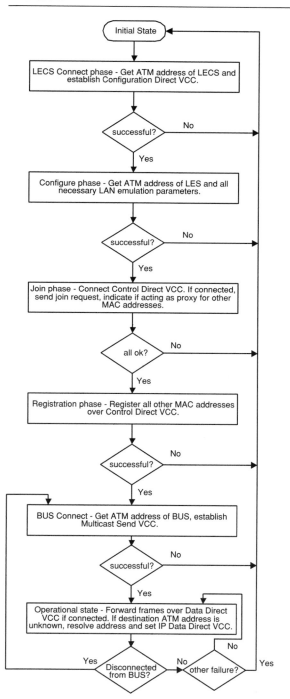

their own ATM addresses. The LEC then begins by establishing a VCC, called a Configuration Direct VCC, to the LECS. Before it can do this, however, it requires the ATM address of the LECS. It attempts to determine this address using the ATM-layer management procedures known as ILMI. If no such address is available, then a well-known ATM address, set aside by the ATM Forum specifications for this purpose, can be used.[4]

After the VCC has been established, the LEC transmits a message (called the CONFIGURE_REQUEST) to the LECS that includes, among other things, its own ATM address, MAC address, LAN type, and the frame sizes that it supports. The LECS, upon validation of these parameters, returns the address of the appropriate LES and the LAN type and frame size to use for this session. This completes the configure phase.

Now that the LEC has the ATM address of the LES, it uses that address to establish a bi-directional VCC, called a Control Direct VCC, to the LES. When it is successfully established, the LEC transmits a LE_JOIN_REQUEST message on the VCC. In the message, the LEC indicates, among other things, whether or not it will act as a proxy[5] for unregistered LAN destinations. It also includes its own MAC and ATM addresses. On receiving the join request, the LES examines all parameters in the message, and if it finds them acceptable, assigns the LEC to an emulated LAN of the requested type. The LES then sends an LE_JOIN_RESPONSE message containing a unique LECID for the LEC. In some cases, however, the LES may first establish a unidirectional Control Distribute VCC back to the LEC before assigning the LEC to an emulated LAN or sending the LE_JOIN_RESPONSE. Hence, the LEC must be prepared to accept a connection request of this VCC. Once this connection has been established, the LES may send the LE_JOIN_RESPONSE on either the Control Direct VCC or Control Distribute VCC. This, in most cases, completes the registration phase. However, if the LEC wishes to register other local unicast MAC addresses and route descriptors, it may do so at this point.[6]

If the registration phase is successful, the LEC establishes a bi-directional Multicast Send VCC to the BUS. To be able to do so, however, it must first determine the ATM address of the BUS. It does this by using the ARP procedures. The BUS follows it up by setting up a unidirectional, point-to-point Multicast Forward VCC back to the LEC. Alternatively, if the BUS has already set up a Multicast Forward VCC to other clients in a point-to-multipoint fashion, it may simply join this LEC as another "leaf" on the VCC. It is on this VCC that an LEC receives broadcast or multicast frames from the LES.

Once the BUS connections have been established, the LEC may then begin forwarding frames. It is important to mention here that unlike an Ethernet end-point that receives and monitors all frames on the Ethernet, an ATM end-point receives, besides broadcast frames,

---

4. This address is 0 x 4700 7900 0000 0000 0000 0000 0000 a03e 0000 0100.

5. An LEC is said to act as a proxy if it agrees to receive LE_ARP requests for a LAN destination that is not registered with an LES.

6. MAC addresses may be unregistered. The LES, if appropriate, adds the LEC as a leaf to its point-to-multipoint Control Distribute VCC.

those and only those frames that are addressed to it. The LES ensures that this indeed is the case.

8.5.2 Control Frames

Frames that are used to request configuration, join or leave an emulated LAN, register with an LES, or resolve an unknown LAN destination by means of the ARP protocol are called control frames to distinguish them from the data frames that are sent in the operational phase. All control frames, except READY_IND and READY_QUERY, have the generic format of Figure 8-15. Some of these fields are common to all frames. Similarly, not all of them are meaningful to all frames.

The op-code indicates the frame type. Some of the frame types are: configure request, configure response, join request, join response, ready_query, ready_ind, register request, register response, unregister request, unregister response, ARP request, ARP response, or topology request. For the op-codes of the frame types, see Reference [1].

The specific values of the marker, protocol, and version fields are shown in Figure 8-15. The status field is meaningful in a response frame only, and indicates whether a request was successful, and if not, why it failed. In the request frame, the status field is filled with all 0's. The transaction ID is set by the requester to an arbitrary value. The same value is returned in the response frame, so that at the receiving end, it can be correctly associated with the request that triggered it. The LECID is an identification number that the LES assigns to an LEC after it has successfully joined an emulated LAN. Thus, it is set to zero prior to the join phase.

In most frames, the flag bits are set to zero. When they are non-zero, each of the bits may have a unique meaning. For example, when sending a join request frame, an LEC may set it to 0×0080 to indicate that it wants to act as a proxy for a non-registered MAC address. Or, when responding to an ARP request frame, the LES may set the flag bits to 0×0001 if the target MAC address is unregistered.

The source LAN destination field is the MAC address of the source that triggered this frame, and is non-zero only if the frame originates at an LEC. The target LAN destination field is used by an LEC when initiating an ARP request frame, and indicates the MAC address that the LEC is trying to resolve. The LAN type is 1 for Ethernet LANs, 2 for IEEE 802.5 LANs, and 0 for all other cases.

The type/length/value (T/L/V) fields are generally used by an LEC and LES in the configure phase to exchange configuration parameters in addition to those which are routinely included in the frame. For example, they may include the control time-out, maximum unknown frame count, VCC time-out period, retry count, etc. If necessary, user- or vendor-specific parameters may also be included.

8.5.3 Initialization

As shown in Figure 8-14, the initialization process consists of five phases: (1) LECS connect, (2) configure, (3) join, (4) registration, and (5) BUS connect.

Figure 8-15   Control frame format.

Header- 4 Bytes	Frame Type-2 Bytes	Fixed-Length Information Elements- 102 Bytes	Additional Information Elements (TLV[7])- Variable Length

Generic Frame Structure

Marker - 2 Bytes (0XFF00)	Protocol Discriminator- 1 Byte (0x01)	LANE Protocol Version - 1 Byte

Header

Information Elements	No. of Bytes	Remarks
Status	2	Set to 0 in a Request Frame. In a Response Frame, set to 0 for a valid request, otherwise a failure cause.
Transaction ID	4	Set by the originator, looped back by the receiver.
LECID	2	Set to 0 if not applicable or assigned.
Flags	2	Extends meaning of frame type.
Source MAC Address	8	Set to 0 if not applicable.
Destination MAC Addr.	8	Set to 0 if unknown or not applicable.
Source ATM Address	20	
LAN Type	1	Indicates if emulated LAN is Ethernet, Token Ring, etc.
Frame Size	1	
Number of Additional Information Elements	1	
Size of ELAN Name	1	
Target ATM Address	20	Set to 0 if unknown or not applicable.
ELAN Name	32	

Fixed-Length Information Field

8.5.3.1 LECS Connect Phase

Before LAN emulation can begin, the LEC and LES must exchange their configuration parameters, which is essential to emulation. For example, the LEC must know the ATM address of the LES so that it can construct an ATM frame. There are two ways to do this: the parame-

---

7. Type/Length/Value.

ters can be either programmed by the user via the network manager at system configuration time or they can be obtained dynamically over a VCC. In the former case, the LECS connect and configure phases are omitted. In the latter case, however, it is necessary to first establish a VCC. This VCC is called a Configuration Direct VCC.

To connect this VCC, the LEC must first obtain the ATM address of the LECS. It does this via the SNMP *get* or *get-next* command. If it can obtain the ATM address this way, it will use the address to establish the VCC. Otherwise, it will re-issue the same SNMP commands to see if another ATM address is available. If it is, it establishes the VCC using that address. Otherwise, it will use a well-known LECS address set aside exclusively for this purpose and then attempt to establish the VCC.[8] If that fails, the LEC will use the well-known PVC (VPI = 0 and VCI = 17) as the Configuration Direct VCC. If that fails, the LEC may be configured via another out-of-band mechanism.

8.5.3.2 Configure Phase

After the LEC has successfully connected the Configuration Direct VCC, the configure phase can begin. The LEC, of course, must know its own ATM address because it is used to establish the Control Direct and Multicast VCCs, and it is also the source ATM address in the client's join request.[9] The LEC issues a CONFIGURE_REQUEST frame to the LECS. The frame has the structure of Figure 8-15, and is constructed by using

1. The correct op-code for the configure request.
2. All 0's for the LECID, flags, target LAN destination, and target ATM address.
3. The MAC address (or route descriptor) for the source LAN destination field.
4. The value for the desired LAN type.
5. The desired maximum frame size.
6. The T/L/V number, indicating how many additional configuration parameters, if any, are included in this frame.
7. The ELAN name.
8. The type, length, and value of each of the items indicated in 6 above.

The control frame, along with the Configuration Direct VCC value, is presented to the AAL5 layer so that an ATM frame is eventually sent out to the LECS.

The response frame, if the configuration request is successful, will include the ATM address of the LES and other configuration parameters such as the control time out, maximum unknown frame count, maximum unknown frame time, VCC time-out period, maximum retry count, aging time, forward delay time, etc.

---

8. Note that although this well-known address is defined, it is not directly supported under UNI 3.x. Therefore, it may be up to switch vendors to implement the functionality of this well-known address.

9. The client may have additional ATM addresses for use with Data Direct VCCs, but does not need to know them when making the join request.

8.5.3.3 Join Phase

Once the LEC knows the ATM address of the LES and all the desired LAN emulation parameters, the join phase begins. The LEC sends a Q.2931 SETUP message to the LES to establish a point-to-point, bi-directional Control Direct VCC, using its own ATM address as the calling party number.[10] If the call attempt fails, the join is aborted and the LEC must go back to the initial state. Otherwise, it sends a join request (i.e., a control frame with the join request op-code) over the VCC with the following parameters:

- The ATM address of the LEC.
- The type of LAN that the LEC is a member of.
- The maximum size of the data frame that the LEC would like.
- Whether or not it will act as a proxy for any unicast MAC address.[11]
- The name of the emulated LAN that the LEC wishes to join.
- One optional MAC address to be registered as a pair. In other words, this registered MAC address will be associated with the source ATM address of the client.

After the LEC has sent its join request, the server itself may initiate call control procedures to establish a unidirectional Control Distribute VCC. Thus, as soon as the LEC has issued the join request, it must be ready to accept a SETUP request from the server. Notice that if the server wants to set up this unidirectional VCC, it must do so before sending the JOIN_RESPONSE message.

The status bits of the join response from the server indicate if the join request was successful.[12] If it was, the frame will provide the following information:

- The type of LAN being emulated.
- The maximum size of the data frame that the LEC and LES should use.
- The emulated LAN name.
- The LECID.

If the LEC accepts these values, the join phase is complete. If it receives no reply from the server within a certain period,[13] it may repeat the entire process all over again. However, it will only retry a certain number of times — if the join phase does not succeed, it will withdraw from the emulated LAN. Furthermore, the join phase must complete within a certain

---

10. Alternatively, if a Control Direct PVC already exists, it can use that PVC and skip the signaling procedures.

11. An LEC is a proxy if it answers an ARP request from an LES for a unicast MAC address that is not registered with the server.

12. The status code indicating success is 0 for all responses.

13. The default value of this time-out period is 15s.

period from the instant that the LEC establishes the Control Direct VCC.[14] Otherwise, the LEC must terminate the join phase and release the VCC. Similarly, if the LES does not receive any join request within the period after the LEC has established the Control Direct VCC, it may terminate the ELAN membership of the LEC. There may be other reasons, not discussed here, why either an LEC or the server may terminate the ELAN membership.

If the LEC receives a SETUP request for a Control Distribute VCC from the server after the join response, it ignores the request. Note, however, that the LES may return the join response on either the Control Direct VCC or Control Distribute VCC. An LES should never issue a join request to an LEC. If the LEC ever gets such a request, it must ignore it.

8.5.3.4 Registration Phase

An LEC may have one or more MAC addresses (or route descriptors for IEEE 802.5 LANs), and they may change during normal operation. After successfully completing the join phase, where the LEC sends just one MAC address associated with its own ATM address, it may register all the other MAC addresses. To register them, the LEC sends over the Control Direct VCC a REGISTER_REQUEST control frame with a transaction ID, its LECID, the unicast MAC address or route descriptor to be registered for the source LAN destination field, and an ATM address for the source ATM address field.[15] In this phase, the LEC must not attempt to register a broadcast or multicast MAC address.

The response frame from the LES is similar to the request frame, except for its op-code and status fields. If the status field indicates success, the address has been successfully registered. The LES may send the response over either the Control Direct VCC or Control Distribute VCC. Thus, the LEC must ignore any response frame received over VCCs other than these two. Notice that an LES will deny a registration request of a given LAN destination address from more than one LEC with different ATM addresses by sending a REGISTER_RESPONSE with the appropriate status code indicating failure. Similarly, a second registration request for a given MAC address with different parameters will be rejected by the LES with a proper status code.

Additionally, the LEC may request one or more address pairs to be removed from the registration by sending an UNREGISTER_REQUEST to the LES.

8.5.3.5 Connecting to the BUS

8.5.3.5.1 General Procedure

The LEC must now connect to the BUS. To do this, the LEC first determines the ATM address of the BUS by sending an ARP request to the LES over the already established Control Direct VCC. When it gets that address from the LES, it initiates a SETUP request for a bidirectional Multicast Send VCC, using the ATM address of the BUS as the called party and

---

14. The default value of this time-out period is 120s.
15. The ATM addresses of an LEC do not change during operation.

its own ATM address as the calling party. After that VCC has been established successfully, the LEC must send all multicast destination packets to the BUS on the VCC.

As soon as the VCC has been established, the BUS sends the LEC a SETUP request to connect a unidirectional, point-to-point or point-to-multipoint Multicast Forward VCC. The LEC must accept the request because the BUS may send some broadcast or multicast frames on this VCC. If the Multicast Send VCC is released for any reason, the Multicast Forward VCC must also be released. After the release, the LEC may try to connect to the BUS again, but must withdraw from the emulated LAN if it has retried a certain number of times but failed to connect.

8.5.3.5.2 Address Resolution Protocol

The term "address resolution" means determining the ATM address to be associated with a given MAC address or route descriptor that is not registered with the server. Both an LEC and an LES may need to resolve an address. For example, we saw in the last section that an LEC uses the ARP to determine the BUS address so that it can connect the Multicast Send VCC.

When an LEC successfully completes the join phase, its MAC address is implicitly registered with the LES. If it has other *local* unicast MAC addresses or route descriptors, they are registered in the registration phase. An LEC may also act as a proxy client for unicast MAC addresses that are not registered with the LES. From the viewpoint of this LEC, these MAC addresses are *remote*. When this is the case, the LES may send an ARP request to the LEC to resolve an unregistered LAN destination. For example, for an IEEE 802.1D transparent bridge, the address to be resolved may be the address of an end station on its other LAN segments.[16]

An LEC sends an ARP request only over the Control Direct VCC. An LES, on the other hand, may send an ARP response or an ARP request on either the Control Direct VCC or the Control Distribute VCC. After an LEC has resolved a unicast MAC address, it must set up a Data Direct VCC to that address.

The ARP is also invoked when a MAC address that is registered by an LEC has been removed from the associated LAN segment. In this case, the LEC sends what is called a NARP request frame to the LES. Similarly, the LEC and LES must notify each other of any changes to their configuration by sending a topology request frame.

An ARP request frame is constructed by setting

- The op-code field to 0×0006.
- The source LAN destination field to the source MAC address of the originator, if present, or to zero otherwise.
- The target LAN destination field to the MAC address or route descriptor for which the ATM address is desired.

---

16. When an LEC sends an ARP response, it clears the FLAGS bits if it is a local unicast MAC address, and sets them if it is a remote MAC address.

- The source ATM address field to the ATM address of the originator.
- The target ATM address field to all 0's.

The ARP response is built by setting

- The op-code field to 0×0106.
- The source LAN destination field to the source MAC address of the originator, if present, or to zero otherwise.
- The target LAN destination field to the MAC address or route descriptor for which the ATM address is desired.
- The source ATM address field to the ATM address of the originator.
- The target ATM address field to the requested ATM address.

8.5.4 Data Transfer Procedures

8.5.4.1 Unicast Frames

When an LEC gets a data frame that has to be forwarded to its destination on the ATM network from the LAN side, it looks up an internal table to see if a Data Direct VCC already exists for that MAC address. If so, it transmits the frame on that VCC. Otherwise, it attempts to establish one. While it is doing so, the LEC may forward the frame to the BUS over the Multicast Send VCC. If the LEC serving the destination is a member of the emulated LAN, the BUS forwards the frame to the LEC using the Multicast Forward VCC. Otherwise, the BUS forwards the frame to all clients or all proxies using the Multicast Forward VCC. If, on the other hand, an LEC gets a data frame from the emulated LAN, it should simply deliver the frame to the LAN side and never forward it back to the emulated LAN over another Data Direct VCC or the Multicast Forward VCC.

If all LAN destination addresses are resolved, a frame will always reach its destination correctly. But, suppose that a frame from the emulated LAN is destined to a station that is connected on a legacy LAN behind a bridge. If the latter is not aware of this station, for the frame to have some possibility of reaching its destination, it must be broadcast on all LAN segments. The BUS must, therefore, forward the frame to all bridges, or at least those that are enabled by the spanning tree protocol, so that each bridge can transmit the frame on the legacy LAN segment. Once the station starts transmitting, the bridge will learn the station's address. Consequently, when this bridge receives an address resolution request for that station in the future, it will respond correctly with its ATM address.

8.5.4.2 Multicast Frames

For multicast frames, the services of the BUS are invoked. Before sending frames to a multicast MAC address, the LEC first obtains the ATM address of the BUS during the initialization process using ARP, and establishes a bi-directional, point-to-point Multicast Send VCC. The LEC then sends the multicast frames to the BUS over the VCC.

The BUS also sets up a Multicast Forward VCC to an LEC so that, when necessary, it can forward multicast frames over the VCC. These VCCs are unidirectional, and may be either point-to-multipoint or point-to-point. The BUS can use either Multicast Send VCC or Multicast Forward VCC to send the multicast or broadcast frames.

An LEC, when sending a data frame, inserts its unique LECID in the header part. When the BUS forwards a frame to an LEC, it includes the same header in the frame. When an LEC receives it, it compares the received LECID with its own ID, and that way filters out any frames that it might have originated itself.

8.5.4.3 Data Frame Format

Before an Ethernet frame is sent out on an ATM cell, the frame is stripped of the preamble, start-of-frame, SYNC bits, and FCS. A 2-octet LANE header, which is the LECID of the sending LEC, is then prepended to the stripped MAC frame as shown in Figure 8-16. The LECID, like a MAC-layer address, is unique for each LEC.

Similarly, for the IEEE 802.5 frame, the start-of-frame sequence, the end-of-frame sequence, and the FCS are removed from the frame. The FCS is really not necessary since the AAL5 frame that contains the LAN emulation frame is itself encoded in a CRC.

The frame format for a token ring LAN is shown in Figure 8-17. The LANE header has the same significance as in the IEEE 802.3 frame. The AC PAD is not used in LAN emulation. It can be set to any value by the transmitter and is ignored by the receiver.

The minimum size of the LANE AAL5 service data unit (SDU) for IEEE 802.3/Ethernet frames is 62 octets. The maximum frame size depends on the LAN type, and may be 1516, 4544, 9234, or 18190 octets.

Figure 8-16   The IEEE 802.3 frame format to be sent over AAL5.

LANE Header 2 octets	Destination MAC Address	Source MAC Address	Type/Length	Data

← ———————————— 802.3 Ethernet Frame ———————————— →

Figure 8-17   The IEEE 802.5 token ring frame format to be sent over AAL5.

LANE Header 2 octets	AC PAD 1 octet	Frame Control	Destination MAC Address	Source MAC Address	Length	Data

← ———————————— 802.5 Token Ring Frame ———————————— →

8.6 Connection Management

As mentioned before, in LAN emulation, it is a more common practice to use SVCs. Standard call control procedures Q.2931, described in Chapter 3, are used to set up SVCs in an ATM network. These procedures have been slightly augmented for LAN emulation applications. The augmented procedure for setting up a Data Direct VCC is shown in the stick diagram of Figure 8-18.

It is necessary to mention here that before the destination LEC sends the CONNECT message to the switch, it must initialize the VCC and associated parameters so that the originating LEC can begin to send the data frames immediately after receiving the CONNECT message from the switch.

When the originating LEC receives the CONNECT message, it initializes the requested VCC and SAR, and may thereafter begin to send data to the called party. However, since the destination LEC receives the CONN_ACK from the local switch and not from the originating LEC (see Figure 8-18), the destination LEC does not know when the source LEC is ready to receive a frame. Consequently, the called party starts a timer and waits for a READY_IND message from the calling party before sending any data packets. The calling party should send a READY_IND message on the newly established VCC as soon as it receives the CONNECT

Figure 8-18   Messages exchanged when setting up a Data Direct VCC.

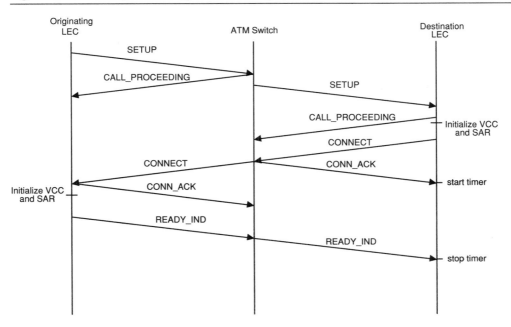

message. If the called party receives the READY_IND before the timer expires, it stops the timer and begins to send data frames. If the timer expires, it sends the calling party a READY_QUERY message on the VCC. Both ends must reply to a READY_QUERY with a READY_IND. Notice that the calling party can send data frames before or after sending the READY_IND message. This does not present any problem to the called party since it is already ready to receive frames.

8.7 LAN Emulation Version 2

LAN emulation that we presented in this chapter is Version 1. We described the interface between an LEC and the different entities of the LAN emulation service (i.e., the LECS, LES, and BUS). Interaction among these entities was not discussed. Reference [3] specifies this interaction. Enhanced capabilities in LAN emulation such as QoS, support for multi-protocol over ATM, etc. are specified in [2].

8.8 Summary

LAN emulation over ATM emulates the services of a traditional LAN so that devices behind Ethernet or token ring LANs running existing protocols such as TCP/IP can communicate across an ATM network or with ATM end-points using the same applications and networking protocols. Consider an Ethernet LAN that is connected to an ATM switch via an Ethernet bridge. In this case, to perform LAN emulation, it is necessary to provide additional functionalities in the form of an LEC in the bridge and LAN emulation service components in the ATM switch. These functionalities are generally implemented in software, but can be designed as stand-alone devices, or integrated into the bridge or switch.

Emulation procedures for a user-to-network interface with Ethernet and token ring LAN types were discussed. On the switch, there are three LAN emulation service components: LECS, LES, and BUS. We presented a brief description of their functions. Before an LEC can begin to send user data across an emulated LAN, it must go through five phases of an initialization procedure: LECS connect, configure, join, initial registration, and BUS connect. We gave a somewhat detailed description of this procedure. Data frames that are sent over a data direct VCC using AAL5, and their formats were discussed as well. In LAN emulation, it is a common practice to use SVCs. Since Q.2931 call control procedures are slightly different for LAN emulation, we illustrated them by means of a message flow diagram for setting up a data direct VCC.

8.9 References

[1] ATM Forum Technical Committee, *LAN Emulation over ATM — Version 1.0*, Jan. 1995.

[2] ATM Forum Technical Committee, *LAN Emulation over ATM Version 2 — LUNI Specification*, July 1997.

[3] ATM Forum Technical Committee, *LAN Emulation over ATM. Version 2 — LNNI Specification, Draft 8*, Feb. 1997.

Problems

8.1 Suppose that we have to design the LAN emulation client of an ATM-Ethernet bridge so that it can interwork with an ATM switch that is emulating the Ethernet LAN. Show in flowchart form the functions that an LEC must perform before it can begin to send a user frame over a data-direct VCC. Be sure to provide enough detail that it can be used in actual implementation. (Recall that the sequence of operations that an LEC goes through to participate in LAN emulation is described in Figure 8-14. However, it does not have the necessary design detail.)

8.2 For Problem 8.1, show in the form of a stick diagram all messages that are exchanged between an LEC and the LAN emulation service components in the initialization phase.

8.3 Encode all messages of Problem 8.2.

8.4 Encode a typical Q.2931 call control message that is used to establish a control VCC (e.g., a configuration-direct VCC, a control-direct VCC, etc.)

8.5 Suppose that you are to design an Ethernet learning bridge. Using either a flow-chart or a C-like language, provide a functional specification of the bridge with enough detail that you can use it in an implementation.

8.6 Show how the message encoding of Problem 8.3 would be different for a token ring LAN.

IP over ATM

9.1 Introduction

We saw in Chapter 7 how an ATM network could emulate Ethernet or token ring LANs by means of the LANE protocol. This protocol, in essence, allows the network layer to exchange packets with the ATM layer in the same MAC format, using the same network drivers (e.g., the Network Driver Interface Specification (NDIS) or Open Data Link Interface (ODI)).

A disadvantage of LAN emulation is that existing applications running above the network layer cannot request a desired QoS, which is an important feature of ATM services. The reason is that existing LANs, because of their inherent latencies, cannot provide a guaranteed QoS, and as such, the network-layer protocols were never designed to support QoS requests. Hence, the only ATM services that are suitable for emulated LANs are UBR and ABR services.

One obvious way to overcome this limitation of emulated LANs is to design new application- and transport-layer protocols which would run directly over ATM and, at the same time, be able to request a desired QoS and receive a guarantee from the network. If an application can directly use ATM in an end-to-end ATM connection, it is referred to as native mode ATM. The protocol stack for this mode is shown in Figure 9-1(d).

An alternative solution would be to modify existing application-layer protocols in a way that would allow them to run over ATM and provide some form of resource reservation. In fact, it is likely that, in the future, many network-layer protocols will be extended to accommodate new services, particularly emerging multimedia applications on different types of networks. Also, IP-based protocols are being developed that will provide some mechanism for exchanging traffic descriptors (such as the average bandwidth, maximum bandwidth, delay variances, etc.), which are very similar to the QoS parameters for ATM. Examples of these protocols are: the Resource Reservation Protocol (RSVP) and IP Version 6 (IPv6). Clearly, it would be desirable to use these protocols in ATM networks, even though some modifications would be necessary before they could be used in an ATM environment.

To allow these IP-based protocols to run directly over ATM without LANE, the Internet Engineering Task Force (IETF) has modified IP. This modified version of IP is called IP over ATM. With this protocol, routers connected over an ATM interface forward packets based on

Figure 9-1 Examples of IP over ATM. (a) An ATM LAN segment. (b) Legacy LAN segments connected to an ATM backbone to form a WAN. For ease of administration, the LAN segments are divided into multiple logical IP subnetworks (LIS). (c) The protocol stack on the IP station and IP router. This is known as IP over ATM. (d) The protocol stack for the native mode ATM.

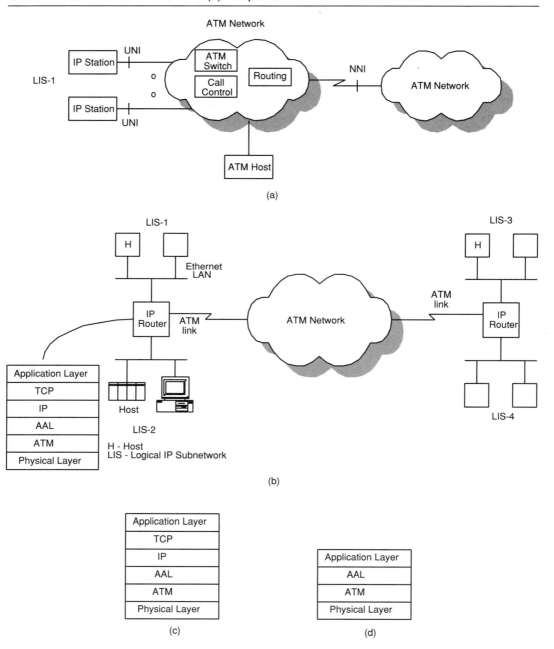

their IP address using AAL5. Some examples of the use of this protocol are shown in Figure 9-1. In Figure 9-1(a), a traditional LAN segment has been replaced by an ATM LAN. However, its end-points (e.g., the stations and host) continue to use TCP/IP protocols. Figure 9-1(b) illustrates the situation where Ethernet LAN segments are connected via IP routers to an ATM backbone. Figure 9-1(c) shows the necessary protocol stack on IP stations and IP routers.

For a network of the type shown in Figure 9-1, IP over ATM provides some advantages, at least in the short term. To see this, consider Figure 9-1(b) again. Assume that hosts[1] H1 and H2 are running two applications, AP1 and AP2, respectively. If AP1 wants to send a packet to AP2, it can use a specially designed, new protocol that allows it to open a direct ATM connection with AP2 and then send the data packets over AAL5. In this case, the two hosts, H1 and H2, and the router must be modified. With IP over ATM, on the other hand, AP1 opens a new ATM connection to the transport address[2] of the desired application on H2 and sends IP packets over AAL5 [1]. With this approach, the only entities in the network that require any changes are the two hosts, H1 and H2.

Significant work has been done in this area by a number of researchers [1]−[6]. Laubach and Halpern [1] proposed initial applications of classical IP and ARP in an ATM environment, and provided details that are useful to implementation. In Reference [6], a method is suggested whereby an IP host, on a request from the application layer, sends IP packets over an ATM connection to another IP host. Cole, et al. [5] discuss different proposals considered by the IP over ATM Working Group and provide a framework for comparing them. The purpose of this chapter is to present an overview of this protocol.

We begin with a description of how IP datagrams can be transmitted over ATM. Since each end-point in an ATM network is identified by a unique ATM address, packets can be forwarded based on their IP addresses only if an ATM address can be found corresponding to a given destination IP address. This is made possible by the ATM address resolution protocol (ATMARP) which, in essence, resolves a given IP address to an unknown ATM address. The inverse ATMARP (InATMARP) protocol does exactly the opposite — it determines an unknown IP address corresponding to a given ATM address [4]. Since these protocols are an integral part of IP over ATM procedures, a brief description of these protocols is included.

9.2 Packet Transmission Procedure with IP over ATM

In the scenario that we have just described, a specific packet type, namely a datagram packet, was assumed to be initiated by the application. There are many other types of packets that the

---

1. In our discussion here, we use the term "host" to mean an end system that sends and receives packets but does not relay them as a router would. A subnetwork is a collection of hosts connected in such a way that any one of them can communicate with any other directly without requiring the services of a router. A glossary of these and other terms used in this chapter may be found in Reference [5].

2. This address identifies the network, the host, and a port at the destination, and is known in the literature as a socket.

protocol may need to handle. For example, there may be an application that may want to resolve an unknown ATM address using ATMARP running on an end-point. Thus, when using IP over ATM, it may be necessary to multiplex multiple packet types at the source and demultiplex them at the receiving end. There are two ways of doing this: (i) use of multiple VCs, and (ii) use of a single VC with appropriate packet encapsulation.

When using multiple VCs, a separate VC is used for each packet type — say, one for an IP datagram packet, a second one for an ATMARP packet, a third one for Appletalk packets, and so on — so that at the destination end-point, it is uniquely identified by the associated VC. Both PVCs and SVCs can be used for this purpose. SVCs are established using the call control procedures of Reference [3], and taken down as needed. This multiplexing procedure seems to be suitable for a large network that can support a relatively large number of VCs, but may not work so well if the number of VCs available between two ATM end-points is limited [5].

With multi-protocol encapsulation, a single VC is used for all applications. To provide multiplexing, an 8-octet header is added to the IP packet. Packet encapsulation is shown in Figure 9-2. Values of logical link control (LLC), organizationally unique identifiers (OUIs), and protocol identifiers (PIDs) are given in Reference [2] for various protocols such as routed ISO, routed IP, bridged Ethernet/802.3, bridged 802.4, etc. Table 9-1 gives these values for two AAL users — IP and ATMARP.

After the header has been added to the packet, it is passed to AAL5. An AAL5 CPCS-PDU is then constructed, as in Figure 9-3, where the payload field contains the LLC-encapsulated IP packet of Figure 9-2. The CPCS-PDU is then passed to the lower layers following standard ATM rules.

These procedures are reversed at the receiving end. On receiving a packet, the AAL on the destination host first removes the header, and then, based on the PID field, delivers the rest of the packet to the appropriate user of the AAL service.

Figure 9-2   Multiplexing with a single VC using multi-protocol encapsulation.

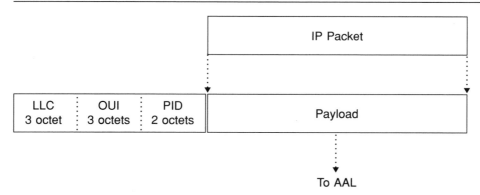

Table 9-1 IP Packet Header Values for IP and ATMARP

AAL User	Logical Link Control (LLC)	Organizationally Unique ID (OUI)	Protocol ID (PID)
IP	0xaa,0xaa,0x03	0x00,0x00,0x00	0x0800
ATMARP	0xaa,0xaa,0x03	0x00,0x00,0x00	0x0806

Figure 9-3 AAL5 CPCS-PDU format.

AAL5 Payload (IP Packet with Header)
PAD: 0 – 47 octets
CPCS User-to-User Indication – 1 octet
Common Part Indicator – 1 octet
Length – 2 octets
CRC – 4 octets

According to Reference [1], IEEE 802.2 logical link control/subnetwork attachment point (LLC/SNAP) encapsulation is the default packet format for IP over ATM, and should be supported in all systems.

9.3 ATMARP

ATM addresses comply with the NSAP ATM End System Address, or E.164 Public-UNI Address coding rules. In the literature, these addresses are also referred to as "hardware addresses."

For ease of configuration and management, an Ethernet LAN can be divided into a number of subnetworks, each identified by a subnet number and address mask. Communication among these subnetworks takes place via a router. In the same way, an ATM network with end-points operating with classical IP can be divided into a number of independent logical IP subnetworks (LISs). If two or more end-points belong in the same LIS, they can communicate directly over ATM links as long as they know the ATM address of the destination end-point. If an end-point does not know the destination address, it must determine the address using the services of an ATMARP server. If end-points belong in two or more different LISs, they must communicate via an IP router, which is an ATM end-point with one or more ATM addresses. An ATMARP server may be implemented either as a separate physical entity or as part of an ATM network element, say, the IP router in the above description. An LIS may have one or more ATMARP servers. If there is just one server in an LIS, all clients of that LIS must be configured to have the same ATM address of that server; if there are more, each client must be configured with the ATM address of the desired server only.

ATMARP queries are initiated only by clients that operate with SVCs. These SVCs are established when necessary using UNI 3.1 signaling procedures. Clients that use PVCs only should never generate ATMARP queries. They may, however, invoke the InATMARP.

The salient features of the ARP are briefly the following:

1. At system administration time, each station in an LIS is configured with its own IP and ATM addresses, and the ATM address of the ATMARP server. Each IP station initially registers with the ATMARP server by sending an ARP request packet on a VC. Thereafter, it may periodically send such packets so that the server can update the station's parameters (e.g., the time-out on an ATMARP table entry) that help determine if the station has been inactive long enough to be considered out-of-service. The request packet contains, among other things, the source ATM address, the source protocol address, the target ATM address, and the target protocol address [1], [2]. If it does not know an address, it is filled with zeros.

2. For each station in an LIS, the server creates and maintains in its cache a table with two entries: the ATM address corresponding to the station's IP address and the associated VC(s) active on the station. The table is built from the address resolution request packets that the server receives from the stations.

   An IP station can register in two ways: (i) It may send a request packet where the target IP address is the same as the source IP address. On receiving the packet, the server examines the table for an ATM address corresponding to the IP address and acts according to the flowchart of Figure 9-2. For example, if the server does not find an ATM address for the given IP address, it creates a new entry with the received ATM address and VC that carries the request packet. Or, if an ATM address entry exists and if its associated open VC is the same as that of the request packet, the table is updated with the received source ATM address. If the server detects duplicate IP addresses, it reports the finding to the network manager. The entry thus created or updated is returned to the requester as part of the ATMARP reply. (ii) The IP station may register and, at the same time, request an unknown ATM address by sending a regular request packet where the target IP address is different from the source IP address. If the table already contains an ATM address entry corresponding to the source IP address, the server proceeds to reply to the request packet following Step 3 below. Otherwise, the server first creates a new entry and then proceeds to reply to the request packet as in Step 3.

3. If an end-point does not know the target ATM address corresponding to a target IP address, it again generates an ATMARP request, but this time, it sets the source and target IP addresses to different values. After receiving the request packet, the ATMARP

server replies in the following way: (i) If there is an entry in the table corresponding to the target IP address, that entry is sent to the requester in an ARP reply packet. (ii) If there is no such entry in the table, it sends a NAK in the reply packet.

These functions of the protocol, as viewed from the server, are summarized in the flowchart of Figure 9-4. Notice that if a separate VC is to be opened for registration or address resolution purposes, it is up to the end-point and not the ATMARP server to do so.

Figure 9-5 shows the format of a request or reply packet for an ARP-PDU. The op-code indicates the packet type (e.g., an ATMARP request or reply packet, InATMARP request or reply packet, NAK, etc.).

From these discussions, one can see what functional entities are required in an ATM end-point to provide routing over ATM. These are shown in the simplified block diagram of Figure 9-6.

9.4 Inverse ATMARP

As the name suggests, this protocol performs an inverse function [4]. In other words, it allows a server to determine the IP address corresponding to a given ATM address. It is almost the same as the ATMARP, except that since the target ATM address is already known, it is not necessary to broadcast an address resolution request. To invoke this protocol, a source station simply inserts its own hardware and protocol address and the hardware address of the desired end-point, fills the target protocol address field with zeros, encapsulates the packet properly for an ATM network, and then sends it out to the server. As in ATMARP, the latter destination, upon receiving the request packet, saves the source hardware and protocol address in a table, and then sends a reply packet to the originating station with either the requested protocol address, if available, or a NAK otherwise.

9.5 Performance of TCP/IP over ATM

At this point, it is appropriate to ask how well IP over ATM actually performs. This topic has been investigated by a number of authors [7], [8], and was also addressed in Chapter 5 in connection with our study of traffic management in ATM networks. For reference, we will summarize these results in this section.

A number of parameters are used to provide a quantitative measure of the performance of a packet-switched network. Among them are: effective throughput, buffer utilization, effective link utilization, and delay. The throughput is defined in terms of the number of packets that have been successfully forwarded. In TCP, if a packet is timed out, that is, if the sender does not receive an acknowledgment within a time-out period, the packet is retransmitted. This clearly diminishes the net throughput. The effective link utilization is also reduced since some bandwidth is wasted when the receiver runs out of buffers and consequently drops newly arrived packets.

Figure 9-4 ATMARP functions at the ATMARP server end.

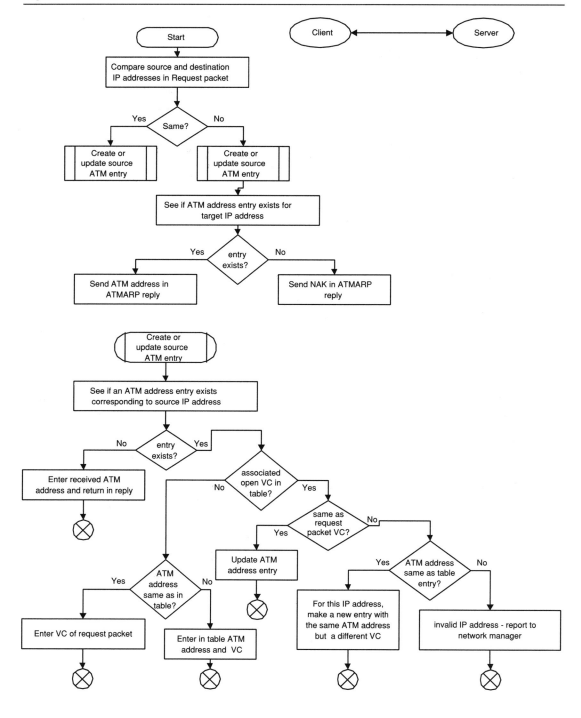

Figure 9-5 ATMARP/InATMARP request and reply packet format.

Hardware Type – 2 octets
Protocol Type – 2
Type and Length of Source ATM address – 1
Type and Length of Source ATM Subaddress – 1
OP-code – 2
Length of Source Protocol Address – 1
Type and Length of Target ATM Address – 1
Type and Length of Target ATM Subaddress – 1
Length of Target Protocol Address – 1
Source ATM Address
Source ATM Subaddress
Source Protocol Address
Target ATM Address
Target ATM Subaddress
Target Protocol Address

A number of factors contribute to the delay experienced by a packet. For example, delays may be caused by TCP processing and operating system overhead, and by segmentation and reassembly at the ATM adaptation layer. In addition, there are switching delays, link serialization delays, and propagation delays. Delays encountered in the ATM switch are generally very small, say in the range of 5–10 microseconds, whereas the TCP processing delay would be on the order of 200 microseconds. However, as far as IP over ATM is concerned, these delays do not significantly vary over the life of a TCP session, and as such, are not considered in our discussion here.

Similarly, we could use other performance indicators such as packet loss ratio or CLR, TCP retransmission rate, etc., but since their effect is already included in the throughput, these parameters are not described here.

Figure 9-6 Functional block diagram of an ATM switch with IP over ATM.

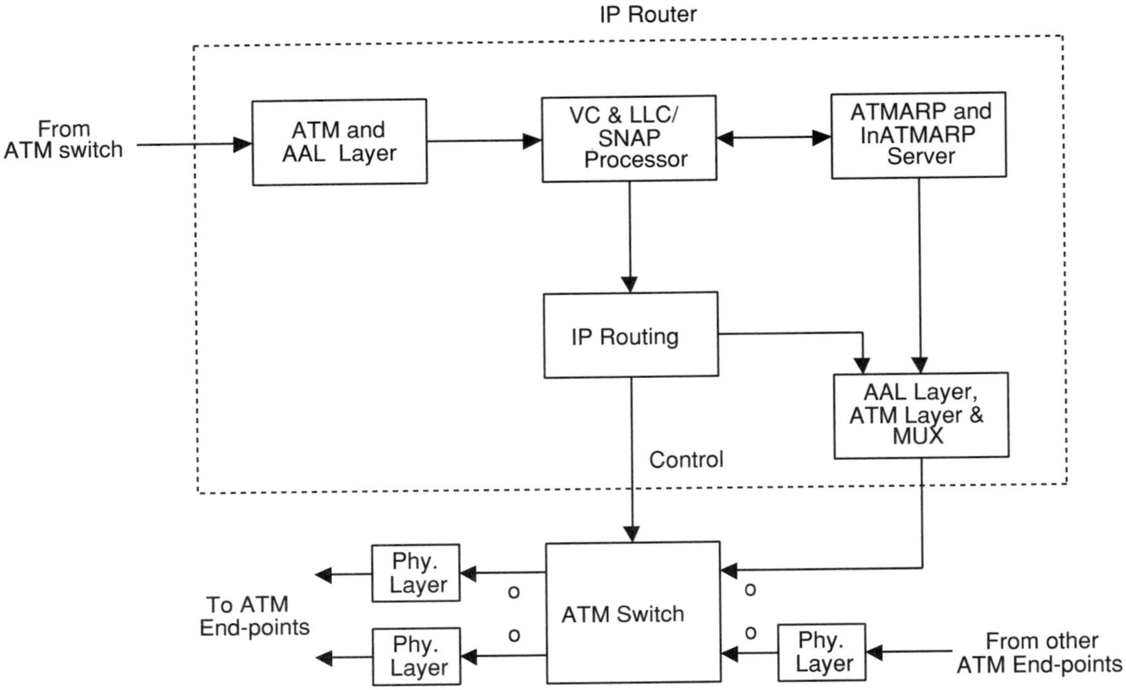

Performance greatly depends on how the ATM network handles congestion. The congestion control mechanisms that have been considered in these papers are listed below.

- *Credit-based flow control* — The credit-based flow control scheme, also known as the back-pressure method, works in the following way: Each VC at a node is allocated a certain number of buffers. The node keeps a count of these buffers, and sends an ATM cell only if a buffer is available at the receiver. Each time it sends a cell, it decrements the count, or the credit, as it is called, by one. When the receiving node has successfully forwarded the cell to the next hop, it sends an acknowledgment back to the sending node, which then increments its credit by one. In the event of congestion, the receiver withholds the acknowledgment. If at any time the credit becomes zero, the sending node stops emitting any more cells. If this flow control is implemented on each VC on each link on an end-to-end basis, each upstream node along the route is back-pressured this way until the source end-point stops originating any more cells. Since no cells are dropped, there is no retransmission as long as all cells constituting a TCP packet have been received before the packet is timed out. Thus, the network never experiences any congestion, and the system throughput very nearly approaches the link bandwidth. For example, suppose that any two adjacent switches are connected by a 155-Mb/s OC-3c link. Further assume that there are no channel errors in the system. Then, since the payload of each ATM cell is 48 octets, the maximum achievable throughput is about $155 \times 48/53$, or 140.38 Mb/s, ignoring overhead at the AAL layers. Also, the number of buffers that would be required in a flow-controlled system would be much smaller than otherwise. For example, Reference [8] uses a credit grant of only five cells per VC. On the other hand, if there were no such flow control, the required buffer size for a TCP packet size of eight kilobytes[3] would be about 170 cells.

- *Simple cell drop scheme* — In this scheme, when an ATM cell arrives at a full buffer, the receiver drops it. If, however, congestion clears at a later time, subsequent cells of the same packet are queued in the buffer. Thus, even though the packet is now totally useless, it continues to use network resources and waits for its turn to be serviced by the switch. Since, at the end of the time-out period, the TCP packet is re-transmitted, it further congests an already congested network. Consequently, the throughput with this scheme is significantly less than that achievable with the traditional packet TCP.

- *Selective cell drop scheme* — Here, two specific schemes have been considered: the so-called drop-tail or partial packet discard (PPD) scheme and the drop-whole or early packet discard (EPD) scheme. In the first scheme, when an ATM cell arrives at a full buffer, the receiver drops not only that particular cell, but all subsequent cells even though the network may no longer be congested. However, cells that arrived before the onset of congestion continue to be queued in the buffer and wait for their turn to be serviced by the switch. Clearly, then, there is some improvement in the throughput; however, it is still not as good as packet TCP. In the second scheme, the switch waits for a complete packet to arrive before forwarding its constituent cells to the next hop. If at any point the VC runs out of its allocated buffers, the switch removes all earlier cells of the packet from the buffers and drops all subsequent ones. Thus, in the absence of any flow controls, this congestion control scheme has the best performance.

Table 9-2 summarizes computer simulation results on the performance of these schemes [7]. The simulations are based on a two-node system — a source node and a destination node — connected via an OC-3c link. The AAL and ATM layer are provided by ATM hosts. The model uses a TCP window size of 64Kb, a TCP packet size of 8Kb, a buffer size of 256 cells

---

3. The default size of a TCP packet for IP over ATM is 9180 octets. For other networks, it is different. For example, it is 512 octets for IP networks and 1500 for Ethernets.

Table 9-2 Throughput as a Function of the Link Bandwidth for Different Congestion Control Mechanisms

Congestion Control Mechanism	Throughput
Simple cell drop scheme	0.65
Tail-drop scheme	0.75
Drop-whole scheme	0.82

per VC, and 6 concurrent TCP sessions. The throughput is expressed as a fraction of the link bandwidth.[4]

The throughput also depends on the per-VC buffer size. Clearly, if the buffer allocated to a VC is too small, there is a high probability that a newly arrived cell will find the buffer full much of the time. As a result, the effective throughput decreases. As the buffer size is increased, the throughput keeps increasing until it reaches the link capacity. Further increases in the buffer size have no effect on the throughput.

9.6 Summary

In LAN emulation, network layers exchange packets with the ATM layer in the same MAC format as is used in the LANs being emulated. A disadvantage of LAN emulation is that existing applications running above the network layer cannot request a desired QoS. One way to overcome this limitation is to modify existing network-layer protocols such that they would be able to support applications that provide some form of resource reservation for ATM. A protocol that has been modified to this end is IP. This modified version of IP is called IP over ATM. To accommodate different application-layer protocols, multiple packet types are multiplexed at the source. This is done in two ways: use of multiple VCs, and use of a single VC with multi-protocol encapsulation by adding an 8-octet header to an IP packet. IP packets thus modified are sent over AAL-5. Since each end-point in an ATM network has a unique ATM address, it is necessary to map an IP address to an ATM address, and vice versa. Two protocols — ATMARP and InATMARP — which are used for this purpose were described. We also indicated how IP would actually perform over ATM. This performance is specified in terms of the throughput. Congestion control schemes are based on dropping a cell when the network is congested and then discarding the affected packets following some rules. The results show that the early packet discard scheme performs the best.

9.7 References

[1] M. Laubach and J. Halpern, "Classical IP and ARP over ATM," RFC 2225, Apr. 1998.

[2] J. Heinanen, "Multiprotocol Encapsulation over ATM Adaptation Layer 5," version 2, RFC 1483, July 1993.

---

4. Notice that the maximum possible throughput is equal to the link bandwidth, and can only be achieved if there is no congestion in the network.

[3] M. Maher, "ATM Signalling Support for IP over ATM — UNI Signalling 4.0 Update," RFC 2331, Apr. 1998.

[4] T. Bradley and C. Brown, "Inverse Address Resolution Protocol," RFC 1293, Jan. 1992.

[5] R. Cole, D. Shur, and C. Villamizer, "IP over ATM — A Framework Document," RFC 1932, Apr. 1996.

[6] W. Almesberger, J. Le Boudec, and P. Oechslin, "Application Requested IP over ATM (AREQUIPA)," RFC 2170, July 1997.

[7] C. Fang, H. Chen, and J. Hutchins, "A Simulation Study TCP Performance in ATM Networks," *Proc. IEEE GLOBECOM* 94, Nov. 1994, pp. 1217–1223.

[8] A. Romanow and S. Floyd, "Dynamics of TCP traffic over ATM networks," IEEE JSAC, Vol. 13, No. 4, May 1995, pp. 633–641.

Problems

9.1 An application gathers real-time data from a system and transfers it over ATM to a central location. The data is monitored and used to control the system. Generally, a real-time transport protocol is used for this kind of application. See, for instance, H. Schulzrinne, et al., "A Transport Protocol for Real-Time Applications," RFC 1889, Jan. 1996.

List the requirements imposed by this application that should be supported by this protocol. How would you transfer this data over ATM? Suggest an appropriate protocol stack. Construct a user data packet and show how it is encoded at different layers of the stack.

9.2 Traditional LANs such as Ethernets and token rings have been designed for data applications. A basic requirement for these applications is that the data be delivered to the destination end-point error-free. This is achieved by using the TCP protocol at the transport layer, which provides for end-to-end error recovery. Since each user must contend with other users for network resources, packets encounter delays that increase as the offered load increases. Thus, the bandwidth available to each user is not constant, but depends on the offered load on the system. However, variable bandwidths and delay variations are generally not a problem for data applications.

Voice applications, on the other hand, require the network to guarantee fixed bandwidths. Bandwidths actually needed for an application depend on the QoS desired. For example, G.723.1, G.729, and G.711 audio require bandwidths of 6 kb/s, 8 kb/s, and 64 kb/s, respectively. They can all tolerate delays. However, for good quality interactive voice, these delays should be around 100 ms or so, and delay variations (or jitter) should be zero or as little as possible; otherwise, packets might be dropped.

The TCP protocol, in general, cannot guarantee these QoSs. New protocols that would meet the QoS requirement on legacy LANs have been suggested. Indicate how IP might be modified to provide the desired QoS for voice over these legacy LANs.

Multi-Protocol Over ATM (MPOA)

10.1 Introduction

We saw in Chapter 7 that an ATM network can emulate an Ethernet or a token ring LAN [1]–[4] using the LAN emulation protocol. Clearly, as we discussed in that chapter, LAN emulation provides some advantages. For example, the ATM network is now capable of running the same applications and protocols as the end-points on legacy LANs. The Multi-Protocol Over ATM (MPOA), which is an ATM Forum standard, further enhances this capability, and makes it possible for ATM networks to operate with a variety of internetwork-layer protocols that are used in today's networks [5].

To understand MPOA, it is helpful to recall the basic ideas of emulated LAN. Consider Figure 10-1, where an Ethernet LAN is connected to a host across an ATM network. The protocol stack on the host is shown on the right-hand side of the figure. The bridge also uses the same protocol stack. The logical entity marked "LEC," which resides in the bridge, performs address resolution and forwarding functions. When the workstation sends a unicast data packet that is destined to the host, the bridge LEC takes the IP data packet, constructs a frame according to the procedures of LAN emulation over ATM, and forwards it to the peer LEC using a Data Direct VCC. The IP data packet for an IEEE 802.3 LAN has the format of Figure 10-2. Embedded in its IP PDU is the internetwork-layer protocol address. However, the LEC does not use it when forwarding the packet to its peer LEC. In MPOA, this protocol address is used for forwarding purposes when some conditions are met.

Now consider the situation where there is more than one emulated LAN, connected together by routers, as depicted in Figure 10-3. The emulated LANs are shown as Subnets 1 and 2. If the host has a data packet to send to the server, its LEC would transmit the packet to the LEC in Router 1. Router 1 would use its routing function to forward the packet to Router 2. While doing so, it would retain the original format of the packet. If Router 2 is connected to more than one subnet, it must invoke its routing function to forward the packet to the LEC, associated with the appropriate subnet, which would then send the packet to the LEC of the destination server. In the MPOA, it is possible to send the packet using a shortcut VCC between the source and the destination, which would make it unnecessary for the routers to invoke their routing functions. Consequently, the source LEC (in the host in this

Figure 10-1   LAN emulation. The workstation-bridge combination and the host run the same protocol stack shown on the right-hand side of the figure.

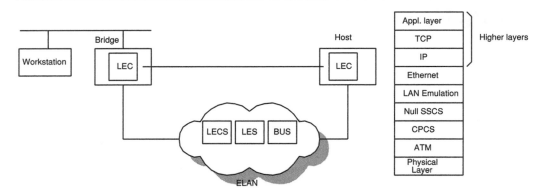

Figure 10-2   The IP data packet that the LEC receives from the higher layers in an IEEE 802.3 LAN.

Destination MAC Address 6 octets
Source MAC Address 6 octets
Length 2 octets
Fixed Pattern 0xaaaa aa03 0000 0008 (8 octets)
IP PDU

Figure 10-3   Inter-subnet data flow. Here, the ATM network consists of a number of IP subnets. In LAN emulation without MPOA, the inter-subnet traffic must go through the routers. With MPOA, on the other hand, the data flow bypasses the routing functions of the routers, and can be sent using a shortcut VCC between the source in one subnet and the destination in the other. Here, packets are transferred across the ATM network using the internetwork-layer address (e.g., the IP address).

example) can strip the incoming packet of all MAC addresses and just send the IP PDU (together with the 8-octet fixed pattern of Figure 10-2). In other words, the MPOA allows the inter-subnet data to be transferred over an ATM VCC, bypassing the routing functions and only using the internetwork-layer protocol addresses for forwarding purposes.

The purpose of this chapter is to present an overview of MPOA [5]. It is organized as follows: First, we define some common terms that are used in MPOA. This is followed by a description of components that make up an MPOA system. Since the resolution of an unknown address is an essential part of the MPOA procedures, an ARP, called the Next Hop Resolution Protocol (NHRP), which is commonly used in non-broadcast multiple access (NBMA) networks, is presented next [6]. Finally, the MPOA procedures are briefly described.

10.2 Some Definitions

Authoritative NHRP Resolution Reply — A reply is authoritative if it comes from the Next Hop Resolution Server (NHS) that serves the destination. Otherwise, it is non-authoritative. A transit NHS, for instance, can only generate a non-authoritative reply.

Cache entry — Information describing data flows in an MPOA system. Ingress cache entry relates to inbound data, while egress cache entry is concerned with outbound data.

Egress — A point where outbound data leaves an MPOA system.

Ingress — A point where inbound data enters an MPOA system.

Internetwork layer — The media-independent layer. An example is the IP layer.

MPC — MPOA client. This functional entity is associated with a host. It performs forwarding functions, and generates service requests to an MPOA server.

MPS — MPOA server. This logical entity is associated with a router, and responds to service requests from an MPC.

NBMA — Non-broadcast multi-access network. This is a network or subnetwork that does not support broadcasting. For example, an X.25 or an ATM network is an NBMA network.

NHC — Next Hop Client. It performs a similar function to an MPC except that it operates with NHRP.

NHRP — Next Hop Resolution Protocol. It is used to determine an unknown NBMA address corresponding to a given protocol address.

NHS–NHRP server. It performs a similar function to an MPS, except that it operates with NHRP.

Station — This is a generic term used for a host or a router with an ARP functionality.

Subnetwork layer — The media-dependent layer. An example is ATM, X.25, etc.

10.3 MPOA Components

A number of logical components make up an MPOA system. Hosts such as the one shown in Figure 10-3 perform some distinct logical functions. One of them, as we already know, is the

Figure 10-4 The various functional entities of a host and a router in an MPOA environment. (a) The MPC in a host, bridge, or edge device. (b) The MPS in a router. (c) An example of an MPC serving two LECs.

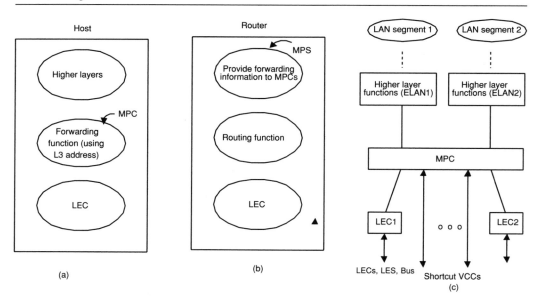

LEC. The second is the layer 3 forwarding function. When a host receives a packet from its upper layer that has to be forwarded toward its destination, it examines whether it can use a shortcut VCC for this purpose. If such a VCC exists, it forwards the packet using the VCC. If there is no such VCC, and if it determines, based on some criteria, that the packet should now be forwarded using a shortcut VCC, it will request such a VCC from the next hop router.[1] Similarly, the host may receive a packet from a server which it must deliver to its local interfaces. The logical entity in a host or edge device that performs this forwarding function is called an MPC. This is shown in Figure 10-4(a). Thus, in MPOA, when an ingress MPC receives an incoming unicast data packet from the upper layers, it sends the packet to its peer MPC on the destination end-point directly over a shortcut VCC using the internetwork-layer protocols. This is shown by the dashed line in Figure 10-5.

Devices marked "Routers" in Figure 10-3 also include an LEC. These devices perform two other logical functions. The first one, of course, is the normal routing function of a router. The second is to provide internetwork-layer forwarding information to a requesting MPC.

---

1. This, of course, assumes that the destination MAC address of the data packet has been already resolved, that is, the ATM address of the destination with the given MAC address has been already determined.

Figure 10-5   Unicast data transfer in MPOA. The dotted line shows that the peer MPCs in the source and destination hosts use a shortcut VCC to transfer the data.

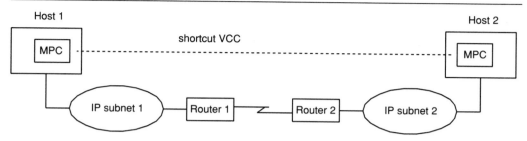

This second function of the router is termed an "MPS." These functions are shown in Figure 10-4(b). Like an MPC, an MPS is also a logical entity. Clearly, an MPC lies between the LEC and the higher layers residing on the host. The MPS function can also be similarly delineated in the router.

In LAN emulation, an ATM network requires the services of the following functional entities: the LECS, LES, and BUS. These functional entities can be either embedded in an ATM network or provided by some stand-alone devices that work in conjunction with the ATM network. Similarly, MPOA requires each MPOA host (i.e., an MPOA edge device) to include, or be associated with, an MPC. Also, each router in an IP subnet (of an ATM network) must include, or be associated with, an MPS. These requirements are in place so that an edge device or router can forward a packet to its destination anywhere within the network using the internetwork-layer protocol address information.

It is possible for a device to have more than one MPC. Each MPC can serve one or more LECs. An LEC, on the other hand, can only be served by one MPC. See Figure 10-4(c). Each MPC should have one (control) ATM address, which may be the same as the ATM address of an LEC that it serves.

10.4 Next Hop Resolution Protocol

A network contains, among other things, a number of stations — both hosts and routers. Depending upon the internals of the network, a given station may not be able to communicate directly with all of the other stations. To do so, it may have to go through one or more routers. Thus, on this basis, it is possible to partition a network into a group of subnetworks such that an inter-subnet communication may be subjected to routing and filtering restrictions, whereas an intra-subnet communication would be free from such restrictions. For example, the network of Figure 10-6 is partitioned into three subnets.

An inter-subnet packet, before it can reach its destination, may have to traverse a number of hops and go through a number of routers in an NBMA network. For example, in the above figure, if Edge Device-1 wants to send a packet to Host-1, it can do so directly without having to traverse a router. On the other hand, a packet to Host-2, for instance, must go

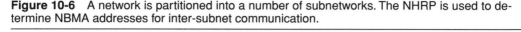

Figure 10-6 A network is partitioned into a number of subnetworks. The NHRP is used to determine NBMA addresses for inter-subnet communication.

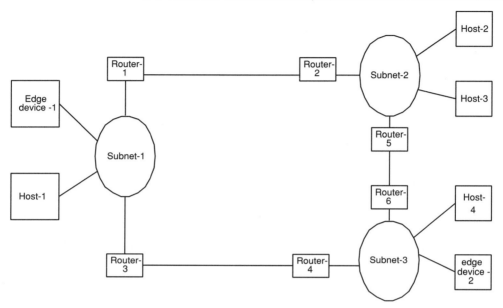

through at least two routers. Here, the edge device first sends the packet to its next hop router, say, Router-1, which then sends the packet to another NHS downstream toward the destination, and so on.

To be able to send a packet to its destination using internetwork-layer address information, the source station must know the NBMA address of the destination. It can know that address in a number of ways. For example, at system configuration time, that address can be manually entered into the system by the user. Thus, in each station's cache memory, one could create a table that provides a binding between an internetwork-layer protocol address and an NBMA address. A better way, of course, would be for a station to generate a request to the next hop asking for the unknown address, build the table automatically, and update its entries, or remove them when needed.

A number of ARPs are available for this purpose. One such protocol is the NHRP, developed by the IETF for NBMA networks. Clearly, for this protocol to work, a router should be able to reply to an address resolution request. This is accomplished by incorporating a logical entity called the Next Hop Server (NHS) that would perform this function in the router. Similarly, a device that requests this service from an NHS must have a functional entity that would generate the address resolution request. That entity is called Next Hop Client (NHC). Clearly, the NHS and NHC are similar in concept to the MPS and MPC, respectively.

A given NHC may be served by more than one NHS. For example, in Figure 10-6, Host 1 is served by NHSs in Routers 1 and 3. When an NHC wants to send a packet to another NHC, it first determines, using normal routing procedures, which of those NHSs the packet is to be forwarded to. As mentioned before, each NHC maintains in its cache a table of *<internetwork layer address, NBMA address>* tuples for each NHS that serves it. The table may also contain the address of a default router that a host could use for its next hop. In the same way, each NHS maintains a table containing its own protocol address and ATM address, and those of each NHC that it serves. There may be instances where an NHS does not directly serve any NHC, but merely routes packets to other subnetworks[2] via a downstream NHS. In these cases, each NHS must maintain a table of *<internetwork layer protocol address, router identification>* tuples for all its downstream NHSs. Furthermore, it should be configured so that it can exchange routing information with them.

10.4.1 Procedures

With these preliminaries out of the way, let us now describe the protocol. For this, we consider a relatively simple case where a source station wants to send a data packet to its destination. The source could be a host or transit router. The following procedures are invoked when an MPC gets a data packet:

1. Upon receiving the packet, the MPC determines the next hop toward the destination using standard routing procedures. If the source is a host, the next hop is one of the routers that serve this source, or it could be simply a default router. If the source is a transit router, the next hop is just the protocol address in the packet. The source then refers to its cache and determines if the table contains the NBMA address corresponding to the protocol address. If it does, there is no need to resolve the address; it simply uses the known address and forwards the packet to the neighboring NHS on its way to the destination.

2. If the NBMA address of the destination does not appear in the table, it forms an NHRP Resolution Request packet containing its own NBMA address, its own internetwork-layer address (i.e., the protocol address), and the destination's protocol address, and sends it to the next hop. As for the data packet itself that was supposed to be sent, the NHC may either discard it as it waits for a reply, save it, or better yet, forward it to the next hop along with the Resolution Request packet so that it can reach the destination following the same route.

3. The NHS at the next hop, on receiving the Resolution Request, first checks to see if it serves the destination station. If it does, the NHS forms an NHRP Resolution Reply packet with the destination's address, appropriately sets a bit[3] to indicate that it is an authoritative reply, and sends the packet to the source. On receiving the packet, the

---

2. In other words, this NHS is an exit point for MPOA data, and may be viewed simply as an egress router.

3. This bit is one of the bits of the Flags field in the mandatory portion of the reply packet.

NHC adds the new NBMA address corresponding to the destination's protocol address to its table.

4. If this NHS does not serve the destination, it may still be able to reach the destination through one of its downstream NHSs.[4] To determine which one to choose, it refers to its table, where it maintains the identification number of router(s) corresponding to each protocol address. If it finds an entry for the desired protocol address, it forwards the Resolution Request packet to that downstream NHS, and returns an NHRP Resolution Reply packet indicating a non-authoritative reply to the source.

5. If there is no match in the table, the NHS sends an NHRP Resolution Reply packet, indicating a negative acknowledgment (NAK).[5]

6. When the NHRP Resolution Request packet finally reaches the NHS that directly serves the destination, the NHS first forms an authoritative NHRP Resolution Reply, inserting its NBMA address in the packet. It then retrieves the source address from the NHRP Resolution Request packet, and sends it to that address. Upon receipt of the reply, the source NHC enters the destination's NBMA address into the table.

Notice that an NHC could initiate other requests as well. For example, it could generate an NHRP Registration Request, asking to register its NBMA address with the NHS, or an NHRP Purge Request, asking the NHS to remove its NBMA address from its list.

Similarly, the possible replies from an NHS are as follows: an NHRP Resolution Reply, NHRP Registration Reply, NHRP Purge Reply, and an NHRP Error Indication. An NHS may be connected logically not only to multiple NHCs, but also to one or more routers. Hence, if a router is not connected to any NHS, then that router cannot handle the NHRP.

In some cases, there may be one or more loops between a source and a destination (see Figure 10-6). The NHRP can detect these loops and prevent a packet from looping indefinitely. Similarly, there are features in the protocol that allow for tracing the route traversed by a packet. It does this in the following way: As a packet traverses in the forward direction to its destination, each intermediate NHS[6] modifies the NHRP Resolution Request packet, which it receives from the upstream NHS, by appending its address to the extension part of the packet as described in Section 10.4.2, and then forwards the modified packet to the downstream NHS. The backward path from the destination to the source can also be traced in a similar way. When the forward path is traced, the extension part of the packet is known as NHRP Forward Transit NHS Record extension. When the backward path from the destination to the source is traced, the extension part of the packet is known as NHRP Backward Transit NHS Record extension.

---

4. This would be the case when the destination station is located in a subnet several hops away from the originating subnet.

5. This is done by setting the code field of the mandatory portion of the NHRP resolution reply packet to a non-zero value. If the value is zero, it indicates a positive acknowledgment. If it is 12, it indicates that the NHS could not resolve the destination's protocol address. For more detailed information, see Reference [6].

6. An intermediate NHS is also known as a transit NHS.

10.4.2 Data Formats

The format of an NHRP packet is shown in Figure 10-7. All packets, whether request or reply, have the same generic format. As shown in Figure 10-7(a), they have three parts: (i) a 20-octet fixed header part, (ii) a variable-length mandatory part, and (iii) a variable-length extension part. All field lengths in the figure are expressed in octets.

The details of the fixed part are shown in Figure 10-7(b). The hop count provides the maximum number of intermediate NHSs that a packet can traverse before being discarded. The packet type indicates whether the packet is a Resolution Request, Resolution Reply, etc. Its values are shown in Figure 10-7(f). Figure 10-7(c) is the mandatory part that consists of a header portion and one or more client information elements (CIEs). The format of each CIE is shown in Figure 10-7(d). The extension part is optional and may be omitted. Its format is shown in Figure 10-7(e).

10.5 MPOA Overview

The MPOA operates in much the same way as LAN emulation. There are five operations in MPOA: configuration, discovery, address resolution, connection management, and unicast data transfer.

10.5.1 Configuration

Each MPC and MPS must be configurable either manually at system administration time or through the LECS of an emulated LAN. Some of the configuration parameters of an MPC are: shortcut setup frame count, the time when an MPC should attempt to forward a packet using a shortcut VCC, and the retry time (i.e., the time after which the MPC should retry the address resolution if it did not receive a reply to its first attempt). Some of the parameters for MPS are: internetwork-layer protocols supported in address resolution, retry time, and the minimum time to wait before abandoning a resolution request.

10.5.2 Discovery

Each MPC should determine the MAC and ATM address of each MPS so that control VCCs that can be used for sending an MPOA ARP request can be established. Similarly, an MPS must learn the ATM address of an MPC. This process of learning addresses is called discovery. In some cases, an ELAN may have multiple MPSs; they too must discover each other. Discovery is accomplished via the registration and address resolution procedures of LAN emulation.

Each LEC must register with the LES entity of an emulated LAN by sending an LE_REGISTER_REQUEST containing its MAC and ATM address. The format of the registration request in the MPOA system differs slightly from that in the LANE protocol — the MPOA device type T/L/V is to be included, indicating whether it is an MPC, MPS, or both.[7] If, later on, the status of the MPOA device changes, each LEC served by that device first unregisters and then re-registers with the new set of device parameters.

---

7. See the chapter on the LANE protocol.

Figure 10-7 The NHRP packet format. (a) Generic format. (b) The fixed part. (c) The mandatory part. (d) The CIEs contained in the mandatory part. (e) The extension part. (f) The various NHRP packet types.

Fixed Part - 20 Bytes	Mandatory Part - Variable Size	Extension Part - Variable Size

(a)

Information Elements	Size in Bytes	Remarks
Link Layer Address Indicator	2	Set to 0x0008 to indicate that NHRP is using an ATM address. For HDLC address, it is 0x0004.
Protocol Type	2	For ATM Forum, it is 0x0400 - 0x04ff.
SNAP Extension of Protocol Type	5	Non-zero only if Protocol Type = 0x0080.
Hop Count	1	If Hop Count > 0, received packet is forwarded. Otherwise, packet is dropped.
Packet Size in Bytes	2	
Checksum	2	
Offset to Start of Extension Part	2	Indicates where the extension part begins.
Address Mapping and Management Protocol Version	1	The value of this field is 1 for NHRP.
Packet Type	1	Indicates if it is a resolution request, reply, etc.
Size of Source NBMA Address	1	
Size of Source NBMA Subaddress	1	

(b)

Information Element	Size	Remarks
Source Protocol Address Size	1	It is address of source in a request packet or address of destination in a reply packet
Dest. Protocol Address Size	1	
Flags	2	Depends on, among other things, whether packet comes from a router or host. For details, see [5].
Request ID	4	Generated by requesting device, copied by receiver.
Source NBMA Address	Varies	
Source NBMA subaddress	Varies	
Source Protocol Address	Varies	
Dest. Protocol Address	Varies	
Client Information Entries	Varies	A Resolution Request packet may have at most one CIE. A Resolution Reply or a Registration Request packet may have more.

(c)

Figure 10-7 *Continued*

Information Element	Size	Remarks
Code	1	Meaningful in a reply packet. 0 if a valid reply, otherwise a failure cause code.
Prefix Length *n*	1	If *n* > 0, it means that there is an equivalence class of addresses that matches first n bits of destination protocol address.
Unused	2	
Maximum Transmission Unit	2	
Holding Time	2	Time for which client information remains valid.
Type and Length of Next Hop NBMA Address	1	This and following entries are omitted in a Resolution Request packet.
Type and Length Next Hop NBMA Subaddress	1	
Length of Client Protocol Addr.	1	
Preference	1	Indicates relative importance of each CIE.
Client NBMA Address	Varies	Omitted in a Registration Request if a device registers only itself, and included if it registers next hops as well.
Client NBMA Subaddress	Varies	
Client Protocol Address	Varies	

(d)

Type - 2 Bytes	Length - 2 Bytes	Value - Variable Length

(e)

Value of Packet Type	Packet Type
1	Resolution Request
2	Resolution Reply
3	Registration Request
4	Registration Reply
5	Purge Request
6	Purge Reply
7	Error Indication

(f)

10.5.3 Address Resolution

The ARP is used to resolve an unknown target address so that VCCs can be established for transferring unicast data. In other words, the ATM address of the destination end-point for a shortcut data VCC, if not known, must be determined. When an MPC determines that an incoming data packet[8] should be sent over a shortcut VCC, but the destination ATM address is not known, its associated LEC sends an LE_ARP_REQUEST containing its ATM address, the destination MAC address, and optionally, the source MAC address from the data packet that triggered the Resolution Request. If the MPS has the requested information, it sends it to the MPC; otherwise, the MPS itself originates a request along the routed path through its local NHS, using its own internetwork-layer protocol address as the source, but copying all the other information elements from the MPC's original request.

10.5.4 Connection Management

Connection management procedures are used to set up VCCs when needed. Recall that there are two types of VCCs: control VCCs and data VCCs. An address resolution request, for instance, would be sent over a control VCC, while a unicast data packet would be sent over a data VCC.

10.5.5 Data Transfer

10.5.5.1 Incoming Data

The transfer of unicast data that comes into an MPOA system at an ingress MPC from the upper layers (e.g., a bridge) involves the following steps.

1. When an MPC receives an incoming packet from the upper layers, it examines if its cache contains the ATM address of an MPS (in a next hop router) corresponding to the destination MAC address contained in the packet. As we said before, ATM addresses are learned via the discovery process. Since there may be more than one LEC served by an MPC, the MPC uses the <*LEC number, MAC address*> pair as an index into the ingress cache to fetch the correct MPS ATM address.

2. For each <*MPS ATM address, internetwork layer protocol address*> tuple, the cache also contains three parameters: (i) the destination ATM address, or so-called shortcut VCC, (ii) information on the internetwork-layer protocol encapsulation,[9] and (iii) some control information. Since different internetwork protocols forward packets in different ways, the encapsulation details may be different from one protocol to another, and even for a given protocol, from one media access type to another. The control information that is often used in the context of incoming packets is the length of time, or a similar count, after which a unicast data packet should be sent over a shortcut VCC.

---

8. A packet that comes to an MPC from upper layers (an ingress point).

9. Remember that the protocol here is not necessarily the IP protocol — it could be other protocols.

Figure 10-8 Ingress cache in MPOA. There are two lookup tables. The first one, when indexed by the LEC number-MAC address combination, gives the MPS ATM address, which is then used along with the internetwork-layer protocol address to index the second table.

Parameters Used to Index the First Table	Cache Entry 1	Parameters Used to Index the Second Table	Cache Entry 2		
			Shortcut VCC	Encapsulated Info	Control Info
LEC-1, MPS MAC Address 1	MPS ATM Address 1	ATM Address 1. Internetwork-Layer Protocol Address 1			
LEC-2, MPS MAC Address 1	MPS ATM Address 1	ATM Address 1. Internetwork-Layer Protocol Address 2			
o	o	o		o	
o	o	o		o	
LEC-n, MPS MAC Address - *m*					

Using the *<ATM address of the MPS* (fetched in Step 1), *internetwork layer destination address>* tuple as an index, the MPC examines if there is an entry in the cache of the above three parameters as depicted in Figure 10-8. If there is no such entry, a new one is created with its shortcut VCC field marked invalid. Its control information field is also initialized. The MPC then transmits the packet to the LEC, which eventually sends it out to the ELAN. We call this the default path. Obviously, the shortcut VCC, which has been marked as invalid, cannot be used at this point.

3. If there is already an entry in the cache, but its direct VCC field is invalid, the above control field is incremented and the data packet is again sent out over the default path.

4. If the direct VCC field is invalid but the count has exceeded a pre-configured value, the MPC sends an MPOA Resolution Request to the MPS, asking for an ATM address so that it can be used to establish a shortcut VCC.

5. When the MPS replies and a shortcut VCC is established, the corresponding entry in the cache is marked valid, and the packet is sent out using the VCC.

When an ingress MPC determines that a packet must take the default path, it retains the DLL encapsulation with which it received the packet from its upper layers. As mentioned before, this encapsulation is different for different medium access protocols. For example, Figure 10-2 shows the DLL encapsulation of an IP packet over an IEEE 802.3 LAN. Figure 10-9 shows the same thing for an Ethernet LAN. When a packet uses a shortcut VCC, the MPC removes the DLL encapsulation and simply sends the multi-protocol packet. As an example, an IP packet, after this removal, takes the format of Figure 10-10.

Figure 10-9   The IP data packet that the LEC receives from the higher layers in an Ethernet LAN.

Destination MAC Address 6 octets
Source MAC Address 6 octets
Ether Type 2 octets
IP PDU

Figure 10-10   The format of an IP data packet over a shortcut VCC in an MPOA system.

Fixed Pattern 0xaaaa aa03 0000 0800 (8 octets)
Internetwork-Layer PDU

10.5.5.2 Outgoing Data

When a data packet comes into an MPC to be forwarded to the upper layers (e.g., a bridge), the following procedures are used: [10]

1. For each combination of the internetwork-layer destination address, the source ATM address and the destination ATM address, the MPC egress cache maintains an entry of three parameters: (i) the LEC number, (ii) DLL header, and (iii) control information. When an MPC receives a packet on a shortcut VCC, it looks for a matching entry in its cache. If it finds one corresponding to the internetwork-layer destination address, the source ATM address, and destination ATM address, and if the destination MAC address is available, the MPC fetches the DLL header field from the table, appends it to the multi-protocol-layer packet received from the MPS, and presents it to the bridge so that it can be delivered to the destination.

2. If there is a matching entry, but if the destination MAC address is not available in the LEC, the MPC may choose to forward the packet to the bridge so that it can learn the address through normal procedures. However, it is allowed to do so only for a limited

---

10. In this case, the data packets are leaving the MPOA system, and hence the MPC is an egress MPC.

length of time (30s). If, by this time, the bridge cannot learn the address, the egress MPC marks the entry in the cache as invalid and sends an egress cache purge request to the MPS, which then initiates an NHRP purge request.

3. If there is no matching entry in the table, the MPC discards the packet, increments an error counter, and sends an NHRP purge request over the shortcut VCC asking the source MPC that originated the packet (i.e., the ingress MPC at the remote end) to remove the corresponding entry from its own ingress cache.

10.6 Summary

MPOA can be understood by recalling the basic ideas of LAN emulation. When an LEC receives a data packet from higher layers that has to be forwarded to an emulated LAN, it takes the IP PDU, together with the source and destination MAC addresses, adds a 2-octet LANE header, and then sends the resulting packet over a data direct VCC. Although the IP PDU contains the internetwork-layer protocol address, the LEC does not use it when forwarding the packet. In MPOA, on the other hand, the LEC strips the incoming packet of all MAC addresses and forwards the IP PDU over a shortcut VCC using that protocol address. Similarly, if an emulated LAN consists of multiple subnets, and if a packet has to be forwarded from one subnet to another, each router must invoke its routing functions. MPOA makes that unnecessary. Thus, with MPOA, it is possible for an ATM network to operate with a variety of internetwork-layer protocols that are used in today's networks.

We defined terms that are commonly used in the description of MPOA. An MPOA system consists of a few logical components such as an MPOA client and MPOA server. We described these components and indicated the functions they perform. All unknown ATM addresses must be resolved before a packet can be forwarded to its destination using the protocol address. In MPOA, this is done using NHRP. We provided a comprehensive description of this protocol, and also described the NHRP packet formats. There are five operations in MPOA: configuration, discovery, address resolution, connection management, and data transfer. We described these operations briefly, and in particular, showed how higher-layer data packets, which have to be forwarded across an ATM network, are treated differently from those which come from the ATM network and have to be passed to the higher layers.

10.7 References

[1] The ATM Forum standard AF-LANE-0021.000, "*LAN Emulation over ATM,*" Version 1.0, Jan. 1995.

[2] The ATM Forum standard AF-LANE-0084.000, "*LAN Emulation over ATM − LUNI Specification,*" Version 2, July 1997.

[3] The ATM Forum standard af-lane-0050.000, "*LAN Emulation over ATM Version 1.0 Addendum,*" Dec. 1995.

[4] The ATM Forum *"LAN Emulation over ATM Version 2 — LNNI Specification,"* Draft 8, Feb. 1997.

[5] The ATM Forum standard AF-MPOA-0087.000, *"Multi-Protocol over ATM,"* Version 1.0, July 1997.

[6] J. V. Luciani, et al., "NBMA Next Hop Resolution Protocol (NHRP)," *Internet Draft,* Sept. 1997.

Switched Multimedia Services

11.1 Introduction

Multimedia services provide an integrated transport of voice, data, image, and video, including graphics. Some examples are:

- *Video conferencing* — Three or more end-points can participate in a video conference using a multipoint control unit (MCU). Currently, video conferencing using a PRI interface and, in some cases, multiple BRI interfaces over an ISDN is quite popular. Many vendors are also offering video conferencing equipment for use over ATM.
- *Multimedia desktop* — This is a real-time teleservice involving voice, data, image, video, and graphics between two or more end-points. In one mode of operation, users can participate in a multimedia conference. If desired, the conferencing can be interactive. In another mode, more than one user can access a multimedia server at the same time and retrieve the desired information. In the third, a multimedia source can broadcast information to all users.
- *Interactive distance learning* — A single source broadcasts multimedia information to a number of end-points with each end-point given the option to interact with the source. The information consists of audio, video, and data.

It is possible to use different data rates for multimedia services. Protocols are available supporting these services over both public and private networks. For example, a multimedia terminal can be connected to a general switched telephone network (GSTN) over a V.34/V.8 modem or over BRI/PRI lines at $n \times 64$ kb/s with $n = 1, \ldots, 30$. Similarly, multimedia services can be delivered to end-users over traditional LANs with or without guaranteed QoS, or over ATM LANs at higher data rates. The different information types — voice, data, image, and video — are combined into a single frame and then transported over a physical channel with the desired bandwidth. Each application may require a different QoS. Also, it is necessary to provide services on a demand basis, and as such, call control procedures must be supported by both networks and end-points.

The purpose of this chapter is to describe generic multimedia services. A number of international standards, known as the H and T series recommendations, have been developed in the last few years that specify the functional requirements of terminal equipment used in multimedia services and their connection procedures [1]–[26]. Our description is based on these standards. Initially, most vendors started designing multimedia services for N-ISDNs and legacy LANs. Presently, the general architecture of ATM terminals supporting multimedia services is very similar to that for N-ISDNs. Hence, it is appropriate to begin the chapter with a description of these services over narrow-band ISDNs. A brief description is included of an MCU, which is an important entity in multimedia services. This is followed by a description of the multimedia services over legacy LANs and ATM. Since we would like to give the reader an understanding of how to go about designing a system, we provide functional architectures of multimedia terminals, the protocol stack used in the system, and some detail of call control procedures.

11.2 Standards Supporting Multimedia Services

Table 11-1 shows multimedia services and corresponding H-series standards on which they are based. As indicated in the third column of the table, each standard invokes many other standards, and for most of the services, many of them are common.

11.3 Multimedia Services over Narrow-Band-ISDN

11.3.1 Network Configuration

Narrow-band-ISDN provides low-speed multimedia services at bandwidths of $n \times 64$ kb/s, where $n = 1, \ldots, 30$. The data rate used in any specific application depends on the QoS de-

Table 11-1 Multimedia services and corresponding standards that define them.

Service Definition	Main Standard	Other Standards Referenced in the Main Standard
Multimedia services over a GSTN using a V.34/V.8 modem	H.324	G.723, H.261, H.263, V.14, LAPM, H.245, H.223
Multimedia services over an N-ISDN	H.320	G.711, G.722, G.728, H.261, H.263, H.264, H.220/AV270, H.230, H.242, H.243, H.221, Q.939
Multimedia services over LANs that guarantee a QoS comparable to that of an N-ISDN	H.322	G.711, G.722, G.728, H.261, H.263, H.264, H.220/AV270, H.230, H.242, H.243, H.221
Multimedia services over LANs that do not guarantee a QoS	H.323	G.711, G.722, G.723, G.728, G.729, H.261, H.263, H.264, R.120, H.245, H.225.0
Multimedia services over B-ISDN	H.321	G.711, G.722, G.728, H.261, H.263, H.264, H.220/AV270, H.230, H.242, H.243, H.221, AAL-5

sired and the cost of the networking equipment. As in B-ISDN, one of the most important multimedia services at data rates up to 2 Mb/s is video conferencing. In private networks, which are mostly composed of T1 lines, the video equipment connects to the network over T1, or fractional T1 lines. Currently, many equipment vendors are offering ISDN access equipment, which provides V.35 and RS-449 interfaces to video codecs, BRI interfaces to desktop PCs, and BRI/PRI interfaces to an ISDN.

Video conferencing may involve only two terminals as shown in Figure 11-1, where the codec connects to the network through a terminal adapter. Figure 11-2 shows a network configuration where more than two terminals can participate in a conference call. An MCU

Figure 11-1 Video conferencing between two terminals in a point-to-point configuration. Depending on the QoS desired, a few BRI interfaces could be used in lieu of a PRI interface.

Figure 11-2 Multipoint video conferencing over an ISDN.

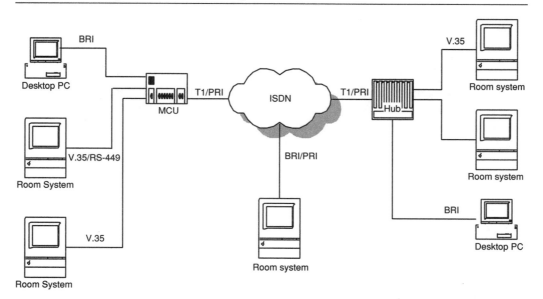

Figure 11-3   Functional block diagram of an H.320 terminal.

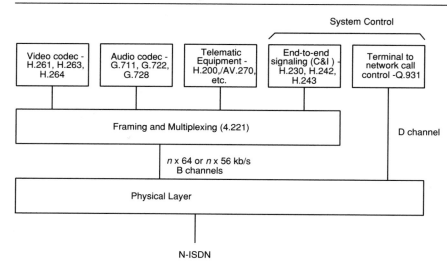

receives multiple channels from its network and codec ports, processes the audio-visual signals according to some rules, and distributes them along with any data to the desired conferees. Connections are established on a demand basis by means of ISDN call control procedures implemented in the hub, which also multiplexes multiple, co-located, room systems into a single PRI interface.

11.3.2 H.320 Terminal Architecture

A functional block diagram of an audio-visual terminal based on CCITT Recommendations H.320 is shown in Figure 11-3. Since video signal processing takes longer, the audio codec adds compensatory delays to audio signals to ensure lip synchronization. The video codec provides redundancy reduction. The data signals include visual aids such as electronic blackboards, still pictures, facsimiles, and documents, and provide enhancements to the basic visual telephone system. There are two types of control signals: out-of-band, Q.931 call controls and in-band control and indication (C&I). The C&I signals allow end-points to exchange terminal capabilities and establish the proper mode of operation according to Recommendations H.230, H.242, and H.243.[1] Signals are multiplexed and demultiplexed using H.221 framing and multiplexing rules.

---

1. C&I are sent over the service channel of H.221 frames.

Figure 11-4   Connection procedures between H.320 terminals in a point-to-point configuration.

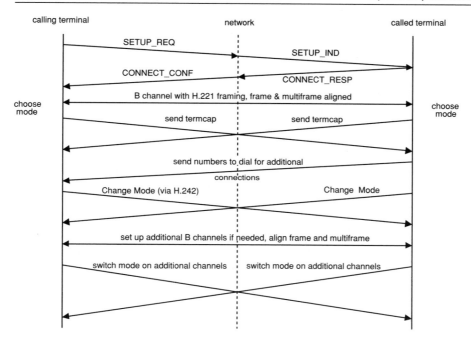

11.3.3 Connection Procedures for a Point-to-Point Call

The connection procedures are based on Recommendations H.242, and are summarized in Figure 11-4. First, the calling terminal establishes a single B channel connection across a public ISDN to the desired remote terminal using call control procedures Q.931. Once this channel is established, the H.221 framing is overlaid, and the in-band procedure (over the B channel) is activated. Since, initially, neither terminal knows the capabilities of the other,[2] they both select default capabilities, send their terminal capabilities over H.221 frames,[3] start a timer, and try to acquire frame and multiframe alignment on the incoming channel. If a ter-

2. A terminal may have many different capabilities. For example, it may be able to decode audio according to G.711 A-law, G.711 mu law, or ISO standard, all at rates up to 384 kb/s. One video codec, for example, may decode both common intermediate format (CIF) and quarter CIF (QCIF), while another just QCIF, but not CIF. Similarly, different terminals may handle different transfer rates. For example, one of them may support a 64-kb/s and a 384-kb/s channel, while another may support a single channel with a bandwidth of 64 — 384 kb/s, and so on. Different visual telephone types and their capabilities are listed in Recommendations H.221 and H.261.

3. Notice that each terminal, when sending its capabilities, indicates what it can receive, not what it can transmit.

minal fails to acquire alignment before the timer expires, the sequence is restarted all over again. Since the capabilities of the terminals must match before they can begin to exchange information, they must choose the highest common set of capabilities.

If additional B channels are required, the calling party establishes them sequentially following the same call control procedures. Frame alignment must be acquired and common capabilities selected on each additional channel following the same procedures as for the first channel. When a call is active, a terminal may request a mode or capability change. This may be the case if, for example, a user turns on an auxiliary telematic machine.

11.3.4 MCU

An MCU allows three or more terminals to participate in a multimedia conference. The number of interface ports on MCUs currently available in the market varies, but 16 — 64 ports are not unusual. Each terminal connected to an MCU port may have different capabilities. Any terminal can control the conference at any time, but only one may be assigned to be the chair control.

An MCU is available either as a stand-alone device or as part of an access hub. A stand-alone MCU provides connections not only to terminals, but also to a network over a PRI, or one or more BRI lines. Its functional block diagram is shown in Figure 11-5.

When an MCU receives signals from the network side, the block designated as "H.221 Frame Mux/Demux" acquires frame and multiframe alignment, separates the signal into audio, video, data, and control signals, and passes them to the appropriate processing units and then to the terminals. If the audio or video signal bandwidth extends over multiple B channels, the demultiplexer buffers them, if necessary, and properly orders them into octets. If encryption is used at the transmitting end, the signal is decoded here. In the other direction, this block multiplexes the audio, video, data, and control signals from a terminal into a single frame.

The audio conferencing algorithm used in an MCU may vary. In one variation, the digitized audio signal received from each port is decoded into linear PCM and applied to the input of a mixer along with a similarly decoded signal from other ports. The output of the mixer is encoded according to the audio capability of each destination terminal and then sent out to each terminal. The video signal received from the terminal that has the conference control at a given time is broadcast to all other terminals, while the control terminal continues to get the video from the same terminal from which it was getting the video before. Alternatively, the video from some or all terminals may be mixed by spatially multiplexing the images into a single, composite image. The resulting output is then sent to the other terminals.[4]

---

4. The chairperson controlling the conference may decide which terminal should transmit the video at any time. This is done by sending a Multipoint Command Visualization (MCV) code from a terminal to force the MCU to broadcast the video signal from the terminal. These C&I codes are listed in Recommendations H.230. T.120 gives other procedures to control a conference from a terminal as well.

Figure 11-5   A functional block diagram of an MCU.

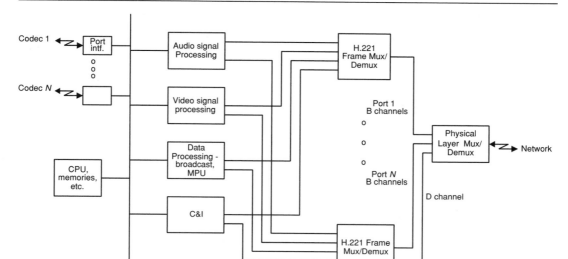

The data processing unit is characterized by the fact that it only accepts data from one port at any time, and ignores inputs from all other ports. It then broadcasts the data to all other ports according to their terminal capabilities. This unit also implements the simplex data protocol as defined in Recommendations H.243 or the multiple layer protocol (MLP) as defined in T.120-series recommendations to process telematic information and conference control signals.[5]

The C&I processing unit processes the conference control functions and provides for, among other things, correct routing, mixing and switching of audio, video, data, and control signals. For example, it ensures that the incoming audio at each port is correctly decoded before it is applied to the mixer input, the audio is encoded according to the capability of each destination terminal before it is transmitted, etc.

---

5. The T.120-series recommendations include T.122, T.123, T.124, T.125,etc. The telematic information is defined in Recommendations T.122 and T1.25. Examples of the conference control signals are request or grant floor, chair control, switching audio/video, etc. These are defined in Recommendations T.124 and T1.28.

Figure 11-6 Functional block diagram of an H.322 terminal. Here, the LAN supports isochronous services.

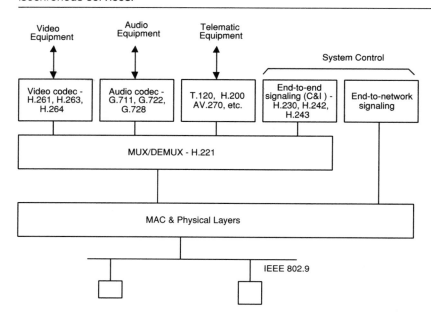

11.4 Narrow-Band Multimedia Services over LANs

11.4.1 LANs with Guaranteed Quality of Service

So far we have described multimedia services over an ISDN. Similar services are available over one or more LANs. Recommendations H.322 define these services over LANs[6] that provide a guaranteed QoS comparable to that of an N-ISDN.

Figure 11-6 shows the functional blocks and associated protocol stacks for an H.322 terminal. In this case, the LAN supports isochronous services, and as such, essentially the same protocol suite is used as for H.320 terminals.

11.4.2 LANs without Guaranteed Quality of Service

Video conferencing over traditional LANs such as an Ethernet 802.3 is fast becoming popular in many applications. The ITU has defined a set of standards for such equipment. Known as H.323, these standards define the protocol and procedures for setting up a connec-

---

6. IEEE 802.9 Isochronous Services with CSMA/CD represent this type of LAN.

Figure 11-7   Functional block diagram of an H.323 terminal.

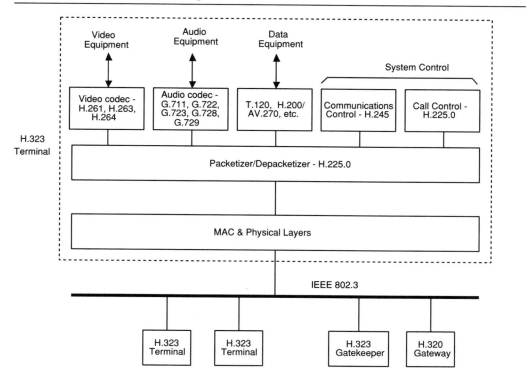

tion between two terminals, multiplexing the various multimedia information types on a single packet stream, and providing a framework for interworking with H.320 terminals.

Figure 11-7 shows the functional block diagram of an H.323 terminal. The data equipment may support file exchange, still image transfer, database access, audiographics conferencing, etc. The communications control provides for terminal capability exchange. The packetizer/depacketizer converts the outgoing audio, video, data, and control signal into packets, retrieves the signal from the incoming packets, and also performs such functions as sequence numbering, error control, and so on.

The purpose of the gatekeeper is to ensure that H.323 terminals wishing to participate in a conference have the correct network addresses, thus preventing terminals with invalid or unsupported addresses from initiating or intruding in a conference call.[7] While setting up a connection, an H.323 terminal can exchange call control messages directly with the destina-

---

7. Hence the term "gatekeeper."

Figure 11-8 The protocol stack of an H.323 terminal.

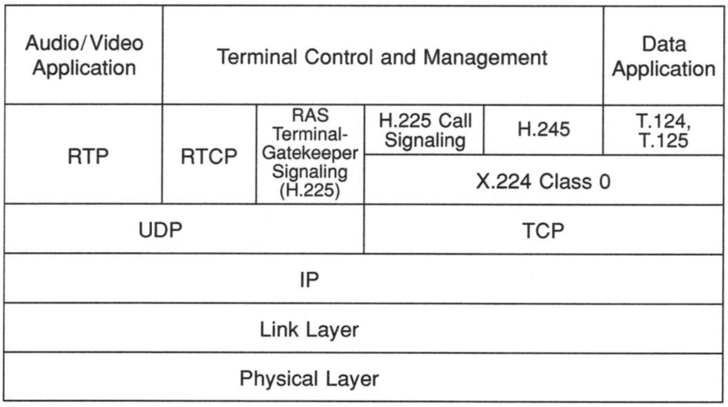

Audio/Video Application	Terminal Control and Management				Data Application
RTP	RTCP	RAS Terminal-Gatekeeper Signaling (H.225)	H.225 Call Signaling	H.245	T.124, T.125
			X.224 Class 0		
UDP			TCP		
IP					
Link Layer					
Physical Layer					

tion terminals. However, such direct exchange is not essential — the call can go through a gatekeeper. In this case, the calling terminal first sets up a connection with the gatekeeper, which then, like a PSTN switch, sets up a connection to the called terminal, allocating the bandwidth requested by the participating terminals. A gatekeeper can optionally provide directory services as well.

An H.320 gateway allows an H.323 terminal to communicate with an H.320, circuit-switched terminal, and hence provides protocol conversion. Conceivably, there could be other types of gateways, for example, an H.321 gateway that would provide interoperability between an H.323 and an ATM terminal.

In an H.323 terminal, the multimedia information — the audio, video, and data signals — is packetized following the procedures of Recommendations H.225. Figure 11-8 is the protocol stack for an H.323 terminal.

The real-time transport protocol (RTP) [27] has been designed specifically for real-time data such as audio and video. It provides end-to-end delivery services such as identification of payload types, sequence numbering, time-stamping, etc., and generally uses the user datagram protocol (UDP) at the transport layer. Consequently, there may be an occasional loss of packets or an out-of-sequence delivery.[8]

There are no procedures in the RTP protocol that guarantee a desired QoS in a system. The real-time transport control protocol (RTCP) allows data to be monitored and provides limited control. According to this protocol, control packets are sent periodically to all partici-

---

8. RTP is not a regular protocol because it is not intended to be implemented at a certain layer. Rather, it is supposed to be part of an application, and can be adapted to many different applications if there is a common set of functions across all applications. Its header can be modified or extended according to an application's needs.

pants in a conference so that they can determine if there is any congestion or flow control in place, and diagnose any possible problems in the system. There are other functions performed by this protocol as well. For example, since a user can leave a conference at any time, the control packets can indicate which terminals are still participating at a given time. Or, a terminal may broadcast a message indicating how well the current speaker is being received at the terminal.

11.5 Multimedia Services over ATM

Multimedia services can be provided over ATM in a number of ways. For example, if H.323 is deployed over IP as in Figure 11-8, we could use IP over ATM, MPOA, or even multi-protocol label switching (MPLS). In this case, multimedia services over ATM become just another IP-based application. One disadvantage of this approach is that it does not provide any means by which an application can request a desired QoS applicable to ATM services.

The second approach is to modify an existing protocol in a way that allows it to run over ATM and provide some form of resource reservation. In fact, CCITT has developed procedures H.321 by modifying Recommendations H.320 to provide multimedia services over native mode ATM. Since an H.320 terminal is circuit-switched and supports CBR services, QoS is not an issue with H.321 terminals. However, one disadvantage of using H.321 procedures is that they require end-to-end ATM.

Finally, it is possible that new protocols will be developed that would allow specifying QoS parameters. As discussed in Chapter 5, multimedia services are sensitive to delays; they can tolerate random bit errors, but not long error bursts. Bandwidths may be fixed or variable depending on the coding used. Thus, the QoS parameters relevant to multimedia services are low cell delays, low cell delay variations, and low cell loss ratios. Examples of new protocols that support QoS requests are RSVP and IPv6. Obviously, it would be desirable to be able to use these native protocols over ATM, even though it may be necessary to modify them to some extent.

Since H.321 offers multimedia services over native mode ATM, we shall describe it in the following section.

11.5.1 Terminal Architecture-H.321 Terminal

An H.320 terminal can be adapted to an H.321 terminal in two ways. The first is to design a B-ISDN terminal adapter that connects to an existing H.320 terminal on one side and an ATM network on the other as shown in Figure 11-9. The second is to design an integrated H.321 terminal with all the functions implied in Figure 11-9.

An integrated H.321 terminal performs circuit emulation with AAL1 for the bearer channels, but is otherwise based on the same audio and video coding and the same H.221 multiplexing procedures as an H.320 terminal. A separate VC may be used for each physical channel in the call. For example, for a call with two B channels, two VCs are established. Multiple VCs, when they exist, are synchronized (for the audio and video signals) by means of

Figure 11-9 The functional block diagram of a B-ISDN H.321 terminal, adapted from an N-ISDN H.320 terminal.

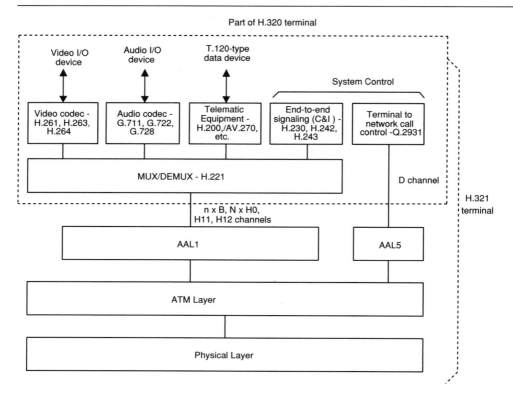

H.221 multiframes. However, it is possible for two H.321 terminals to use a single VC for the aggregate bandwidth of a call, provided the ATM network allows user-to-user signaling between the two end-points.

11.5.2 ATM Cells for User Data in H.321 Terminals

As shown in Figure 11-9, the AAL1 protocol is used in an H.321 terminal to transfer H.221 frames over ATM1. For a detailed description of AAL1, refer to Chapter 2. Here, however, we will repeat the basic ideas.

First, consider the user data. The simplest way to design an H.321 terminal is to circuit-emulate an H.320 terminal. The terminal operates with a constant bit rate, and is connected to the network over multiple, circuit-switched B or H0 channels, an H11 channel, or an H12 channel. The application layer collects a block of data from these channels as described in Chapter 7, and it passes it to CS. The CS constructs a CS-PDU with 46 octets of user data, and adds a 1-octet pointer field. This forms the SAR-PDU payload. On receiving this PDU, the SAR sublayer adds one octet of the SAR-PDU header with the CSI bit set to 1, and passes the resulting 48-octet SAR-PDU to the ATM layer. This layer then adds the 5-octet ATM header and sends it out as an ATM cell. This is shown as the P format in Figure 11-10(b). The SDT feature of the ATM standards requires that the P-format alternate with the non-P format of Figure 11-10(a), where the SAR-PDU payload consists of 47 octets of user data from the H.320 terminal. For this payload, the SAR-PDU header field sets the CSI bit to 0.

Normally, the SDT mode should be used when an H.321 terminal connects to an H.320 terminal or another H.321 terminal. It is not used when a single B channel (i.e., only 64 kb/s)

Figure 11-10 Constructing ATM cells in an H.321 terminal. Following Recommendations I.363, the two formats shown here are used in alternate ATM cells.

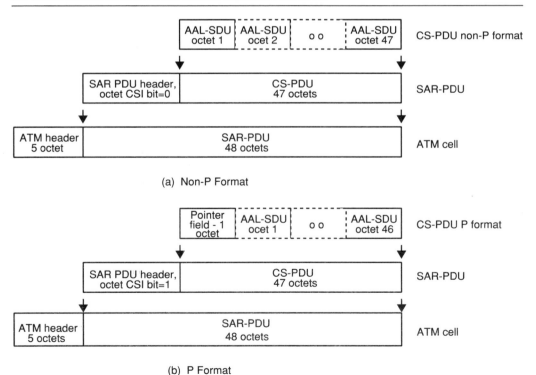

(a) Non-P Format

(b) P Format

is used or when multiple VCs are established over multiple B or H0 channels. In an H.321 terminal, the SRTS method is not used.

11.5.3 Call Control

Call controls used by an H.321 terminal are based on the Q.2931 procedures of Chapter 3. Since the terminal is a CBR, circuit-switched device, it must include bearer capabilities very similar to those of an N-ISDN call in the SETUP message. The following information elements must be present in that message:

- AAL parameters.
- ATM traffic descriptor.
- Broadband bearer capability.
- End-to-end transit delay.
- Narrow-band bearer capability.
- Narrow-band high-layer compatibility.
- Narrow-band low-layer compatibility.
- OAM traffic descriptor.
- QoS parameters.

Fields in each information element must be set appropriately when a call is initiated. For example, some information elements are shown in Tables 11-2 — 11-4.

11.6 Interworking of Multimedia Terminals

Figure 11-11 shows various multimedia terminals interworking with each other. This is made possible by means of gateways. Each gateway that connects one network to another provides the required protocol conversion between the two networks. For example, Gateway G1 does the protocol conversion between the H.320 and H.323 terminals. Similarly, two or more H.323 terminals connected to an Ethernet LAN can communicate with an ATM network via Gateway G3. Here, the ATM network emulates an Ethernet LAN.[9]

11.7 Summary

In multimedia services, voice, data, image, video, and graphics are combined into a single frame and transported over a physical channel with a desired bandwidth. Examples of these services are video conferencing, multimedia desktop, interactive distance learning, etc. Depending on the desired QoS, different data rates can be used. Presently, the general architecture of ATM terminals supporting multimedia services is similar to that for narrow-band

---

9. Refer to Chapter 8 for a description of the LAN emulation procedures.

Table 11-2 Narrow-band Bearer Capability Information Element for an H.321 Terminal

Fields	Permissible Values
Information Transfer Capability	Unrestricted digital information Restricted digital information 3.1 kHz audio Unrestricted digital information with tone/announcement
Information Transfer Rate	64 kb/s 2 × 64 kb/s 384 kb/s 1536 kb/s 1920 kb/s n × 64 kb/s (multi-rate)
Rate Multiplier	2—30
User Information Layer 1 Protocol	G.711 mu-law H.711 A-law Recommendations H.221 and H.242

Table 11-3 Broadband Bearer Capability Information Element for an H.321 Terminal

Fields	Permissible Values
Bearer Class	BCOB-A
Susceptible to Clipping?	Yes
Call Configuration	Point-to-Point

Table 11-4 AAL Parameters

Fields	Permissible Values
AAL Type	AAL-1
Subtype Identifier	Circuit transport
CBR Rate	64 kb/s n × 64 kb/s
Multiplier	2—30
Source Clock Frequency Recovery Method	No (i.e., synchronous) Adaptive clock method
Error Correction Method	No
Structure Data Transfer Block Size	Variable—depends on delays that can be tolerated
Partially Filled Cells Method	47

Figure 11-11   Interworking of various multimedia terminals.

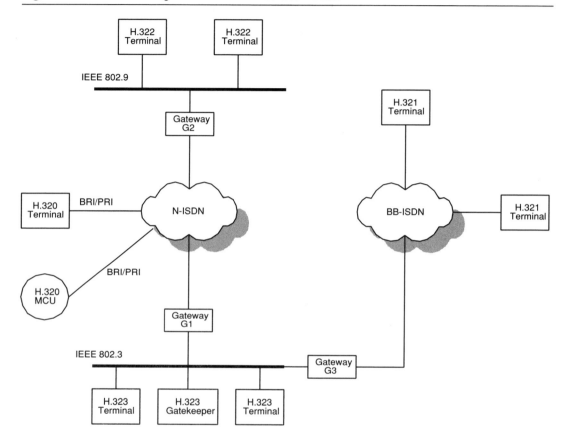

ISDNs. We, therefore, began with a description of these services over N-ISDNs and legacy LANs. More specifically, we discussed the multimedia terminal architectures for N-ISDNs, LANs such as IEEE-802.9 with a guaranteed QoS, and LANs such as IEEE-802.3 that do not guarantee any QoS. Architectures were described in terms of functional blocks using the relevant protocol stacks as a basis.

Multimedia services can be provided over ATM in a number of ways. For example, an IP-based H.323 terminal for an Ethernet LAN could be adapted to ATM using IP over ATM, LANE, or MPOA. However, in this case, users cannot request any QoS, which is an important feature of ATM. The second approach is to implement Recommendations H.321, whereby an N-ISDN H.320 terminal is adapted to ATM using circuit emulation for the user information and AAL-5 for the system control. Here, since an H.320 terminal is circuit-switched, QoS is not an issue. As such, an H.321 terminal which offers multimedia services over native mode ATM was described in some detail.

11.8 References

[1] CCITT Recommendation G.711, *Pulse Code Modulation (PCM) of Voice Frequencies*, Nov. 1988.

[2] CCITT Recommendation G.722, *7kHz Audio Coding within 64 kb/s*, Nov. 1988.

[3] CCITT Recommendation G.728, *Coding of Speech at 16 kb/s Using Low-Delay Code Excited Linear Prediction*, Sept. 1992.

[4] CCITT Recommendation G.728, *Coding of Speech at 16 kbit/s Using Low-delay Code Excited Linear Prediction (LD-CELP)*, May 1992.

[5] CCITT Recommendation G.729, *Coding of Speech at 8 kb/s Using Conjugate Structure Algebraic Code-Excited Linear Prediction*, Mar. 1996.

[6] ITU-T Recommendation H.221, *Frame Structure for a 64 to 1920 kb/s Channel in Audio-visual Teleservices*, 1995.

[7] ITU-T Recommendation H.224, *A Real Time Control protocol for simplex applications using the H.221 LSD/HSD/MLP channels*, 1995.

[8] Draft for H.225.0 Media Stream Packetization and Synchronization for Visual Telephone Systems on Non-Guaranteed Quality of Service LANs, Jan. 24, 1996.

[9] ITU-T Recommendation H.230, *Frame Synchronous Control and Indication Signals for Audiovisual Systems*, 1995.

[10] ITU-T Recommendation H.231, *Multipoint Control Units for Audiovisual Systems Using Digital Channels up to 1920 kb/s*, 1996.

[11] ITU-T Recommendation H.233, *Confidentiality System for Audiovisual Services*, 1993.

[12] ITU-T Recommendation H.242, *System for Establishing Communication Between Audiovisual Terminals Using Digital Channels up to 2 Mbit/s*, 1996.

[13] ITU-T Recommendation H.261, *Video Codec for Audiovisual Services at p x 64 kb/s*, 1993.

[14] ITU-T Recommendation H.263, *Video Coding for Low Bit Rate Communication*, 1996.

[15] ITU-T Recommendation H.310, *Broadband and Audiovisual Communications Systems and Terminals*, 1996.

[16] ITU-T Recommendation H.320, *Narrowband Visual Telephone Systems and Terminal Equipment*, 1996.

[17] ITU-T Recommendation H.321, *Adaptation of H.320 Visual Telephone Terminals to B-ISDN Environments*, 1995.

[18] ITU-T Recommendation H.322, *Visual Telephone Systems and Terminal Equipment for Local Area Networks which Provide a Guaranteed Quality of Service*, 1995.

[19] ITU-T Recommendation H.323, *Visual Telephone Systems and Terminal Equipment for Local Area Networks which Provide a Non-Guaranteed Quality of Service*, 1996.

[20] ITU-T Recommendation H.324, *Terminal for Low-Bit Rate Multimedia Communication*, 1995.

[21] ITU-T Recommendation T.120, *Overview of the T-Series (Draft). Determination scheduled for February 1996*, 1996.

[22] ITU-T Recommendation T.122, *Multipoint Communication Service for Audiographics and Audiovisual Conferencing Service Definition*, 1993.

[23] ITU-T Recommendation T.123, *Protocol Stacks for Audiovisual and Audiographic Teleconference Applications*, 1993.

[24] ITU-T Recommendation T.124, *Generic Conference Control*, 1995.

[25] ITU-T Recommendation T.125, *Multipoint Communication Service Protocol Specification*, 1994.

[26] ITU-T Recommendation T.128 (draft), *Multipoint Application Sharing*, 1998.

[27] "RTP: A Transport Protocol for Real-Time Applications," *Internet Engineering Task Force Audio-Video Transport WG draft-ietf-avt-rtp-08.txt*, Nov. 20, 1995.

Problems

11.1 In 1994, MPEG-2 was approved as an ISO standard for compressed digital audio and video. Subsequently, it was accepted as part of the H.310 standard to provide two-way digital audio and video communication over ATM. See, for instance, B. G. Haskell, A. Puri, and A. N. Netravali, *Digital Video: An Introduction to MPEG-2*. New York: Chapman & Hall, International Thomson Publishing, 1996, for a detailed description of MPEG-2.

Briefly, compressed audio and video signals are digitally encoded, packetized, and then multiplexed with user data. There are two types of packet streams in MPEG-2: the transport stream and the program stream. The transport stream is composed of short, fixed-length packets, each consisting of 184 bytes of data and 4 bytes of header. Packets are encoded into error-correcting codes to ensure satisfactory operation over a noisy channel such as coaxial cables in television networks and satellite transponders. The program stream is intended for a digital storage medium, where audio, video, and user data are multiplexed into larger packet sizes, usually on the order of 2–64 kbytes, and carry such information as copyright indication, fast forward, fast reverse, packet sequence numbers, necessary fields for network performance testing, and so on. A number of separate programs, thus encoded and packetized, may be multiplexed into a single bit stream. MPEG-2 is backwards-compatible with its predecessor, MPEG-1. The bandwidths needed for MPEG-1 and MPEG-2 are, respectively, 1.5 Mb/s and 6.0 Mb/s.[10]

Suppose that a cable TV network broadcasts its MPEG-2 multimedia programs to its customers over ATM. The maximum bandwidth available to a customer equipment terminal (i.e., a digital TV) is ~155 Mb/s. Draw a block diagram of the network in terms of major functional elements and show how customers access the network.

11.2 Figure 11-P.1 shows a functional block diagram of the entities used by a customer terminal and ATM network to request and provide QoS, respectively. On the terminal side, the application requests the desired QoS from the network. The block designated as RSVP on the terminal maps the QoS request from the terminal or the QoS response

---

10. H.323-based interactive video on legacy LANs requires much smaller bandwidths. For example, 128 kb/s, 384 kb/s, and 768 kb/s provide, respectively, good-, high-, and top-quality video.

Figure 11-P.1 Multimedia service over ATM with RSVP in the native mode.

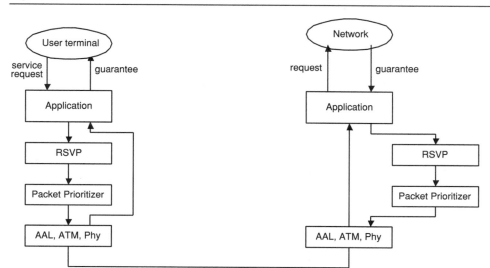

from the network to a corresponding ATM function. For each packet received from the application, the packet prioritizer determines its priority based on the QoS and schedules it for transmission over the link layer. On the network side, the RSVP block determines if the network has enough resources to guarantee the QoS requested, and verifies if the user terminal is authorized to request the service. If the network is a transit node, the QoS may even imply a specific route. Define an appropriate set of QoS parameters that describe the desired quality for the above multimedia service.

11.3 Refer to Figure 11-P.2. Examine if the RSVP protocol can be used in this application. Assume that only SVCs are supported. If RSVP is adequate, show how the RSVP reser-

Figure 11-P.2 Mapping between RSVP and ATM.

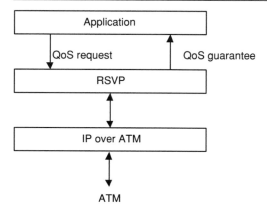

vation and guarantee map to ATM QoS. Otherwise, how would you modify the protocol so that it is usable here? See the following references: R. Braden, et al., "Resource Reservation Protocol (RSVP)," *RFC 2205*, Sept. 1997; L. Berger, "RSVP over ATM Implementation Guidelines," *RFC 2379*, Aug. 1998; and L. Berger, "RSVP over ATM Implementation Requirements," *RFC 2380*, Aug. 1998.

11.4 Design an admission control algorithm to be implemented on the network that would provide the user with the requested QoS. The QoS for the existing connections should be maintained.

11.5 Referring to Figure 11-P.1, write two application programs, one showing how the terminal requests the QoS and the other showing how the network responds using either a flow chart or C/C++-type structures.

Wireless ATM

12.1 Introduction

In the last few years, wireless LANs (WLANs) and wireless ATM (WATM) have been subjects of extensive research. Reference [1] summarizes the current status of wireless access technology. The driving force behind this activity is the inherent advantage of wireless access — the mobility of the terminals and the avoidance of expensive, and in some environments, cumbersome coaxial cables. Although in recent years coaxial cables have been replaced, in some cases, by twisted wire pairs, the mobility of terminals will continue to be an attractive feature as the rapidly growing wireless telephony and personal communications system (PCS) services demonstrate. Also, there is a good possibility that, in the future, ATM will be used extensively in long-haul networks, and as such, should be capable of providing both wired and wireless interfaces.

One of the important requirements for the efficient operation of a WATM network is a well-designed medium access control (MAC) protocol. Over the years, a number of multiple access schemes have been suggested for wireless data networks and personal communications systems [11], [12]. Reference [3] presents a comparative analysis of the currently available protocols for WATM networks and the general problems associated with a WATM interface, and discusses a generic medium access protocol. Passas, et al. [2] have studied the performance characteristics of the MAC protocol and its associated scheduling algorithms for project Magic WAND (Wireless ATM Network Demonstrator).

Broadly speaking, one can use frequency division multiple access (FDMA), code division multiple access (CDMA), or time division multiple access (TDMA). In FDMA, the available RF spectrum is divided into a number of channels. The network assigns these channels to mobile users on a demand basis in much the same way as in the cellular advanced mobile phone service (AMPS).

In CDMA, or the so-called spread spectrum system, multiple users may transmit on the same radio channel at the same time. In a direct sequence spread spectrum (DSSS) system, each user's data is distinguished from all other users by encoding it in a unique random sequence before modulating the RF carrier. The DSSS system has a number of advantages, e.g., very little channel access delay, efficient utilization of bandwidth, and a fairly large number of users for a given a signal-to-noise ratio. However, it needs sophisticated power control mechanisms and complex base station designs.

References [4] and [11] give an excellent description of the packet broadcasting data networks that have been used since the 1970's, and provide theoretical results on their performance. Most of these broadcasting networks are based on the TDMA scheme, where the entire radio channel is available to all users all the time. Any user with a packet to send can seize the channel at any time and begin to transmit. This is the so-called random access TDMA scheme. Since the traffic at any terminal originates randomly, packets from two or more terminals may overlap either partially or completely. When the users detect a collision, they back off, wait a random period of time, and then retransmit. This protocol has been used in the ALOHA system [4]. Clearly, it is not a very efficient scheme since the channel throughput is significantly reduced because of the collisions. Furthermore, the delay increases with channel traffic. The throughput increases if the carrier sense multiple access scheme with collision detection (CSMA/CD) is used.

A comparative study of the CDMA and TDMA schemes in personal communication networks can be found in Reference [12]. A variation of the above TDMA approach is the slotted TDMA scheme. Here, based on a reference clock, time is divided into a number of equal slots. Each user is assigned one or more time slots on a permanent basis. This fixed assignment scheme may work quite well for a relatively small number of users and for CBR services, but not if there are a large number of users or if the services use VBRs. Also, it is not a very efficient utilization of bandwidth since a user may not use its allocated bandwidth all the time.

A random access procedure that overcomes the limitations of the fixed time slot assignment scheme is the so-called slotted ALOHA scheme. Here, if there is a packet to send, a user can begin to transmit, but only at the beginning of a time slot rather than at any arbitrary instant of time. Notice that even though the users are now somewhat synchronized, there is some probability that two or more of them could begin to transmit at the same time. However, the probability of collision is now less since packets from contending users either overlap completely or do not overlap at all. Thus, the channel throughput increases in this access scheme. However, this scheme is still not very efficient, since there is loss of bandwidth due to collision and the associated access delays may be too long, particularly for the VBR services that seem to be the most common service type in ATM.

More recently, a number of other MAC protocols have been proposed for various applications [2], [5]—[10]. While they differ in their details, they all use some form of packet reservation scheme, whereby terminals request bandwidths according to their needs, and in response, the network dynamically assigns bandwidth.

The purpose of this chapter is to introduce the reader to the concept of WATM and the associated emerging technology. We begin with some network examples where a wireless interface is useful. This is followed by a discussion of the necessary features of a WATM interface. We then present a MAC protocol that appears to be suitable for WATM. Since the details of this protocol and its variations are still evolving, no quantitative results on their performance in terms of delays and throughput are presented.

Figure 12-1 Wireless ATM terminals connecting to an ATM network.

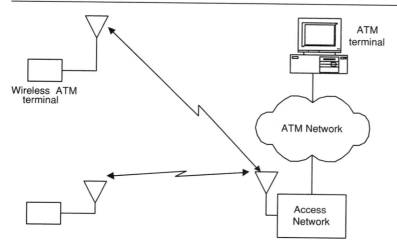

12.2 WATM Networks

Currently, two emerging technologies providing wideband wireless local access (WWLA) are taking shape: WATM and WLAN. As shown in Figure 12-1, WATM allows WATM terminals to be connected to an ATM network, and ensures end-to-end ATM connectivity. An example of a WATM application includes, among other things, a high-bandwidth data transfer for multimedia applications with a guaranteed QoS in an office, campus, hospital, or research environment.

Figure 12-2 shows a public ATM network providing mobile ATM service. Its architecture is very similar to cellular telephony and PCS networks. Notice the protocol stack at different interface points. At this point in time, however, no WATM MAC protocol has been standardized, and there are no products available in the market that support this WATM-to-ATM connection.

In WLAN, on the other hand, a mobile terminal connects to legacy LANs using the IEEE 802.11, which has been specially designed for this purpose [14]. Currently, products are available in the market that support these WLAN-to-legacy LAN connections.[1]

An interesting application of WATM involves accessing an ATM backbone from a legacy LAN via a WLAN interface. The network configuration, together with the protocol stack at various interface points, is shown in Figure 12-3. The MAC protocol used at the air interface is once again the IEEE 802.11. Notice that the ATM network is using the LANE protocol.

---

1. At the physical layer, these products use both DSSS and frequency-hopping spread spectrum (FHSS) techniques.

Figure 12-2 Mobile ATM terminals connecting to a public ATM network via a base station. Also shown is the protocol stack at different interface points.

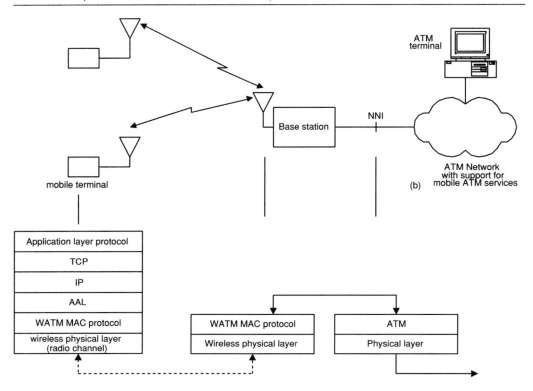

12.3 Wireless ATM Interface

12.3.1 Limitations of the Wireless Medium

The ATM protocol, which was originally designed for wired access, may not work quite so well in a wireless environment. There are a number of reasons for this. First, in a wireless service, only limited bandwidths are available. For example, the IEEE 802.11 standard for wireless LANs has been granted a bandwidth of only 83.5 MHz around 2.4 GHz.[2] The maximum data rate supportable with these bandwidths is in the range of about 34 Mb/s, which may not be sufficient for many of the multimedia services defined for ATM. Second, the ATM protocol was designed to operate over a relatively robust, error-free channel. A mobile radio signal, on the other hand, may suffer severe channel impairments. For one thing, the signal un-

---

2. In January 1997, the FCC granted a bandwidth of 300 MHz around 5 GHz for use by the unlicensed national information infrastructure (U-NII).

Figure 12-3 Legacy LANs connecting into an ATM backbone over wireless interfaces.

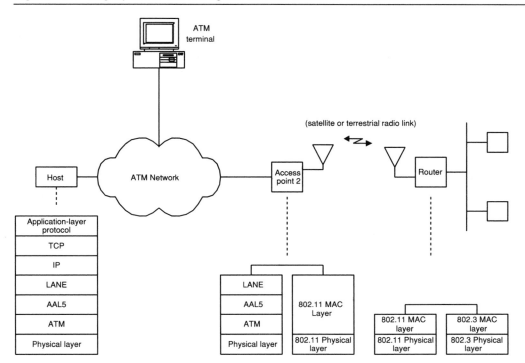

dergoes fast fades due to multipaths that manifest themselves as long burst of errors. For another, there is interference from a reused or adjacent channel.

12.3.2 Desired Features of the Wireless MAC Protocol

Some of the basic requirements for the MAC-layer protocol for wireless ATM are:

- It should be able to interwork with upper-layer protocols seamlessly. In other words, it should not require any changes or modifications to the upper layers, and it should deliver the PDUs to those layers without much added delay.
- Recall that in an ATM network, error recovery is provided by the upper layers on an end-to-end basis. In the case of IP-over-ATM, the transport-layer protocol provides this function. Since the average bit error rate on a mobile radio channel may be as high as 3×10^{-3}, if we continue to use the same error recovery procedures at the transport layer, it may be necessary to retransmit rather long packets too frequently, thereby re-

ducing the channel throughput significantly and causing even more congestion in the network. Thus, either the transport-layer error recovery procedures must be changed or the MAC protocol must include some link-layer procedures that would detect and correct errors on ATM cells. Again, care must be taken to avoid introducing long delays.

- The medium access protocol must be designed to use bandwidth efficiently so that it can accommodate a reasonably large number of users. The probability of packet loss should be low and net throughput high. This may require the network to dynamically allocate its resources among a number of simultaneously contending users. This, in turn, may lead to variable channel access delays. However, many of the ATM service requirements are rather stringent, and these delays must necessarily be held as low as possible.

- The protocol must be designed so that the network can guarantee a certain QoS to the user for various data types — CBR, rt-VBR, nrt-VBR, ABR, and UBR. One way to do it is to use an admission control mechanism that would allow new users to be connected to the network only if they can be provided the QoS they requested without any noticeable decline in quality for already-established connections.[3]

- While this is true for both wired and wireless ATM networks, an additional factor that one must consider in the WATM is the need for handoff. When a mobile moves from the coverage area of one base station (or one antenna sector) to another, it is necessary for the mobile to be switched to a new frequency. That is called handoff. To allow for the possibility of handoff in a WATM network, a base station must set aside a fraction of its available bandwidth for these "roaming" mobiles. Since this bandwidth is limited, the admission control mechanism in an ATM network with wireless interfaces must be designed to be adaptive to handoff needs. However, these functions — handoff and enhanced admission control — may be provided at the upper-layer protocols instead of the MAC layer.

12.3.3 MAC Protocol for WATM

A wireless access scheme that appears to be suitable for various classes of ATM services is described in Reference [3]. This scheme is fundamentally very similar to the MAC protocol of the WAND system of Reference [2],[4] and is based on assigning bandwidths according to demands. Here, data is transmitted in frames, each frame consisting of a number of time slots. Some of these time slots are used for transmitting data to mobile terminals (i.e., downstream), while the rest are used by terminals for transmitting information to the base station (i.e., up-

---

3. Refer to the chapter on IP over ATM to see how the throughput of TCP/IP in an ATM network is affected by the congestion control mechanism used.

4. The MAC protocol of the WAND system is also known in the literature as the Mobile Access Scheme based on Contention and Reservation for ATM (MASCARA).

Figure 12-4 Medium access protocol for a WATM interface based on reservation and dynamic allocation of time slots.

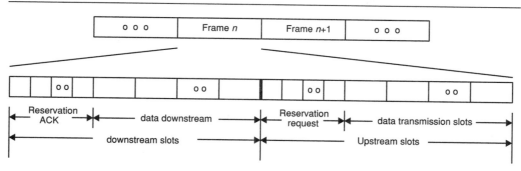

stream). Both the upstream and downstream time slots are divided into two groups: one for control packets such as reservation requests from the mobile or acknowledgments from the base station, and the other group for data packets only (see Figure 12-4).

In the upstream direction, the control slots are random access. In other words, whenever a terminal has some data to send, it transmits a reservation request to the central controller on any of these time slots asynchronously with respect to all other terminals. In reply, the controller reserves some bandwidth for the requesting terminal and informs it over the acknowledgment time slots. Based on the reservation scheme used, the controller may assign a fixed number of time slots to a given terminal, or if a terminal has subscribed to a VBR service, it may determine its average burst length for the particular terminal and assign an appropriate number of time slots accordingly.

Clearly, in this protocol, a request packet can experience a collision. As in CSMA/CD or the collision avoidance (CSMA/CA) scheme of the IEEE 802.11 protocol, a collision is handled using a *backoff* algorithm. Once a terminal has been assigned its time slots, it can transmit its data packets without any possibility of collision. When the terminal is finished with its transmission, the controller can assign those time slots to other terminals that have made similar reservation requests.

As we indicated before, there is a need for a data link control (DLC) protocol that would provide error detection and correction for an ATM cell. With this protocol, as each ATM cell at a mobile terminal is delivered to the MAC layer, a few octets of a DLC header are added. Packets formed this way with a sequence of n ATM cells are then concatenated to construct a MAC layer protocol data unit payload. The latter is prepended with a header of appropriate size[5] and then transmitted upstream in the time slots assigned to the mobile. This is shown in Figure 12-5.

---

5. In Reference [2], this header is assumed to be one time slot in length.

Figure 12-5 Construction of MAC-layer frames in a wireless ATM interface. A DLC header is added to provide error detection.

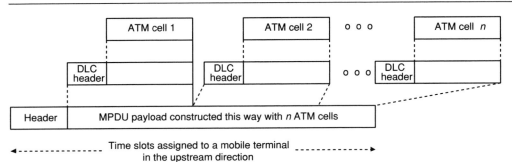

In the downstream direction, the DLC protocol is straightforward. Whenever the base station controller wishes to transmit a packet to a terminal, it simply uses any of the available time slots marked "data downstream," addressing the packet to the desired terminal. Since transmission in this direction is free from collision, performance is not an issue. Also, since the control time slots in the upstream direction are usually much shorter than the ones used for sending data packets, very little bandwidth is lost due to collision.

For this protocol to work well for VBR or UBR services, the access point in the network (e.g., a base station) must allocate time slots to requesting terminals according to a scheduling algorithm. This algorithm should be designed so that the available bandwidth is efficiently utilized and the desired QoS for CBR and VBR services is maintained.[6] Since the cell loss ratio, cell transfer delays,[7] and cell delay variations are indicative of the QoS, the effectiveness of the protocol can be measured in terms of the following parameters:

- Throughput.
- Cell loss probability and probability of cell retransmissions.
- Average delay and its distribution.

A useful means for measuring these parameters is computer simulation [13]. For some MAC protocols, limited simulation results are available in the literature [2].

---

6. See, for instance, the scheduling algorithm used in MASCARA [2].

7. For the MAC protocol that we discussed, there are two components of the cell delay parameter: the request access delay encountered by a terminal during transmission of its reservation request and the packet access delay measured from the instant a terminal sends its reservation request to the instant it can begin to transmit its data packets on assigned slots. Clearly, the packet access delay would depend on the scheduling algorithm used by the controller. Since real-time services are time-critical, they must be allocated as much bandwdith as possible.

12.3.4 Other Access Protocols

Clearly, variations of this protocol are possible. For example, one could use an adaptive polling algorithm [2], whereby the network assigns a time slot periodically to each mobile according to its expected traffic even though a mobile may not have requested any bandwidth. It is possible to improve the performance of this scheme up to a certain extent by optimizing the polling period based on the channel capacity, expected traffic from each user, and subscribed QoS. However, there are cases such as those involving VBR services where it may not work very well. Similarly, one can combine features of different schemes to design a new protocol that may work better for some services than others.

12.4 Summary

Since wireless access provides mobility of terminals, avoiding the use of wires and coaxial cables, considerable work is being done in the areas of WATM and WLAN. WATM allows wireless ATM terminals to be connected to an ATM network, and ensures an end-to-end ATM connectivity. An example of a WATM application involves an office, campus, hospital, or research environment that requires terminal mobility and high-bandwidth data transfer for multimedia services with a guaranteed QoS. In WLAN, mobile terminals connect to legacy LANs using IEEE 802.11 specifications.

An important requirement for an efficient operation of a WATM network is a well-designed multiple access protocol. Over the years, a number of these protocols have been suggested for wireless data networks and personal communications systems. These were briefly reviewed in this chapter. Network configurations were presented in which mobile ATM terminals, or legacy LANs with wireless interfaces, connect to an ATM network. At this point, however, no WATM MAC protocol has been standardized.

A wireless medium has a number of limitations. For example, the bandwidth in WATM is smaller than that available with wired access for which ATM was originally designed. Also, a mobile radio signal is generally subjected to severe channel impairments such as fades due to multipaths and co-channel or adjacent channel interference. We discussed the basic requirements of a MAC protocol suitable for this channel, and described a wireless access scheme that has been suggested as a possibility for various classes of ATM service. According to this scheme, data is transmitted in frames, each consisting of a number of time slots. When a terminal has some data to send, it contends with other similar terminals to send a bandwidth reservation request to a central controller on one of these time slots. Based on some criteria, the controller assigns an appropriate number of time slots to the requesting user. Variations of this access scheme were also discussed.

12.5 References

[1] K. Pahlavan, et. al, "Wideband local access: wireless LAN and wireless ATM," *IEEE Commun. Mag.*, Nov. 1997, pp. 34–40.

[2] N. Passas, et. al, "Quality-of-service-oriented medium access control for wireless ATM networks," *IEEE Commun. Mag.*, Nov. 1997, pp. 42–50.

[3] O. Kubbar, et. al, "Multiple access control protocols for wireless ATM: problem definition and design objectives," *IEEE Commun. Mag.*, Nov. 1997, pp. 93–99.

[4] N. Abramson, "The throughput of packet broadcasting channels," *IEEE Trans. Commun.*, Vol. COM-25, Jan. 1977, pp. 117–128.

[5] D. J. Goodman, et al., "Packet reservation multiple access for local wireless communications," *IEEE Trans. Commun.*, Vol. 37, No. 8, Aug. 1989, pp. 885–890.

[6] D. Raychaudhuri, "Wireless ATM networks: architecture, system design and prototyping," *IEEE Pers. Commun.*, Aug. 1996, pp. 42–49.

[7] B. Walke, et al., "Wireless ATM: air interface and network protocols of the mobile broadband system," *IEEE Pers. Commun.*, Aug. 1996, pp. 50–56.

[8] D. Raychaudhuri, et al., "ATM-based transport architecture for multiservices wireless personal communications networks," *IEEE JSAC*, Vol. 12, No. 8, Oct. 1994, pp. 1401–14.

[9] D. Raychaudhuri, et al., "WATMnet: a prototype wireless ATM system for multimedia personal communication," *Proc. ICC '96*, Dallas, TX, June 23–27, 1996, pp. 469–477.

[10] M. J. Karol, et al., "Distributed-queueing request update multiple access (DRQUMA) for wireless packet (ATM) networks," *Proc. ICC '95*, Seattle, WA, June 1995, pp. 1224–31.

[11] N. Abramson, "Multiple access in wireless digital networks," *Proc. IEEE*, Vol. 82, No. 9, Sept. 1994, pp. 1360–69.

[12] N. D. Wilson, et al., "Packet CDMA versus dynamic TDMA for multiple access in integrated voice/data PCN," *IEEE JSAC*, Vol. 11, No. 6, Aug. 1993, pp. 870–83.

[13] C. Fang, et al., "A simulation study of TCP performance in ATM networks," *Proc. IEEE, GLOBECOM '94*, pp. 1217–1223.

[14] IEEE 802.11D3, "Wireless LAN Medium Access Control (MAC) and Physical Layer (PHY) Specifications," IEEE Stds. Dept., Jan 1996.

Multi-Protocol Label Switching (MPLS) in ATM

13.1 Introduction

We indicated in Chapter 1 that ATM technology is inherently capable of label switching, and mentioned some of its advantages. The idea behind label switching is very simple. In a traditional packet-switched network, when a network-layer packet arrives at a router, it analyzes the layer 3 header of the packet, and depending on the outcome, forwards the packet to the next hop along an appropriate route. As the packet traverses the network, this process is repeated at each hop. Since the layer 3 header generally contains much more information than would be required in making the routing decision, layer 3 forwarding is relatively complex. In label switching, when a packet first enters the network,[1] its layer 3 destination address is analyzed and mapped for forwarding purposes to a shorter, fixed-length identifier called a label. When the packet is forwarded to the next hop, the label is sent along with it so that the receiving router can use it as an index into its memory to derive subsequent routing information. Thus, with label switching, packet forwarding becomes simpler. Labels can be used to perform other functions as well. For instance, two adjacent routers in a network may agree to use different labels to indicate different service classes, or specify different scheduling disciplines and discard thresholds[2] in the treatment of a packet. Similarly, it is easier to implement a high-speed, label-switched router than one using IP-based forwarding. The label switching is called multi-protocol because it can operate with different network-layer protocols. However, most of the work that has been done on MPLS is concerned with the Internet protocol.

Examples of existing technologies that lend themselves to label switching are ATM and frame relay. In ATM, labels are formed with the VPI / VCI field. Similarly, in a frame relay network, Data Link Control Identifiers (DLCIs) are used to construct a label. Thus, label switching takes place at layer 2. Clearly, before label switching can be used to forward a packet, it is

---

1. For the purpose of this discussion, we are defining a network as a set of routers that use a common routing protocol to exchange their routing information. The router at which a packet enters the network is called the ingress router. Similarly, the router at which it leaves the network en route to its destination is called the egress router. Sometimes the term "node" is used for a router.

2. These parameters are called the packet's "precedence levels."

necessary first to create the labels and then distribute them throughout the network. Labels are assigned as each router builds its routing table and distributed to the peer routers by means of a Label Distribution Protocol (LDP).

MPLS is still evolving in the IETF. General issues related to multi-protocol label switching are presented in great detail in Reference [1]. Reference [2] describes general architectural requirements for multi-protocol label switching, and also discusses how an ATM switch can operate as a label-switching router (LSR). Davie, et al. [3] provide detailed procedures for distributing labels among ATM LSRs, using References [1] and [2] as the basis. The purpose of this chapter is to present the basic concepts of label switching. In particular, we will discuss MPLS insofar as it relates to ATM switches.

13.2 Some Definitions

We begin with the definition of a few terms that are often used in the description of the MPLS paradigm.

Router — A packet switch that forwards packets on the basis of layer 3 addresses.

Autonomous System (AS) — A set of routers which, for administrative purposes, may be considered a single entity. The routers within an AS exchange routing information through an interior gateway protocol. Two subnetworks (e.g., two Ethernet LANs) in an AS may be connected either directly by means of a single router or via two routers over a point-to-point link. When two autonomous systems are connected together, the routers on their borders exchange their routing information using an exterior gateway protocol. Sometimes we will use the term "domain" to mean the same thing as an AS.

Broadcast network — If a network is connected to more than two routers, and if it can address all of them over a single message, it is called a broadcast network. A well-known example of such a network is an Ethernet. In a non-broadcast network, of which an X.25 network is an example, if a particular message has to be "broadcast", it must be sent to each router separately.

Forwarding equivalence class (FEC) — A set of all layer 3 packets which, for forwarding purposes, can be treated the same way. For instance, if a group of packets can be forwarded along the same route as in Figure 13-1(a), they may be considered as forming an FEC. Thus, it is valid in MPLS to describe an FEC in terms of a label associated with its packets.

Label — A short, fixed-length identifier that identifies a data stream. A stream, in turn, is defined as one or more "data flows, treated as an aggregate for the purpose of forwarding" at a layer 2 or layer 3 node [3]. In ATM, labels may consist of a VCI or a combined VPI/VCI value, and have only local significance.

Label-switching router (LSR) — A label-switching router, also known as an MPLS router, is one that forwards packets using labels. Normally, an ATM switch forwards packets based on a VP/VCI combination. If, instead, it uses labels, it is called a label-switching router. In this

Figure 13-1 Label switching. (a) An example of a forwarding equivalence class. Packets 1–4 that arrive at Node 1 along four different routes are forwarded to Node 2 along the same route. As such, these packets, by definition, form an FEC. (b) Label swapping. The MPLS node shown in this figure indexes its memory with Label 1 to fetch Label 2. Label 2 is swapped with Label 1 and the resulting packet is forwarded to the next hop. In this case, LSR 1 is the upstream router and LSR 2 the downstream.

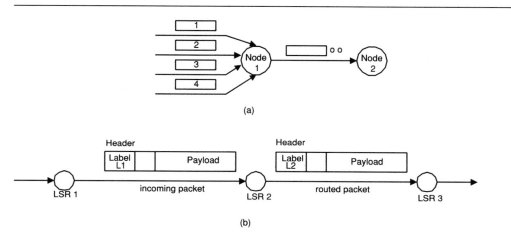

case, the switch runs network-layer routing protocols to determine how packets should be forwarded.

Label stack — Sometimes, a packet may arrive at an MPLS node with multiple labels. The collection of all these labels is called a label stack. The label at the top of the stack is taken to be the incoming label.

Label merging — When packets of a given FEC entering a node with different incoming labels are routed to the next hop with a single outgoing label, we say that the labels have merged.

Label swap — This term refers to forwarding procedures based on MPLS, and includes the following functions: replacing an incoming label of a packet with an outgoing one and encapsulating the latter in the packet header.

Upstream and downstream LSR — If LSR 1 sends an MPLS packet to its neighbor, LSR 2, LSR1 is called the upstream LSR and LSR2 the downstream LSR. For example, in Figure 13-1(b), LSR 1 sends a packet to LSR 2. In this case, LSR 1 is the upstream router and LSR 2 the downstream router.

VC merge — When cells coming over multiple VCs are merged into a single outgoing VC, it is called VC merge.

VP merge—When cells coming over multiple VPs are merged into a single outgoing VP, it is called VP merge.

13.3 Principles of Operation

In multi-protocol label switching, routes are determined on a hop-by-hop basis. Once labels have been assigned, a label distribution protocol is used to distribute them to all MPLS nodes. Consider an autonomous system with a number of LSRs that are mutually connected over ATM interfaces (i.e., ATM LSRs). The label-based packet forwarding process involves the following steps:

1. If a packet arriving at a node is unlabeled, in other words, if it is an IP packet and does not contain any label, the node analyzes the network-layer address of the packet. If it is determined that the node is the destination, the packet is presented to the upper layer.

2. If the address analysis indicates that the node is not the destination for the unlabeled packet and the router is MPLS-capable, the router may extend the IP forwarding information base (FIB) to indicate that the packet ought to be labeled when forwarded, and may also indicate the outgoing label to be used along with the other outgoing interface information. This label is encapsulated in the header, and the resulting packet is sent out to the next hop router. In ATM, a label generally consists of the VCI field or a combined VPI/VCI field. Sometimes, it may also be constructed with the VPI field when two adjacent ATM LSRs are connected by a VP.

   The outgoing packet is constructed in the following way: The network-layer packet is mapped to the PDU of an AAL, say AAL5, which is then segmented according to the procedures of the SAR sublayer. Each SAR PDU consists of an integral number of 48 octets, which are passed to the ATM layer, where each block of 48 octets is mapped into an ATM cell where the label is encapsulated in its header portion. The ATM cells are then routed to the next hop in the same sequence in which they arrived. Notice that it is necessary to preserve this sequence. Otherwise, the ATM cells cannot be re-assembled into the upper-layer PDUs. The reason for this limitation is that there is simply not enough information in the header portion of an ATM cell to re-assemble out-of-sequence cells correctly.

3. If the packet is already labeled, the receiving router indexes its memory with the incoming label and determines the route to the next hop. There are a number of possibilities here: (i) If the packet is to be forwarded to another router within the same domain, labels are simply swapped. In other words, an appropriate outgoing label is obtained from the lookup table and substituted for the incoming label, and the resulting packet is sent out to the next hop router. Label swapping is shown in Figure 13-1. (ii) If the packet is destined to a subnetwork within this domain and therefore does not have to be routed to another LSR, the incoming label is removed and the packet is presented

Figure 13-2 Label merging.

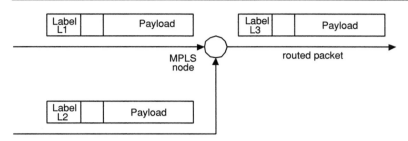

to the upper layers. (iii) The third possibility arises when the packet passes through a transit network (also called a transit domain) with the multi-protocol label switching capability. In this case, as the packet traverses the transit domain, it carries two labels, say L1 and L2, in the form of a stack, L1 for routing internally within the domain and L2 for inter-domain routing.[3] When the packet reaches the exit router in the domain, label L1 is removed, and the packet is presented to the boundary router of the next domain with only label L2 encapsulated in the header. If, on the other hand, the transit domain does not have the MPLS capability, the packet carries only one label as it passes through the domain. Clearly, in this case, the exit router of the transit domain must forward the packet to the boundary router of the next domain on the basis of its IP header. This is further explained in Section 13.6.

Suppose that two packets arriving at an MPLS transit node along two routes with labels, say L1 and L2, respectively, have to be routed along the same path. One way of doing this is for the router to transmit the two packets using a single label, say L3, as shown in Figure 13-2. This is called label merging. If the router is not label-merge-capable, it can use two separate labels, say L3, for the first packet and L4 for the second, and route the packets as if they were two different routes to the next hop. While merging, the contiguity of the cells of an incoming packet must be preserved in the outgoing packet. This can be done easily by making sure that entire packets, associated with the labels to be merged, are received at the MPLS node before attempting to merge the labels. Thus, it is necessary to provide sufficient memory for each of the incoming routes so that packets can be stored temporarily.

It can be noticed from Figure 13-2 that a given FEC can be associated with multiple labels. The converse is generally not true. In other words, the same label should not be assigned to more than one equivalence class of IP packets unless it is possible for the MPLS node to

---

3. There is only very limited capability to do label-stacking in ATM-MPLS networks [12].

Figure 13-3   Example of an FEC where packets from many edge nodes travel to the same node over multiple label-switched paths that look like the branches of a tree.

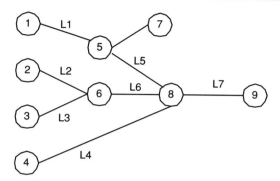

distinguish them by some other means. For example, if there is a situation where packets arrive at a node over two distinct physical interfaces that the node can uniquely identify, using the same label for two different FECs may be valid.

To further clarify the concept of an FEC, consider Figure 13-3, where labels are shown along the routes. Packets originating from nodes 1 — 4 and terminating at node 9 are forwarded using different sets of labels along different routes. However, they are all forwarded in the same manner, and as such belong to the same FEC.

In a given autonomous system, an MPLS node may co-exist with a non-MPLS node. In other words, to use the MPLS paradigm, it is not necessary that all nodes support label switching.

13.4 Hierarchical Labels

When multiple autonomous systems are connected together, it is possible to perform label switching with hierarchical labels. Hierarchical labels are nothing but label stacking. Consider, for example, Figure 13-4, which shows three domains, D1, D2, and D3, each representing, say an Internet Service Provider (ISP). Assume that all three domains use label switching. Assume also that a packet originates from subnet X in D1, passes through domain D2, and terminates on destination Y in D3. Thus, D2 is a transit domain. On receiving the packet from X, router R1 encapsulates label L2 in the header and sends the packet to router R2. Labels L2 and L3, which are used for routing packets within D1 only, are internally generated in D1 using, say, the Open Shortest Path First (OSPF) Internet routing protocol. Labels LB and LC, which are derived in D2 and D3, respectively, are distributed to the boundary routers of the neighboring domains using the Border Gateway Protocol (BGP). Thus, when R3 sends the packet to the boundary router R4 in D2, it encapsulates label LB in the header. As the packet traverses D2 through routers R5, R6, and R7, the header contains two labels, one an inter-

Figure 13-4   Use of hierarchical labels in multiple label switching.

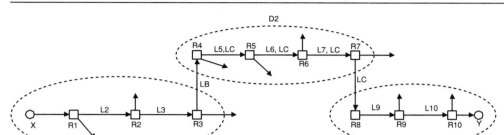

nally derived label for routing within domain D2 and the other LC. The two labels form a stack, and are referred to as two hierarchical labels.

When the packet arrives at router R7, label L7 is popped out of the stack and the packet is presented to R8 with only label LC. If the packet is destined to a subnetwork within D3, R8 replaces label LC with label L9, and forwards the packet to R9. Finally, when R10 receives the packet with label L10, it removes that label and presents the packet to higher layers.

If D3 is a non-MPLS domain, then of course LC does not exist, and the packet traverses the transit domain with a single label that provides routing internally within D2. Each router in D3, in that case, must determine the routing path on the basis of the IP address of the packet.

13.5 Label Assignment

As in traditional networks with IP-based routing, each LSR in an MPLS network must also determine how it is connected to all other routers. Once it has determined a route between itself and other routers, it must perform the additional task of assigning a label to each route.

Broadly speaking, there are three types of label assignment:

1. Topology-driven label assignment — In this procedure, label assignment takes place in the course of normal processing of the routing protocol control traffic. It is called topology-driven because labels are assigned as each LSR builds its routing table using the information on the network topology learned from the routing protocol. Labels are assigned to all routes that exist between any two nodes.

   A protocol that is often used to generate routing tables is the Open Shortest Path First (OSPF) protocol [4],[5].[4] We will describe this protocol in some detail later in this chapter. Suffice it to say here that this protocol calculates the shortest paths from a

---

4. IS-IS is another popular protocol.

router to all other routers to which it is connected. Since a requirement imposed on the protocol is that paths not contain any loops, the calculated routes from any node form a tree with this node as the root. If there are changes in the topology of the AS, the protocol determines those changes and updates the routing table accordingly. Since, in a general case, a packet may have to traverse a number of autonomous systems, a suitable protocol must also be used to exchange the routing information among the routers that are located along the borders of adjacent autonomous systems. The Border Gateway Protocol (BGP) is one such protocol for exchanging inter-AS messages [7].

2. Request-driven label assignment — In this procedure, labels are assigned during normal processing of request-based control traffic. As an example, suppose that a host desires a certain QoS from the network for a particular application. To this end, it sends an appropriate service request to the next hop router. On receiving the request, the router reserves necessary network resources, and in the process, assigns the labels. A protocol that is used in this case is the RSVP [8]—[10].

3. Traffic-driven label assignment — In this scheme, label assignment and distribution take place when an MPLS node receives a data packet and processes it as necessary. In this procedure, there is always some delay between the arrival of the first packet of a given FEC and the assignment of a label to the FEC. One possible way to minimize the effect of this latency is to forward the packet during the setup phase on the basis of its layer 3 address [3].

Reference [1] discusses three types of label allocation : (i) downstream label allocation, where the label is allocated by a downstream LSR, (ii) upstream label allocation, in which an upstream LSR allocates the label, and (iii) domain-wide unique allocation, where each node in an MPLS domain is assigned a label that is unique in the domain. Regardless of how the label is allocated, it is always the downstream LSR that uses the label as an index into its memory to determine how the packet is to be treated.

13.6 Label Distribution in ATM

Once a label has been assigned, it must be distributed to other MPLS nodes so that they can use the label when forwarding a packet of the associated FEC. A label distribution protocol (LDP) is currently under development by the MPLS Working Group. This section presents a brief description of the label distribution procedures for an ATM network.

Since most ATM switches do not support multipoint-to-point and multipoint-to-multipoint VCs, VC merge, generally, is not supported. To accommodate non-merge-capable ATM hardware, "downstream-on-demand" label distribution is used, whereby an upstream LSR explicitly requests a downstream LSR to allocate a label for a given FEC [2]. To understand how labels can be distributed, refer to Figure 13-5. Assume that all LSRs in a given domain are connected over ATM interfaces. If LSR 1 determines that LSR 2 is its next hop router for a certain FEC, it requests an outgoing label from downstream LSR 2. In response, LSR 2 takes the following actions: (i) First, it examines if it has an outgoing label for the

Figure 13-5 Label distribution in ATM LSRs. The LSRs are shown as circles. Adjacent LSRs are connected over ATM interfaces.

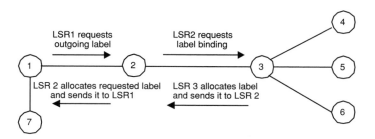

FEC to the next hop router, LSR 3. If it does not have one, it sends a label binding request to LSR 3. (ii) When LSR2 receives a reply from LSR 3, it allocates the requested label and sends it to LSR 1.

In each label binding request received by an LSR, there is a hop count field that indicates how many hops the LSR is from the upstream LSR that first originated the request. The purpose of this field is to detect any loop in a network.[5] When a router receives a binding request (e.g., LSR 2 in the above example), it must check the hop count field. If it is less than the maximum value that has been configured for the FEC, it increments the field by one and then sends the binding request to its next hop router (e.g., LSR 3 above). If the hop count equals or exceeds the allowed maximum value, the router no longer generates a binding request to the next hop, and instead simply returns an error message to its upstream peer. In the example of Figure 13-5, LSR 1, which first initiated the request, sets the hop count field to 1.

Reference [3] suggests that LSR 2 may choose to allocate a label and send it to LSR 1 before receiving the binding from downstream LSR 3. But in this case, it should set the hop count field to 0 indicating that the actual hop count is unknown. Once LSR 2 receives the binding reply from LSR 3, it may notify LSR 1 about the actual hop count.

If an LSR cannot, for some reason, allocate a label, it must indicate that to its upstream peer. For instance, if LSR 2 does not receive an outgoing label from LSR 3, but has already sent an allocated label to LSR 1, it should de-allocate the label and ask the upstream LSR to remove the label as well. There are other exceptional situations where an allocated label may be removed or a label binding request ignored. For details, see Reference [3].

If, for a particular FEC, there is a change in the route, it is necessary to remove the associated bindings. Suppose, for example, that LSR 2 has determined that for a given FEC, LSR 3 is no longer the next hop. In that case, LSR 2 notifies LSR 3 so that LSR 3 de-allocates

---

5. Recall that in IP, a similar function is performed by the time to live (TTL) field of the IP header. The initial value of this field is set by the originating router. When the next hop router receives the IP datagram, it examines the TTL field, and if its value is greater than zero, it decrements the field by 1 and forwards the packet to the next hop. If, on the other hand, its value is 0, it discards the packet and notifies the originating router that the packet cannot be forwarded.

the label, and, in turn, informs its next hop router for the FEC that the associated binding is not required anymore. Similarly, when a route has changed, new bindings must be created for the affected portions of the route and distributed using the LDP.

It is possible that for a given FEC, an ATM LSR may receive more than one label binding request from the same upstream LSR. In that case, for each request, the receiving router must allocate a new label as its resources permit.

As we said before, most ATM LSRs cannot merge VCs. However, an LSR that has this capability forwards all incoming packets of a given FEC to the next hop router using a single outgoing label. Similarly, for a given FEC, it must always reply with the same label to all upstream routers that generate binding requests to this router. In all other respects, the label distribution procedures for these ATM LSRs are similar.

Since labels must be distributed before label switching can take place, a control VC must be established to carry IP packets for label distribution. Any VPI/VCI value can be used for this purpose as long as both LSRs engaged in the label distribution agree. The default is VPI = 0 and VCI =32. The LLC/SNAP encapsulation must be used on this VC [13]. Labels may be distributed explicitly as control messages specially designed for this purpose, or they may be piggybacked on other control messages.

13.7 Routing Table Construction

Since labels are generated from routing tables, it is necessary that we understand how the routing tables are constructed. A number of protocols are available for this purpose. For instance, the well-known Routing Information Protocol (RIP), which is based on the distance vector or Bellman-Ford algorithm, has long been used for computer communications in ARPANET, and has been implemented by many network equipment manufacturers in their IP gateways [6]. Recently, the IETF has specified another TCP/IP Internet routing protocol called the OSPF protocol [4], [5]. We will now present a brief description of this protocol.

An AS generally consists of a number of routers, subnetworks, and networks. A router may be connected to one or more subnetworks directly at a LAN interface port or to a remote network over dedicated links through, say, modems. The AS can then be represented by a graph where each router is a node. Adjacent nodes are connected by the edges of the graph. Starting from a given node, it may be possible to reach any other node along one or more paths provided the graph has no disjoint parts. In this case, we say that the graph is connected. If there are no loops in the system, then there is one and exactly one route between any two given nodes. The graph of the network is then said to form a tree. Generally, however, it is useful to design a network with two or more separate routes between a given node pair so that a congested node or a failed link or interface can be bypassed when necessary. Thus, loops are almost unavoidable in a network. Since a direction is also implicit in the definition of an edge, this direction being the same as that of the packet flow, the graph is actually a directed graph. In the most general case, two nodes may be connected by two directed edges, meaning that packets can flow in both directions, or by a single edge, indicating that packets can flow in one direction only. In our discussion here, we will assume that all links are bi-directional, but rep-

Figure 13-6 A network that is used to illustrate how routes can be determined in the OSPF or a similar routing protocol.

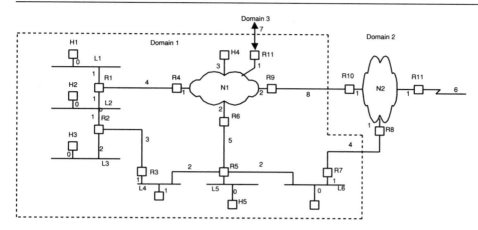

resent each edge by a single, undirected line instead of two directed links. An excellent presentation of these concepts may be found in Reference [11].

If there are multiple paths between a given node pair, it is possible to set some criteria for selecting the most preferred path. For example, selection may be based on the minimum distance between two nodes, the shortest propagation delay, the maximum supportable bandwidth, or a weighted combination of all of the above parameters. Thus, to choose the preferred path, we can associate each edge with a cost function or a metric in terms of these parameters, determine all paths between the two desired nodes using the network graph, and then, for each path, compute the total cost by summing the individual costs associated with its constituent edges.[6] The path for which the total cost is smallest may be called the shortest path. There are procedures in the OSPF protocol that allow each node to discover its neighbors and create a database which, in essence, provides a network graph indicating how it is connected to other nodes. Using this graph, it is then possible to determine the shortest path between any two nodes, say, x and y, by simply constructing all possible trees that stem from x and terminate on y and choosing the one with the smallest cost function.

To pursue these ideas, consider the network of Figure 13-6. The network in the dotted box constitutes a domain. It is connected to two other domains: to Domain 2 via routers R7 and R9 and to Domain 3 via R11. Routers R1 — R6 are internal routers and R7, R9, and R11 are boundary routers of Domain 1. The OSPF protocol, which is an internal gateway protocol, is used in this figure to determine all routes between any two internal nodes in the same domain. Costs have been assigned arbitrarily and are shown alongside each edge. We have assumed that all costs are the same in both directions.

---

6. A bi-directional edge may be assigned a different cost function for each direction. This would be the case if, for instance, the bandwidth is used as a cost function and it is different in each direction.

Figure 13-7 Alternate routes between R1 and R9 constructed using the concept of trees. Figure 13-7(a) is the shorter of the two paths.

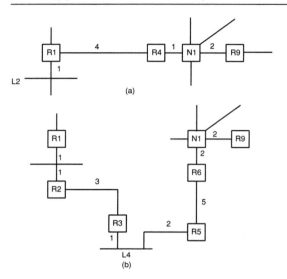

Suppose that using the OSPF protocol, R1 needs to determine the routes to destination router R9. Two paths between these nodes are shown in Figure 13-7. The first one, shown in Figure 13-7(a), has a cost of 7 units, and the second one of Figure 13-7(b) has a cost of 17 units. R9 will, in this case, use the first path as the shortest route. We notice that there are other paths between the two nodes, namely, through routers R7, R8, network N2 and R10. But, because they traverse a different domain, these paths are invisible to R1. It is possible, however, that when R11 wants to send a packet to R1, it may, based on some criteria internal to Domain 2, choose to send the packet via, say, R8 to R7 to R5. R5 may then choose the shorter of the two paths between itself and R1 as determined by the OSPF protocol.

The protocol works in the following manner: In an attempt to discover its neighbors, each router periodically sends out packets over all its interfaces, and waits for acknowledgments.[7] If it does not receive any acknowledgment within a prescribed period from a given adjacent router, it assumes the link to that router to be broken, and accordingly marks the state of that link in its database. These local link states are then distributed to other routers *one hop away from the origin* so that each router knows not only its immediate neighbors, but all other routers that are reachable within the domain as well.[8] In this way, nodes can construct a network topology and maintain a copy of the database, which is the same at all nodes in a

---

7. In the OSPF protocol, the packet types that are used to discover neighboring routers are called Hello packets.

8. This distribution, or flooding of the link states, is called the link state advertisement (LSA).

domain. The distribution of the link states takes place over a special packet, called the Link State Update Packet type, which was designed for this purpose.

Since an identical network topology is to be maintained at all nodes throughout a domain, each time a router initializes itself or one or more of its links, it is necessary for that router to exchange the link state database with its neighbors. The packet type that is used for this purpose is called the Database Description Packet. To send the complete database, a router may require more than one packet. When a router receives a Database Description Packet, it must send an acknowledgment to the originator over a Link State Acknowledgment Packet type. Similarly, if a router, after having exchanged the link state database, discovers that some link states are out-of-date or finds other inconsistencies in one or more link states, it may request more up-to-date information about those links from adjacent routers. A Link State Request Packet is used to send these requests.

13.8 Summary

In this chapter, we presented an overview of multi-protocol label switching (MPLS) in ATM. A label is defined as a short, fixed-length identifier that can be used to identify a packet. When an MPLS router forwards a packet to another MPLS router, it encapsulates the label in the header. The receiving router uses the incoming label as an index into its memory to derive the subsequent routing information, replaces it with an outgoing label, and then forwards the packet to a downstream router. Since a label is shorter than the layer 3 header of a packet, label switching is simpler than IP-based forwarding. In ATM, a label may consist of a VCI, or a combination of a VPI and VCI, and has only local significance.

Hierarchical labels, or label stacking, can be used when multiple MPLS-based, autonomous systems are connected together. As in any traditional network with IP-based routing, each LSR in an MPLS network must determine its routes and then assign a label to each route. After a label has been assigned, it must be distributed to other MPLS nodes so that they can use it when forwarding a packet of the associated FEC. We briefly described the label assignment procedures and a label distribution protocol.

Since labels are generated from a routing table, it is necessary to understand how a routing table is constructed. A number of protocols are available for this purpose. Recently, another routing protocol called the OSPF protocol has been specified by IETF. We presented a brief description of this protocol.

13.9 References

[1] R. Callon, P. Doolan, N. Feldman, A. Fredette, G. Swallow, and A. Viswanathan, "A Framework for Multiprotocol Label Switching," *Network Working Group Internet Draft,* Nov. 1997.

[2] E. C. Rosen, A. Viswanathan, and R. Callon, "Multiprotocol Label Switching Architecture," *Network Working Group Internet Draft,* July 1998.

[3] B. Davie, et al. "Use of Label Switching with ATM," *Network Working Group Internet Draft,* Sept. 1998.

[4] J. Moy, "OSPF Version 2," RFC 2328, April 1998.

[5] J. Moy, "OSPF Protocol Analysis," RFC 1245, July 1991.

[6] C. Hedrick, "Routing Information Protocol," RFC 1058, June 1988.

[7] Y. Rekhter and T. Li (Eds.), "A Border Gateway Protocol 4 (BGP-4)," RFC 1717, Mar. 1995.

[8] R. Braden, et al., "Resource Reservation Protocol (RSVP)—Version 1 Functional Specification," RFC 2205, Sept. 1997.

[9] L. Berger, "RSVP over ATM Implementation Guidelines," RFC 2379, Aug. 1998.

[10] L. Berger, "RSVP over ATM Implementation Requirements," RFC 2380, Aug. 1998.

[11] W. H. Kim and R. T. Chien, *Topological Analysis and Synthesis of Communication Networks*. New York: Columbia University Press, 1962.

[12] A. Viswanathan, *private communication*.

[13] J. Heinanen, "Multiprotocol Encapsulation over ATM Adaptation Layer 5," RFC 1483, July 1993.

Problems

13.1 The network of Figure 13-P.1 is an AS where blocks designated as H denote hosts. Similarly, routers are marked with an R. Beside each link is shown its associated cost function, which is identical in both directions.

For each node in the network, construct a routing table based on the shortest path as determined by the specified cost function.

Figure 13-P.1   Network used in Problem 1.

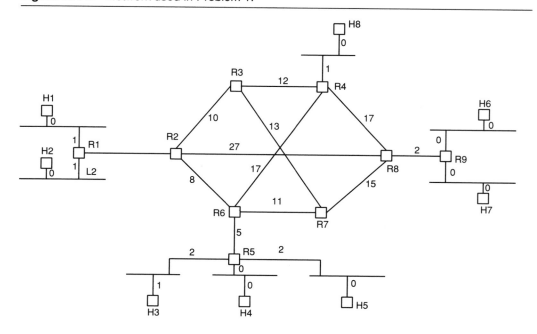

13.2 In the above problem, augment the routing table to show the next best alternate route between any two nodes.

13.3 Referring to Problem 13.1, write an application program showing how each node can discover its neighbors. Ignore the details of constructing packets used in the exchange of link states.

13.4 Referring again to Figure 13-P.1, show in flowchart form how every node distributes the link states to other nodes so that each can construct a routing table that is identical at all nodes.

13.5 In Figure 13-P.2, switches forward packets based on MPLS. Assume that the ATM network permits VC merge and VP merge, but not multicasting or broadcasting. The entire network is to be treated as a single AS. Develop an algorithm to map a protocol address to an ATM label.

13.6 For Problem 13.5, write an application program performing label distribution.

13.7 Continuing with Problem 13.5, write two application programs performing label switching, one for SW-5 and the other for the end-switches.

Figure 13-P.2 An MPLS-based network. SW-5 forwards packets from any end-switch to any other end-switch depending on the destination address using labels.

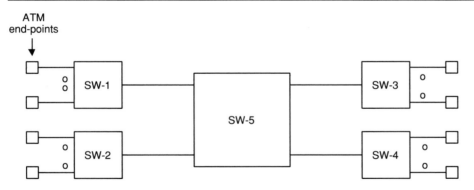

An Overview of T1 and E1 Interfaces

A.1 T1 Overview

The 1.544-Mb/s T1 carrier is a North American standard that was originally designed to replace two-wire and four-wire inter-office toll trunks between central offices in long-haul networks. Its application has now extended to subscriber loops in this country and many other areas. For example, T1 is a common interface between public and private networks for integrated voice and data transmission. For a detailed description of this interface, see Reference [1].

Briefly speaking, a T1 frame for voice telephony is constructed in the following manner: Prior to transmission, the analog voice signal from each channel is band-limited to 4 kHz, sampled 8,000 times a second (i.e., once every 125 μs), and converted by an A/D converter (with proper companding) into standard 8-bit PCM words. This results in a 64-kb/s digitized voice. A 192-bit frame is constructed by byte-multiplexing 24 of these channels. A framing bit is then added to the beginning of each frame to help identify the frame boundaries. This is shown in Figure A-1. Frames, thus constructed, are transmitted at a rate of 8000 frames/s. Since each frame contains 193 bits, the T1 clock rate is 1.544 Mb/s. The composite channel is called a DS1 channel and the constituent channels are known as DS0 channels. The 64-kb/s clocks used in the DS0 channels are all derived from the same source. Thus, the multiplexing scheme used in T1 is inherently synchronous.

In a T1 carrier, consecutive frames may be grouped together to provide different T1 formats. There are three such T1 formats: the most common, D4, or superframe (SF) format, the extended superframe (ESF) format, and the non-signaling (NS) format. In the D4 format, 12 frames form a superframe structure. The framing bits in this format are shown in Figure A-2. As shown there, they form two sequences: a 101010 pattern, called the terminal framing bits (Ft) at the beginning of each odd frame, and a 001110 pattern, called the signaling framing (Fs) bits at the beginning of each even frame. The Fs bit pattern uniquely identifies the superframe boundary. Notice that once the receiver has achieved frame synchronization and maintains it thereafter, the Fs bit pattern is no longer needed. Instead, user data can be sent at the Fs bit positions. This provides the customer with an additional 4-kHz data channel.

An ESF consists of 24 frames. As shown in Figure A-3, the framing bit positions in the

Figure A-1 A T1 frame.

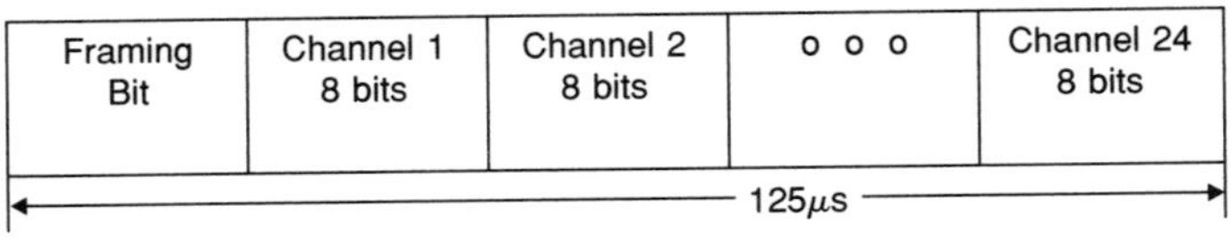

Framing Bit	Channel 1 8 bits	Channel 2 8 bits	o o o	Channel 24 8 bits

← ——————————————— 125µs ——————————————— →

Figure A-2 The framing bits in a D4 or SF format. Twelve frames form a superframe.

Frame Number	Framing Bit	
	Ft	Fs
1	1	–
2	–	0
3	0	
4	–	0
5	1	–
6	–	1
7	0	–
8	–	1
9	1	–
10	–	1
11	0	–
12	–	0

ESF carry three types of information: user data bits designated as m at the beginning of each odd-numbered frame, a 001011 framing pattern (FP) at frame numbers 4, 8, 12, 16, 20, and 24, and a 6-bit CRC for error detection at the remaining bit positions. The m bits form a 4-kHz facility data link (FDL) for diagnostics and maintenance. The 6-bit CRC transmitted in any ESF covers the previous superframe.

In the NS format, a multiframe consists of only four frames, where the framing bits form two sequences: the 1010. sequence and a 4-kHz FDL. This format is generally used for propri-etary applications.

For normal voice telephony applications, the digital carrier system must transmit not only the encoded audio, but also the signaling information such as on-hook and off-hook states, dialed digits, and other call control information.[1] The signaling information for any

---

1. The signaling information may be of the following types: (i) Supervisory signals. They distin-guish between idle and busy states of a channel, and hence change rather infrequently (much less than 8 kHz). They are typically dc signals and are used to seize a circuit when a user initiates a call, control the flow of address information from the originating switch to the destination switch, and indicate to the

Figure A-3 The framing bits in the ESF format.

Frame Number	Framing Bits		
	FDL Bit	FP Bit	CRC Bit
1	*m*		
2			CRC–1
3	*m*		
4		0	
5	*m*		
6			CRC–2
7	*m*		
8		0	
9	*m*		
10			CRC–3
11	*m*		
12		1	
13	*m*		
14			CRC–4
15	*m*		
16		0	
17	*m*		
18			CRC–5
19	*m*		
20		1	
21	*m*		
22			CRC–6
23	*m*		
24		1	

channel on a T1 line is transmitted in-band along with the encoded audio of the channel. This is called channel-associated signaling (CAS). In D4 framing, the so-called A and B bit signaling information for any channel is sent by replacing the least significant bit of the PCM code in every sixth and twelfth frame of a superframe as depicted in Figure A-4. This is known as robbed-bit signaling.

In ESF, the A, B, C, and D bit signaling information is sent in every 6th, 12th, 18th, and 24th frame using robbed-bit signaling. Clearly, this signaling procedure will cause some im-

---

originating switch when the call is answered and terminated for billing purposes. In T1 carrier systems, these signals are transmitted using robbed-bit signaling. (ii) Address signals (dial pulses). They represent the called party address, and are transferred from the source switch to the destination switch over the T1 carrier facility in the same way as the supervisory signals. Generally, they change at a higher rate. (iii) Alerting. These signals indicate to the called party that a message is waiting. Generally, this is a function of the local switch to which the called party is connected. The digital carrier is therefore not involved. But, if it is to be controlled from a remote office, it must be transmitted over the T1 carrier facility by means of a second channel similar to the supervisory channel.

Figure A-4   Robbed-bit signaling.

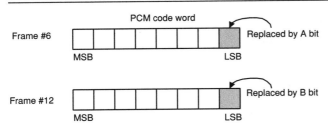

pairments to audio quality. However, for regular voice telephony applications, the effect is imperceptible. Obviously, robbed-bit signaling is not permissible when digital data, instead of digitized voice, is being sent over the T1 carrier.

Instead of using robbed-bit signaling, we could convert the signaling information for all user channels into digital messages and transmit them over a channel that is set aside exclusively for this purpose. This is called message-oriented, or common channel signaling. In N-ISDN, channel 24 is used for this purpose.

A number of alarm conditions have been defined for a T1 link. For maintenance purposes, each incoming DS1 signal must be monitored for these alarm conditions. To achieve full synchronization, the receiver must detect both the frame and multiframe alignment. After it is synchronized, it monitors the Ft bits for errors. If, at any time, two out of five consecutive Ft bits are in error, it loses frame alignment and generates a red alarm, whereupon the transmitter sends a yellow alarm to the remote end. In D4 mode, the yellow alarm is generated by sending a zero in bit position 2 in all data channels, or by setting the Fs bit to 1 in frame 12. In ESF mode, the yellow alarm is generated by repeatedly sending a pattern of 8 ones followed by 8 zeros. A loss of carrier occurs if 31 or more consecutive zeros are received. When the receiver receives an unframed all-1's pattern, it generates an alarm (called a blue alarm) locally.

At the line level, a logical zero is transmitted as a nominal zero volt signal. Logical 1's, on the other hand, are transmitted alternately as a positive and a negative pulse. This is called alternate mark inversion (AMI) line coding. A bipolar violation occurs if two or more pulses of the same polarity follow each other. It is necessary to maintain 1's density on the T1 line so that the receiving end has enough transitions to recover the clock. This is accomplished by using a line coding called B8ZS, whereby any group of eight consecutive zeros is replaced by a certain violations pattern.[2]

---

2. B8ZS coding is applied to the line-level signal (i.e., the alternate pulses) without altering the data itself. To be more specific, the B8ZS coding is implemented in the following way: If the last (alternate mark inversion) pulse before the group of 8 zeros is inserted is positive (+), the inserted code is 000+−0−+. Thus, there are two violations. If the last pulse is negative (−), the inserted code is 000−+0+−. In both cases, the bipolar violations occur in the fourth and seventh bit positions of the inserted code. Thus, if the customer equipment uses B8ZS coding but the carriers do not support it, errors will be introduced in the user data.

Figure A-5 An E1 frame.

Ch. 0 Framing Channel	Ch. 1	Ch. 2	o o o	Ch. 16 – Signaling Channel	o o o	Ch. 31
←				125μs		→

A.2 E1 Overview

The European equivalent of T1 is E1, and it is specified in CCITT Recommendation G.734 [2]. An E1 frame consists of 32 8-bit words, each corresponding to a channel, and is transmitted at a rate of 8000 frames/s. Thus, the data rate is 2.048 Mb/s.

An E1 frame is shown in Figure A-5. Channel 0 is used for frame synchronization and channel 16 for signaling purposes. A 7-bit frame synchronization pattern, 0011011, is sent over the framing channel in every other frame.[3] When the framing channel does not carry the frame sequence, it can be used to transport alarm indications or user data if necessary. Frame alignment is achieved when the framing pattern is detected correctly in, say, frames N and $N+2$, and bit 7 of frame $N+1$ is 1. This assumes that the most significant bit is bit 8. The receiver loses frame alignment when it detects errors in three or more consecutive frame alignment signals. A special form of line coding called HDB3 is used on the E1 interface.

A.3 References

[1] CCITT Recommendation G.733, "Characteristics of Primary PCM Multiplex Equipment Operating at 1544 kbit/s," 1980.
[2] CCITT Recommendation G.734, "Characteristics of 2048-kbit/s Frame Structure for Use with Digital Exchanges," 1980.

---

3. The eighth, or most significant bit of the framing word, is set to 1 by convention.

An Overview of DS3

B.1 Introduction

In Appendix A, we discussed T1 and E1 digital carriers. The next two digital hierarchies are DS2 and DS3, and they are described in detail in References [1]—[4]. The DS2 signal operates at 6.312 Mb/s and is obtained by multiplexing four DS1 streams using a bit-interleaved multiplexing procedure. These DS1 signals are called tributaries. A DS3 signal is generated by multiplexing seven DS2 streams in a similar way. The data rate of a DS3 signal is 44.736 Mb/s ± 20 parts per million.

B.2 Bit Stuffing at DS2 Level

The incoming tributaries of a DS2 or DS3 signal may not all be synchronous to each other. There may be various reasons for that. For example, they may not have exactly the same clock frequency. Or, their clock frequencies may not have the same stability and thus may drift with respect to each other over time. Thus, it is necessary to synchronize all incoming DS1 signals by bringing them up to a common frequency prior to bit-interleaving. This is achieved by a procedure called bit stuffing. In bit stuffing, the clock frequency of the multiplexer output is made a little higher than the sum of the maximum expected rates of all the multiplexer inputs. If, at some instant, the data rate of an incoming DS1 signal is less than the maximum expected value, the multiplexer "stuffs" a bit at a known bit position , say s, of the input channel in the multiplexer output stream. The multiplexer, of course, must now indicate to the receiving end that bit stuffing has been used in the frame. If the demultiplexer determines that bit stuffing has taken place on a channel, it constructs the output data by discarding bit s from the channel. Otherwise, it treats bit s as part of the user data. Each of the seven DS2 streams that comprise a DS3 frame is separately bit-stuffed so that all of them can be synchronized at the DS3 clock rate. The maximum number of stuff bits for each DS1 stream in a DS2 signal is 1796 b/s.

B.3 DS2 Multiplexing

As mentioned before, four DS1 streams are multiplexed into a DS2 signal by bit-interleaving them in the following way: First, 12 consecutive bits of each DS1 stream are interleaved on a

Figure B-1   A 48-bit data block formed by bit-interleaving four DS1 streams. For convenience, this data block is called *d*.

ch 1 bit 1	ch 2 bit 1	ch 3 bit 1	ch 4 bit 1	ch 1 bit 2	ch 2 bit 2	ch 3 bit 2	ch 4 bit 2	o o o	ch 1 bit 12	ch 2 bit 12	ch 3 bit 12	ch 4 bit 12

Figure B-2   The DS2 M-subframes, each containing six overhead bits and six blocks of user data defined as *d* in Figure B-1.

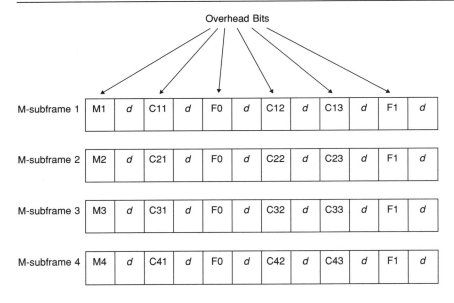

Figure B-3   The DS2 frame format.

M-subframe 1 294 bits	M-subframe 2 294 bits	M-subframe 3 294 bits	M-subframe 4 294 bits

bit-by-bit basis to form a 48-bit block. For convenience, we call this data block *d* in Figure B-1, where ch 1 refers to the first DS1 stream, ch 2 to the second DS1 stream, and so on. A second block of data is built the same way except that it contains bits 13 through 24 of the four DS1 streams. An overhead bit is then added to each block. Six of the resulting blocks, each containing 49 bits, are concatenated as shown in Figure B-2 to form four M-subframes. Thus, each M-subframe contains 294 bits. A DS2 frame is then formed with four DS2 M-subframes as shown in Figure B-3.

The overhead bits perform specific control functions and are given different names. Referring to Figure B-2, bits F0 and F1 are for frame synchronization. F0 is set to 0 and F1 to 1. Bits M1 — M4 provide multiframe synchronization. The multiframe framing pattern is M1 = 0, M2 = 1, M3 = 1, and M4 = either 0 or 1.

The purpose of the C bits is to indicate whether a stuff bit is being used in a DS2 frame at the multiplexer end. Bits C11, C12, and C13 correspond to the first DS1 input, C21, C22, and C23 to the second DS1 input, and so on. The multiplexer indicates the presence of a stuff bit by setting the C bits to one. As an example, if a stuff bit is to be used for the second DS1 stream, bits C21, C22, and C23 are all set to 1. In this case, the first information bit following bit F1 is a stuff bit. If there is no need for a stuff bit for a given DS1 tributary, its associated C bits are set to 0 and an information bit is transmitted in the first bit position following bit F1. At the demultiplexer, if the C bits are all 1 or a majority of them are 1, the first information bit following the F1 bit is taken to be a stuff bit and is therefore discarded. Otherwise, it is taken to be part of the user information.

B.4 DS3 Multiplexing

A DS3 frame is built in a similar way by bit-interleaving seven DS2 frames and inserting framing bits, multiframe alignment bits, bit stuffing control bits, and a few parity bits for in-service error detection.[1] To build a DS3-frame, an 84-bit data block, D, is formed by interleaving 12 consecutive bits of each of the seven DS2 streams. M-subframes are then generated from eight D blocks by inserting an overhead bit ahead of each block as shown in Figure B-4. Thus, each M-subframe consists of 680 bits. A DS3 frame is then constructed by concatenating the seven M-subframes as depicted in Figure B-5.

Each DS3 frame contains 56 overhead bits and 4,704 information bits. Bits F1 — F4 provide M-subframe alignment, and the framing pattern used is 1001. M1 — M3 are multi-frame alignment bits with M0 = 0, M1 = 1, and M2 = 0.

The C bits have the same significance as in a DS2 frame, and indicate whether bit stuffing is being used in a channel. Bits X1 and X2 are in-service message bits very similar to the facility data link message bits in a DS1 frame in the ESF mode. The two X bits in any DS3 frame must be the same — either both 0 or both 1 — and must not change more than once per second.

The P bits are parity bits that provide limited error detection capability. They are computed over the information bits of a DS3 frame and do not cover the overhead bits. Both P bits must be set to the same value. In any DS3 frame, they are set to 1 if the information bits in the previous DS3 frame contain an odd number of ones. Otherwise, they are both set to zero. It is important to note here that since these parity bits are recomputed at every node, they merely provide error detection on a per-section basis and not on an end-to-end or path basis.

---

1. This DS3 framing format is known as the M13 format.

Figure B-4   M-subframes in a DS3 frame. Here, *D* represents an 84-bit interleaved data block.

M-subframe 1	X1	D	F1	D	C11	D	F2	D	C12	D	F3	D	C13	D	F4	D
M-subframe 2	X2	D	F1	D	C21	D	F2	D	C22	D	F3	D	C23	D	F4	D
M-subframe 3	P1	D	F1	D	C31	D	F2	D	C32	D	F3	D	C33	D	F4	D
M-subframe 4	P2	D	F1	D	C41	D	F2	D	C42	D	F3	D	C43	D	F4	D
M-subframe 5	M1	D	F1	D	C51	D	F2	D	C52	D	F3	D	C53	D	F4	D
M-subframe 6	M2	D	F1	D	C61	D	F2	D	C62	D	F3	D	C63	D	F4	D
M-subframe 7	M3	D	F1	D	C71	D	F2	D	C72	D	F3	D	C73	D	F4	D

Figure B-5   A 4760-bit DS3 frame.

M-subframe 1 680 bits	M-subframe 2 680 bits	o o o	M-subframe 7 680 bits

B.5 C Bit Parity Format

As discussed in the last section, all the overhead bits in a DS3-frame have been used up for specific functions. As such, there is no bandwidth left for end-to-end performance monitoring over the physical layer. Since this monitoring capability is important in applications involving DS3 facilities, the X bits and C bits of Figure B-4 must be redefined. The resulting format is called the C-bit parity format.

Since bit stuffing has already been done at the DS2-level, the seven DS2-inputs are now fully synchronous, each operating at 1,545,796 b/s. Therefore, there is no reason for further bit stuffing at the DS3 level. In actual practice, both X bits and C bits are redefined to provide a data link as well as an end-to-end path performance monitoring capability. The 56 overhead bits of a DS3 frame with the redefined C-bit parity format is shown in Figure B-6.

In Figure B-6, the F, M, and P bits are the same as in Figure B-4. However, the X bits have a new meaning. If the far end receives an out-of-frame or alarm indication signal during

Figure B-6   The overhead bits of a DS3 frame with the C-bit parity format.

X1	F1	AIC	F2	NA	F3	FEAC	F4
X2	F1	DL	F2	DL	F3	DL	F4
P	F1	CP	F2	CP	F3	CP	F4
P	F1	FEBE	F2	FEBE	F3	FEBE	F4
M1	F1	DL	F2	DL	F3	DL	F4
M2	F1	DL	F2	DL	F3	DL	F4
M3	F1	DL	F2	DL	F3	DL	F4

any 1-s period, it sets both X bits to 0, indicating a "degraded second," and then transmits the frame to the near end. Otherwise, both X bits are set to 1.

The AIC bit is the application identification channel. It is used by DS3 terminal equipment to identify a DS3 framing format. With the C-bit parity format, it is always set to 1. The NA is reserved for a future network application. The FEAC bit is the far end alarm and control channel. It serves two purposes. First, the remote end can use it to send an alarm or status message. Second, it can be used to initiate from the near end a DS1 or DS3 line loopback at the remote end. Each message is a repeating 16-bit codeword of the form 0xxxxxx0 11111111, where x is a message bit. If no codewords are to be transmitted, the bit must be set to 1 in all frames.

The DL bits form a 112,780-b/s data link for end-to-end path maintenance and user-specific applications. The CP bits are parities that detect line errors on an end-to-end basis. They are computed in the same way as the P bits, and like the P bits, all three CP bits are set to the same value at the transmit end. However, unlike the P bits, they pass through the network unchanged and are not recomputed at every section.

The three FEBE (far end block error) bits are used by the near end to provide an indication of line errors to the far end. If the near end detects such errors, it sets the bits to 0 before transmitting the frame to the far end. Otherwise, they are all set to 1. Thus, the performance of an end-to-end DS3 path can be monitored through the CP, FEBE , FEAC, and DL bits.

B.6 References

[1] ANSI T1.107, Digital Hierarchy — Format Specifications, 1988.

[2] ANSI T1.404, Network-to-Customer Installation — DS3 Metallic Interface Specification, 1994.

[3] CCITT Recommendation G.703, Physical/Electrical Characteristics of Hierarchical Digital Interfaces, 1991.

[4] Telecommunications Techniques Corporation, Application Notes, "The Fundamentals of DS3," 1992.

An Overview of SONET

C.1 Introduction

In 1988, the CCITT adopted a new standard called SONET (Synchronous Optical Network) for user-to-network (UNI) and network-to-network (NNI) interfaces at line rates from 51.84 Mb/s to 9953.28 Mb/s. Subsequently, in the same year, ANSI accepted SONET as an optical interface standard for the US. Ballart and Ching provide an excellent description of the evolution of SONET in their paper [1]. The details of the ANSI standard appear in the ANSI T1.105 series documents [2]. The CCITT Recommendation G.707 describes the related synchronous digital hierarchy bit rates [3]. Currently, the SONET interface is available on many networks and ATM switches. The purpose of this appendix is to briefly describe this interface. For a detailed description, readers are referred to Reference [2].

C.2 SONET Rates

The SONET interface defines a synchronous optical hierarchy. The basic building block, which is the first level of this hierarchy, is the Synchronous Transport Signal — Level 1 (STS-1), operating at a line rate of 51.84 Mb/s. The higher-level signals are denoted as STS-n, and are obtained from n lower-level signals using a byte-interleaved multiplexing procedure. The optical carrier-level n (OC-n) is an optical equivalent of STS-n. For example, to obtain OC-1, the STS-1 frame, with the exception of the framing and STS-1 ID bytes, is first scrambled[1] and then converted into an optical signal. The different levels of the optical signals are listed in Table C-1.

C.3 STS-1 Frame Structure

Each STS-1 frame is 125-μs long and consists of 810 octets, which are arranged in 9 rows and 90 columns as shown in Figure C-1. Bytes are sent out row-by-row, from left-to-right, with the most significant bit of each byte transmitted first.

---

1. The purpose of scrambling is to maintain a proper 1's density on the line so that the receiver at the remote end can recover the clock.

Table C-1   Different Hierarchies of the Optical Carrier Signal

Level	Frequency (Mb/s)
OC-1	51.84
OC-3	155.52
OC-12	622.08
OC-24	1244.16
OC-48	2488.32
OC-192	9953.28

Figure C-1   The STS-1 frame structure.

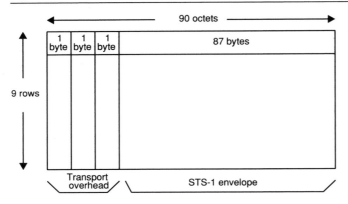

Each STS-1 frame includes framing information so that the receiving equipment can correctly identify the beginning of a frame. Also, since user information may start anywhere in a frame, some additional information must be provided so that the receiving equipment can retrieve its desired channels without having to decode the entire frame. These and other functions such as operations, administration, and maintenance are provided in the first three columns of each STS-1 frame. These 27 bytes are called the transport overhead.

To facilitate equipment design, the transport overhead is partitioned into section and line overhead. The first three rows of the overhead (i.e., the first nine octets) constitute the section overhead and the remaining six rows (that is, 18 octets) comprise the line overhead (see Figure C-2). The section overhead, which is processed by all SONET equipment, consists of two framing bytes, an STS-1 identification byte (which is used to identify the desired STS-1 frame when a number of STS-1 frames are multiplexed into a broadband payload), a bit-interleaved parity byte (BIP-8) to detect section errors if any, an orderwire byte to provide a voice channel between hubs and remote terminals for maintenance, another byte for user-specific applications (say, operations), and three bytes (designated as D1, D2, and D3) to provide data communications for section-level maintenance and provisioning.

Figure C-2   The transport overhead in an STS-1 frame.

Framing −1	Framing −2	STS−1 ID
BIP−8 (B1)	Orderwire	Network User
D1	D2	D3
Pointer 1	Pointer 2	Pointer Action
BIP−8 (B2)	APS −1	APS −2
D4	D5	D6
D7	D8	D9
D10	D11	D12
Sync	REI	Orderwire

Section Overhead covers the first three rows; *Line Overhead* covers the remaining rows.

The line overhead, which is processed by all SONET equipment except regenerators, includes two octets of an STS-1 payload pointer. Since the user information, i.e., the synchronous payload envelope (SPE), can appear anywhere in an STS-1 frame, this pointer specifies an offset, in bytes, between itself and the point where the SPE begins. Usually, the payload begins in one STS-1 frame and ends in the next as shown in Figure C-3. However, it is possible for an entire SPE to be contained in each STS-1 frame.

Since differences may exist between the transmitter's and receiver's clocks, the incoming data in each frame is held in a buffer at the receiving end. The function of the pointer action byte is to indicate to the receiver how this buffer is to be adjusted. This byte is followed by another octet of a bit-interleaved parity byte for detecting any possible errors in the line overhead. The next two octets are for automatic protection switching in the event of a failure. The next nine bytes of user data, D4 through D12, provide a 576-kb/s facility data link for maintenance and administration purposes. The sync byte conveys the quality of the synchronization source. The REI (Remote Error Indication) byte is used by the receiving end to indicate to the source that it has detected an error in a data block.

The remaining 87 columns (i.e., 9×87 octets) carry user information, and thus determine the synchronous payload or maximum bandwidth available to the user. The SPE consists of a 9-octet path overhead (POH) and variable-rate user information. The POH, which is depicted in Figure C-4, is an essential part of the SONET STS-1 payload and is always transmit-

Figure C-3   The SPE in STS-1 frames. Here, two adjacent frames are shown, where the payload begins in the first and ends in the second.

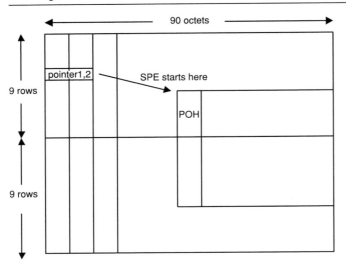

Figure C-4   The path overhead of an SPE.

Trace
BIP−8
Signal Label
Path Status
User Channel
Multiframe
Growth
Growth
Growth

ted along with the payload. The trace byte carries a known pattern so that the receiver can determine if it is connected to the desired transmitter. The BIP-8 parity byte, which is generated over the previous SPE, provides error indication on an end-to-end basis. The signal label specifies the type of the associated payload. The path status byte is returned unmodified by the receiving end so that the sending end can determine if any error has occurred on the full duplex path. The multiframe alignment byte identifies a superframe boundary of smaller pay-loads (see below). The last three bytes have been reserved for future use.

C.4 Sub-STS-1 Payloads

The user information may consist of a variety of channels. For example, it may be a clear, 44.736-Mb/s DS3 channel or a number of lower-bit-rate (i.e., sub-STS-1) payloads. These smaller payloads, are transported over an STS-1 frame using structures called virtual tribu-taries (VTs). The SONET standard specifies four VTs corresponding to the four payloads: 1.728 Mb/s, 2.304 Mb/s, 3.456 Mb/s, and 6.912 Mb/s. Each VT occupies a certain number of columns depending on its bandwidth and is properly interleaved by VTs of other groups. For example, a VT corresponding to 1.728 Mb/s takes up three columns of an STS-1 frame.

C.5 Multiplexing Multiple STSs

The higher-level signal, STS-n, is obtained by byte-interleaving n lower-level signals. Be-fore they are multiplexed, it is necessary to frame-align the transport overhead bytes of each STS-1 frame. The transport overhead of the composite signal consists of the first $3n$ columns, of which only the first three are used for the usual framing and maintenance purposes. The re-maining $3(n-1)$ columns are left unused at this time. Notice that since we continue to use the payload pointers in the multiplexed signal, there is no need to align the SPEs of the indi-vidual STSs.

C.6 References

[1] R. Ballart and Y. Ching, "SONET — Now It's the Standard Optical Network," *IEEE Comm. Mag.*, Mar. 1989, pp. 8–15.
[2] ANSI T1.105, Synchronous Optical Network (SONET) — Basic Description including Multiplex Structure, Rates and Formats, 1995.
[3] ITU-T Recommendation G.707, "Synchronous Digital Hierarchy Bit Rates," 1993.

ADSL

D.1 Introduction

The asymmetrical digital subscriber line (ADSL) provides physical-layer transport of digital data at rates up to 6.144 Mb/s over distances of up to 6 km between a central office and an end-user using the existing two-wire twisted pair cables in the subscriber's loop plant. This is achieved by using specially designed modems at the two ends that essentially convert the existing telephone loops into digital subscriber lines. These modems are based on either carrier-less amplitude modulation (CAM) or the more common discrete multitone modulation (DMT), also known as orthogonal frequency division multiplexing (OFDM).[1] The symbol rate for the DMT modulator is about 4 kHz. A similar technology, called very high-speed digital subscriber line (VDSL), can support data rates as high as 50 Mb/s, but only over very short distances (up to about 1.5 km). ADSL is now a well-defined standard, and can be used by an end-user device to access a variety of networks, including ISDN and ATM networks. In this appendix, we will give an overview of the ADSL technology. For details, see Reference [1].

D.2. ADSL Data Transfer Capability

Figure D-1 shows how an ADSL transceiver unit provides connections to customer equipment and networks. The set-top box or its equivalent provides the user with the capability of accessing multimedia services interactively in real time. As shown in the figure, it may connect to various types of networks (e.g., ISDN, ATM, etc.); however, its interface to a network is defined only in terms of logical functions.

Bandwidths used by an ADSL unit are generally asymmetrical — the data rate is higher in the network-to-user direction (downstream) than in the other direction. Altogether, it supports up to seven channels simultaneously, of which four are simplex in the downstream direction and three are duplex. However, in any ADSL system, the latter three channels can be configured to operate in the simplex mode in either direction. Data rates on these channels

---

1. Presently, OFDM is being used in other communications systems as well. For example, it is used in the Digital Audio Broadcasting (DAB) system in Europe.

Figure D-1   Interfaces of an ADSL transceiver unit to customer equipment and networks.

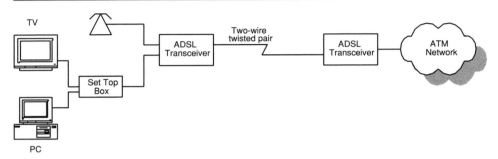

Table D-1   Data Rates Supported in an ADSL System in the Simplex Mode (Downstream)

Transport Class	Range	Data Rates
1	Shortest range	Up to four channels; the aggregate rate is up to 6.144 Mb/s
2	Mid range	Up to three channels with an aggregate rate up to 4.608 Mb/s
3	Mid range	One or two channels with a total rate of up to 3.072 Mb/s
4	Longest range	One channel at 1.536 Mb/s

Table D-2   Data Rates Supported in an ADSL System in the Duplex Mode

Transport Class	Range	Data Rates
1	Shortest range	One channel at 576 kb/s or two channels, one at 160 kb/s and the other at 384 kb/s.
2 or 3	Mid range	Two channels, one at 160 kb/s and the other at 384 kb/s.
4	Longest range	One channel at 160 kb/s

can be programmed in steps of 32 kb/s. The multiplexing format used is flexible enough to transport channelized data such as in T1, PRI, and SONET. The maximum data rates supported depend on the distance over which the data has to be transported and the type of the existing subscriber loops.

Table D-1 shows various transport classes supported by an ADSL system in the simplex downstream mode. As for duplex operation, there may be at most three channels in an ADSL system. One of them is the mandatory 16- or 64-kb/s control channel that carries signaling information for call controls and selection of service options available to the user. The allowed data rates of the remaining two channels are shown in Table D-2. An ADSL system allows the user to select any valid combination of data rates from the two tables simultaneously.

Figure D-2 A functional block diagram of an ADSL transmitter.

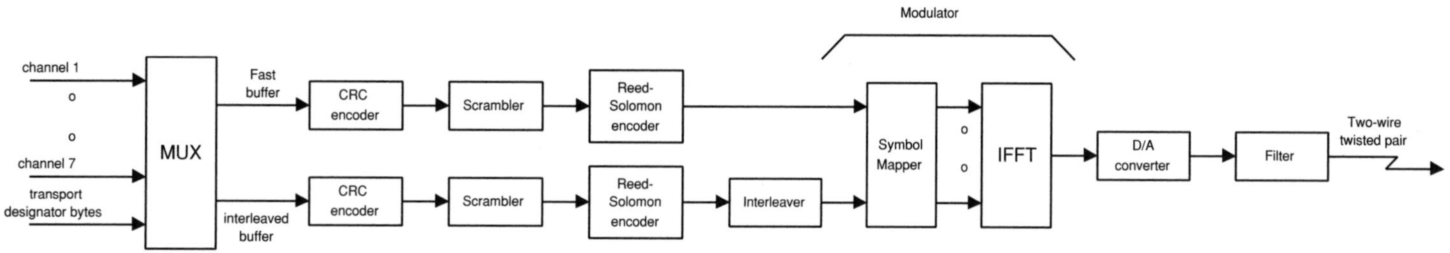

Figure D-3   The generic frame structure for the fast and interleaved data buffers in an ADSL system.

Sync byte, or eoc or oc byte	Simple Channel 1	Simple Channel 2	Simple Channel 3	Simple Channel 4	Duplex Channel 1	Duplex Channel 2	Duplex Channel 3	Duplex Channel 4	1 or 2 bytes (Channel Designator)

Figure D-4   The superframe format in an ADSL system. The length of the superframe is 17ms. A frame is 68/69 × 250 microseconds long. Reproduced by permission of ANSI.

Frame 0	Frame 1	Frame 2	. . .	Frame 67	Synch Symbol

D.3 Functional Description of ADSL Transceiver

Figure D-2 is a functional block diagram of an ADSL transmitter based on the DMT modulation technique. Complementary functions are performed in the receiver. The block designated as "MUX" multiplexes up to four downstream, simplex, user data channels and up to three duplex channels into frames, adding a so-called sync byte at the start and one or two channel designator bytes that indicate transport types at the end.[2]

A generic frame structure is shown in Figure D-3. Each frame is roughly one symbol period. The symbol rate in DMT modulation is 4,000 baud; thus, the symbol period is 250 microseconds. Sixty-eight of these frames, followed by a synchronization symbol, constitute a superframe. The superframe format is shown in Figure D-4.

Referring to Figure D-2, the output of the "MUX" block is actually two streams, each constructed by splitting the incoming user data symbols into two groups: the fast data buffer and the interleaved data buffer. The two streams are subsequently processed and used in the modulator in much the same way, except that the interleaved data buffer stream is later passed through an interleaver, where the data bits are interleaved according to a certain rule.

As indicated in Figure D-2, the first byte of the first frame in a superframe is the sync byte that is generated by CRC code over the preceding superframe. The first byte of each of the other frames in a superframe is used for sync control, embedded operations, or overhead controls.

The fast and interleaved data stream outputs from the CRC encoder are separately scrambled by means of a shift register with a feedback loop. The scrambled output is encoded into a forward error-correcting Reed-Solomon code. The resulting encoder output for the fast data stream is then fed into the symbol mapper. The interleaved data stream, on the other

---

2. These added bytes indicate the transport type being carried, whether it is simplex or duplex operation, and the number of individual channels in each.

Figure D-5 The tones modulated by data symbols in ADSL. The symbol rate is set equal to the frequency of separation between adjacent subcarriers (f_s = 4.3125 kHz).

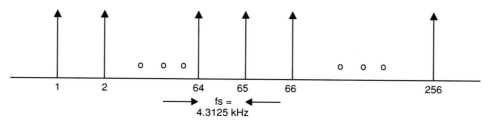

hand, is first byte-interleaved before being converted into symbols. Interleaving can be performed in a number of ways. ADSL uses what is called convolutional interleaving, whereby all data bytes over a given interval are delayed in proportion to their position in the interval. For example, if the interval chosen is long enough to contain only four bytes, say, then its first byte is delayed one byte, the second byte is delayed two byes, and so on, with the interleaving bytes being filled with the data bytes of the previous interval.

In the symbol mapper,[3] the data bits are converted into symbols, following some rules, prior to modulation. Given the fixed bandwidth of the channel, the incoming data rate determines the number of bits in each symbol. For example, we can construct a symbol with two bits, whereby the bit pair (0,0) is assigned to the first symbol, bits (0,1) to the second, bits (1,0) to the third, and bits (1,1) to the fourth. This gives a 2-bit constellation. If the data rate is higher, more bits can be used per symbol. For instance, a 4-bit constellation can be used in which incoming data bits (0,0,0,0) are mapped to the first symbol, (0,0,0,1) to the second, and so on. In this case, there are 16 different symbols. These symbols, which are subsequently used to modulate the discrete tones (or subcarriers as they are called), are each represented by a complex quantity with an amplitude and an associated phase angle.

The modulation scheme used in the ADSL system is briefly the following: In frequency modulation, the carrier frequency is modulated by the information bits. The output signal has a continuous spectrum, its bandwidth depending on the maximum frequency deviation. In the modulation scheme that is used in ADSL, there are 256 discrete subcarriers numbered 1 through 255, spaced 4.3125 kHz apart (see Figure D-5).

To eliminate or reduce inter-symbol interference, signals associated with adjacent subcarriers are made orthogonal to each other. Two signals with frequencies f_1 and f_2 are orthogonal over a symbol period T if

$$\int_{-T/2}^{T/2} e^{j2\pi f_1 t} e^{j2\pi f_2 t} \, dt = 0$$

---

3. In the ADSL literature, it is called a constellation encoder.

From the above, it can be shown that orthogonality is achieved if the symbol rate is equal to the frequency of separation between adjacent tones.

Each tone, with the exception of tone 64, is modulated by a certain number of bits of the digital data stream that constitute a symbol. To modulate a tone with a given symbol, the tone is simply assigned a unique complex quantity depending on the symbol. Subcarrier 64 ($f = 276$ kHz) is used as a pilot tone; the data modulating the pilot subcarrier is a constant quantity with zero amplitude and phase. The sequence of 256 complex quantities formed this way during each symbol period are then summed, converted into an analog signal by a D/A converter, filtered, and then applied to the line.

The principles of multitone modulation are well-documented in the literature [2]−[5]. Suppose that a complex symbol is represented as

$$c_k = a_k + jb_k$$

When a subcarrier is modulated by this symbol, the time domain signal is given by

$$\text{Re}[c_k e^{j2\pi f_k t}] = a_k \cos(2\pi f_k t) - b_k \sin(2\pi f_k t)$$

where Re stands for the real part of a complex quantity, and f_k is the k-th subcarrier. If there are K subcarriers, the time domain signal $x(t)$ at the input of the D/A converter due to all subcarriers is

$$x(t) = \sum_{k=0}^{K-1} \text{Re}[c_k e^{j2\pi f_k t}] \tag{D.1}$$

$$= \sum_{k=0}^{K-1} [a_k \cos(2\pi f_k t) - b_k \sin(2\pi f_k t)]$$

If the symbol period is T_s, then, because of orthognality, adjacent subcarriers are separated by $\Delta f = 1/T_s$. Thus, assuming that the first subcarrier starts at 0, $f_k = k/T_s$. Hence, omitting the term Re for convenience, Equation D.1 can be written as

$$x(t) = \sum_{k=0}^{K-1} c_k e^{j2\pi kt/T_s} \tag{D.2}$$

Suppose that this signal is now sampled at a rate of N samples per symbol period. If the sample period is T, $T_s = NT$. From Equation D.2, the n-th sample is given by

$$x(nT) = \sum_{k=0}^{K-1} c_k e^{j2\pi knT/NT} = \sum_{k=0}^{K-1} c_k e^{j2\pi kn/N} \tag{D.3}$$

Dropping the term T, Equation D.3 reduces to

$$x(n) = \sum_{k=0}^{K-1} c_k e^{j2\pi kn/N}, \qquad n = 0, 1, \ldots, N-1 \tag{D.4}$$

Recall that Equation D.4 is the inverse fast Fourier transform (IFFT) of sequence $\{c_k\}$. Thus, as shown in Figure D-2, a sampled version of the modulated signal can be generated by simply passing the output of the symbol mapper through the IFFT.

In ADSL, $N = 511$. Since $K = 255$, it is necessary to derive an augmented sequence $\{c_k'\}$ from $\{c_k\}$. It is done in the following way:

$$c_k' = \begin{cases} c_k, k = 0, 1, \ldots, K - 1 \\ c_{512-k}^*, k = 257, 258, \ldots, 511 \end{cases}$$

where c_k^* is the complex conjugate of c_k. In other words, the sequence $\{c_k'\}$, which gives the amplitude and phase of the tones, has Hermitian symmetry.

System performance can be improved by convolutionally encoding the data stream and then using trellis code. However, this additional coding is not mandatory in an ADSL system.

D.4 References

[1] ANSI Standard T1.413, "Network and Customer Installation Interfaces — Asymmetric Digital Subscriber Line (ADSL) Metallic Interface," 1995.

[2] M. Saito, et al., "Transmission Characteristics of DQPSK-OFDM for Terrestrial Digital Broadcasting Systems," *IEICE Trans. Commun.*, Vol. E77-B, No. 12, Dec. 1994.

[3] J. A. C. Bingham, *The Theory and Practice of Modem Design.* New York: John Wiley and Sons, May 1988, pp. 109–121.

[4] J. A. C. Bingham, "Multicarrier Modulation for Data Transmission: An Idea Whose Time Has Come," *IEEE Comm. Mag.*, May 1990, pp. 5–14.

[5] R. D. Wesel, et al., "Fundamentals of Coding for Broadcast OFDM," *Proc. of 29th Asilomar Conf.*, 1990, pp. 2–6.

Abbreviations

AAL	ATM Adaptation Layer
ABR	Available Bit Rate (also known as "Best Effort" service)
ABT	ATM Block Transfer
ACR	Allowed Cell Rate
ADSL	Asymmetrical Digital Subscriber Line
AIC	Application Identification Channel
AIN	Advanced Intelligent Network
AMI	Alternate Mark Inversion
AMPS	Advanced Mobile Phone Service
AP	Adjunct Processor
ARP	Address Resolution Protocol
AS	Autonomous System
ATM	Asynchronous Transfer Mode
ATMARP	ATM Address Resolution Protocol
AUU	ATM layer User-to-User
B8ZS	Bipolar Eight Zero Substitution
BCD	Binary Coded Decimal
BECN	Backward Explicit Congestion Notification
BGP	Border Gateway Protocol
BIP	Bit-Interleaved Parity
B-ISDN	Broadband-ISDN
BRI	Basic Rate ISDN
BS	Base Station
BUS	Broadcast and Unknown Server
CAC	Connection Admission Control
CAS	Channel-Associated Signaling
CBR	Constant Bit Rate
CCITT	International Telegraph and Telephone Consultative Committee
CCR	Current Cell Rate

CDMA	Code Division Multiple Access
CDV	Cell Delay Variation
CDVT	Cell Delay Variation Tolerance
CE	Circuit Emulation
CI	Control and Indication
CIE	Client Information Element
CIF	Common Intermediate Format
CLP	Cell Loss Priority
CLR	Cell Loss Ratio
CPCS	Common-Part Convergence Sublayer
CPE	Customer Premises Equipment
CRC	Cyclic Redundancy Check
CTD	Cell Transfer Delays
CS	Convergence Sublayer
CSI	Convergence Sublayer Indication
CSMA/CA	Carrier Sense Multiple Access with Collision Avoidance
CSMA/CD	Carrier Sense Multiple Access with Collision Detection
DL	Data Link
DLCI	Data Link Control Identifier
DLC	Data Link Control
DMT	Discrete Multi-Tone modulation
DQDB	Distributed Queue Dual Bus
DS0	Digital Signal Level 0
DS1	Digital Signal Level 1
DS2	Digital Signal Level 2
DS3	Digital Signal Level 3
E1	European Transmission Level 1
E3	European Transmission Level 3
EFCI	Explicit Forward Congestion Indication
EPD	Early Packet Discard
ER	Explicit Rate
ESF	Extended Super Frame
ESI	End System Identifier
FDDI	Fiber Distributed Data Interface
FDMA	Frequency Division Multiple Access
FEAC	Far End Alarm and Control
FEBE	Far End Block Error
FECN	Forward Explicit Congestion Notification
FEC	Forward Error Control, Forward Equivalence Class
FTP	File Transfer Protocol
GFC	Generic Flow Control
GSM	Global System for Mobile Communications

HDLC	High Level Data Link Control
HEC	Header Error Control
HLR	Home Location Register
HOL	Head Of the Line
IAB	Internet Activities Board
ICR	Initial Cell Rate
IETF	Internet Engineering Task Force
ILMI	Integrated Local Management Interface
IME	Interface Management Entity
InATMARP	Inverse ATM Address Resolution Protocol
IP	Internet Protocol
IPv6	IP Version 6
ISDN	Integrated Services Digital Network
ITU	International Telecommunication Union
IWF	Interworking Function
LAN	Local Area Network
LANE	LAN Emulation
LAPD	Link Access Procedure on the D Channel
LATA	Local Access and Transport Area
LDP	Label Distribution Protocol
LEC	LAN Emulation Client
LECID	LAN Emulation Client Identifier
LES	LAN Emulation Server
LECS	LAN Emulation Configuration Server
LIS	Logical IP Subnetworks
LLC	Logical Link Control
LNNI	Lan Emulation Network-Network Interface
LSR	Label Switching Router
LUNI	LAN Emulation User-Network Interface
MAC	Medium Access Control
MAN	Metropolitan Area Network
MBS	Maximum Burst Size
MCR	Minimum Cell Rate
MCS	Multicast Server
MCU	Multipoint Control Unit
MIB	Management Information Base
MPC	MPOA Client
MPLS	Multi-Protocol Label Switching
MPOA	Multi-Protocol Over ATM
MPS	MPOA Server
NBMA	Non-Broadcast Multiple Access
NDIS	Network Driver Interface Specification

NHC	Next Hop Client
NHRP	Next Hop Resolution Protocol
N-ISDN	Narrowband ISDN
NMS	Network Management Station
NNI	Network Node Interface, Network-to-Network Interface
NS	Non-Signaling Format
OAM	Operations, Administration & Maintenance
OC	Optical Carrier
ODI	Open Data link Interface
OSPF	Open Shortest Path First
OFDM	Orthogonal Frequency Division Multiplexing
OUI	Organizationally Unique Identifier
PCR	Peak Cell Rate
PDU	Protocol Data Unit
PID	Protocol Identifier
POH	Path Overhead
POTS	Plain Old Telephone Service
PPD	Partial Packet Discard
PPP	Point-to-Point Protocol
PRI	Primary Rate ISDN
PROM	Programmable Read-Only Memory
PSTN	Public Switched Telephone Network
PT	Payload Type
PTI	Payload Type Indicator
PVC	Permanent Virtual Circuit, Permanent Virtual Connection
QCIF	Quarter CIF
QoS	Quality of Service
RC	Routing Control
RD	Routing Descriptor
REI	Remote Error Indication
RI	Routing Information
RIP	Routing Information Protocol
RM	Resource Management
RSVP	Resource Reservation Protocol
RTP	Real-time Transport Protocol
RTCP	Real-time Transport Control Protocol
RTS	Residual Timestamp
SAR	Segmentation and Reassembly
SCR	Sustainable Cell Rate
SDT	Structured Data Transfer
SDU	Service Data Unit
SEL	Selector

SF	Super Frame
SMTP	Simple Mail Transfer Protocol
SN	Sequence Number
SNAP	Subnetwork Attachment Point
SNMP	Simple Network Management Protocol
SONET	Synchronous Optical Network
SPE	Synchronous Payload Envelope
SRTS	Synchronous Residual Timestamp
SS7	Signaling System 7
SSCS	Service Specific Convergence Sublayer
STM	Synchronous Transfer Mode
STS-1	Synchronous Transport Signal-Level 1
SVC	Switched Virtual Channel
SVPC	Switched Virtual Path Connection
TCP	Transmission Control Protocol
TDMA	Time-Division Multiple Access
TELNET	Telecommunication Network Protocol
TFTP	Trivial File Transfer Protocol
TTL	Time-To-Live
UBR	Unspecified Bit Rate
UDP	User Datagram Protocol
UNI	User-to-Network Interface
UPC	Usage Parameter Control
UTP	Unshielded Twisted Pair
VBR	Variable Bit Rate
VC	Virtual Channel
VCC	Virtual Channel Connection
VCI	Virtual Channel Identifiers
VLR	Visitor Location Register
VP	Virtual Path
VPC	Virtual Path Connection
VPCI	Virtual Path Connection Identifier
VPI	Virtual Path Identifier
VDSL	Very high-speed Digital Subscriber Line
VT	Virtual Tributary
VTOA	Voice and Telephony over ATM
WAN	Wide Area Network
WATM	Wireless ATM
WFQ	Weighted Fair Queuing
WLAN	Wireless LAN
WWLA	Wideband Wireless Local Access

Index

A

AAL-SDU, 25–26
Abbreviations, 285–89
ADD PARTY ACKNOWL-
    EDGE message, 44
ADD PARTY message, 43–
    44
ADD PARTY REJECT
    message, 44
Address Registration MIB,
    133–34
Address resolution protocol
    (ARP), 176–77
ADSL (asynchronous digital
    subscriber line), 30,
    277–83
    data transfer capability,
        277–80
    functional description of
        ADSL transceiver,
        280–83
Advanced intelligent net-
    works (AINs), 13
Advanced mobile phone ser-
    vice (AMPS), 12–13,
    233
ALERTING message, 37–38
Allowed cell rate (ACR), 99
ALOHA system, 234
Alternate mark inversion
    (AMI) line coding,
    262

AMPS (Advanced Mobile
    Phone Service), 12–
    13, 233
ARPANET, 252
ARP-PDU, 189
Associated signaling, 36
Asynchronous transfer mode
    (ATM), *See* ATM
ATM:
    advantages of, 5–8
        bandwidth-on-demand,
            8
        high-speed/high-
            bandwidth, 7
        integrated access from
            customer premises, 7
        integrated network, 7
        interworks with exist-
            ing protocols/legacy
            LANs, 7–8
        label switching, 5–6
        low latency, 6–7
    defined, 3–5
    evolution of, 1–3
    example applications,
        8–15
        central office ATM
            switch, 8–10
        high-bandwidth ATM
            backbone, 8
        mobile communications
            systems, 10–13
        video conferencing, 13

ATM adaptation layer
    (AAL), 4–5, 23–24
ATM adaptation-layer pro-
    tocol, 23–30
    AAL Type 1, 24–25
    AAL Type 2, 11, 26
    AAL Type 3/4, 26–27
        convergence sublayer
            format, 27–28
        SAR sublayer format,
            28–29
    AAL Type 5, 11, 29–30
        convergence sublayer
            format, 29
        SAR sublayer and ATM
            layer, 30
    service types, 24
ATMARP packet (ATM
    address resolution
    protocol), 186, 187–
    89
ATM Forum, 3, 3fn, 7, 88,
    90, 95, 99, 131, 155
    congestion control scheme
        for ABR services,
        98–102
    congestion control
        mechanism, 101–2
    RM cell format, 99–
        100
    LAN Emulation Sub
        Working Group
        (SWG), 158

ATM layer, 4, 18–23
  generic flow control, 19–21
  payload type (PT) field, 22–23
  virtual path/virtual channel, 21–22
ATM layer user-to-user (AUU) bit, PT field, 23
ATM network management, 119–39
  ATM interface MIB, 132–35
    Address Registration MIB, 133–34
    auto-discovery, 136–37
    Link Management MIB, 132–33
    protocol stack in ILMI, 135–36
    Service Registry MIB, 134–35
    system requirements, 137
  network management functions, 119–21
    configuration management, 120
    fault management, 120
    performance management, 121
    security management, 17–32, 119, 121
  network-network manager interface, 121–23
  Simple Network Management Protocol (SNMP), 123–30
    defined, 123–24
    get-next operator, 126

get-next(sysDescr.0) operator, 126–27
get request operator, 126
get response operator, 127
operators, 124
organization of MIB, 128–30
overview, 123–24
set operator, 127
trap operator, 127
ATM ports, 120
ATM protocol, 17–32
  ATM adaptation-layer protocol, 23–30
  ATM layer, 4, 18–23
  ATM protocol stack, 4, 17–18, 34
  physical layer, 30–31
ATM routing table, 120
ATM switching systems, 53–86
  buffering, 71–81
    completely shared buffering, 79
    input buffering, 72–76
    input bus and output buffering, 80–81
    output buffering, 76–79
  cross-point switch, 55–59
  self-routing switches, 59–67
    banyan network, 59–60
    Batcher-banyan networks, 67–69
    blocking in, 62–64
    cascaded banyan networks, 65–67
    omega networks, 60–62
    replicated banyan network, 64

tandem banyan network, 64–65
    time-division switches with common memory, 69–71
ATM system parameters, 120
Authoritative NHRP Resolution Reply, 199
Auto-discovery, 136–37
Autonomous system (AS), 244, 252
Available-bit-rate (ABR), 91
Available-bit-rate (ABR) services, 95, 108–14
  congestion control scheme for, 98–102

B

B8ZS coding, 262
Backoff algorithm, 239
Back-pressure method, 98, 192–93
Backward Explicit Congestion Notification (BECN) scheme, 98
Band allocation, 2
Bandwidth-on-demand, 8
Banyan network, 54, 59–61
Base station (BS), 10–11, 13
Basic Rate ISDN (BRI), 2
Batcher-banyan networks, 54, 67–69
Bellman-Ford algorithm, 252
Benes network, 66
Binary coded decimal (BCD) digits, 45
Border Gateway Protocol (BGP), 250
Bridge, compared to router, 164fn

Broadband-ISDN (B-ISDN), 3, 20
Broadcast network, 244
Broadcast and Unknown Server (BUS), 164
connecting to, 175–77
address resolution protocol (ARP), 176–77
general procedure, 175–76
Buffering, 71–81
completely shared buffering, 79
input buffering, 72–76
input bus and output buffering, 80–81
output buffering, 76–79
Buffer utilization, 88

C

Cache entry, 199
Call admission control (CAC), 93
Call control procedures, 33–62
call control message coding example, 49–51
end-point addressing, 45–46
general procedures, 33–34
message construction, 40–42
meta-signaling, 33
out-of-band signaling, 33–34
point-to-multipoint signaling, 42–45
point-to-point signaling, 35, 36–40
user-to-user signaling, 34

voice and telephony over ATM (VTOA), 46–48
CALL PROCEEDING message, 37–38, 41fn
Carrier sense multiple access scheme with collision detection (CSMA/CD), 234, 239
Cascaded banyan networks, 65–67
CCITT Study Group XVIII, 1, 3fn
CCITT X.213, 45
CDMA (Code Division Multiple Access), 12–13, 233
Cell delay variation (CDV), 89, 97
Cell delay variation tolerance (CDVT), 97
Cell loss priority (CLP) bit, 18, 49
Cell loss ratio (CLR), 49, 89
Cells, 2–3, 23
Cell transfer delay (CTD), 89
Central office ATM switch, 8–10
Channel-associated signaling (CAS), 48, 261
Circuit emulation over ATM, 141–58
clock recovery at receiving end, 154
emulation procedure, 145–50
$N \times 64$kb/s with CAS, 148–50
$N \times 64$kb/s structured without CAS, 145–48
64-kb/s service, 145

example of, 150–51
functions to emulate, 143–45
alarms, 144–45
bit-oriented messages, 145
channels, 143
clocking, 144
facility data link (FDL), 144
framing, 143
signaling, 143–44
generating source clock information, 151–53
Common channel signaling, 262
Common-part convergence sublayer (CPCS), 18
Completely shared buffering, 79
Configuration management, 120
Congestion control, 91–102
early work, 93–95
preventive controls, 95–97
reactive controls, 97–98
CONNECT ACKNOWLEDGE message, 37
Connection management, 179–80
CONNECT message, 38
Constant bit rate (CBR), 141
Constant-bit-rate (CBR) service, 90–91, 92
Convergence sublayer (CS), 17
Convergence sublayer protocol data unit (CS-PDU), 23, 25–29, 225
CPCS-CPU format, 29

CPCS PDU (common-part convergence sublayer protocol data unit), 103
CPCS-UU field, 29
Credit-based flow control scheme, 98, 192–93
Cross-point switch, 55–59
CS-PDU, *See* Convergence sublayer protocol data unit (CS-PDU)
Current cell rate (CCR) field, 100
Customer premises equipment (CPE), 141

D

Database Description Packet, 255
Data frame format, 178
Data link control (DLC) protocol, 239–40
Data Link Control Identifiers (DLCIs), 243
Delays, and traffic management, 89
Delta class, 54
Direct sequence spread spectrum (DSSS) system, 233
Distribution network, 66
Downstream LSR, 245
DROP PARTY ACKNOWLEDGE message, 45
DROP PARTY message, 44–45
Drop-tail packet discard scheme, 193
DS1 interface, 142–43
DS2 multiplexing, 265–67

DS3, 265–69
    bit stuffing at DS2 level, 265
    C bit parity format, 268–69
    multiplexing, 267–68
Dual queue distributed bus (DQDB), 7

E

E1 interface, 142, 263
Early packet discard (EPD), 106, 193
EFCI-marking switches, 101fn
Egress, 199
Egress router, 243fn
Email, 1
Emulated LAN types, 161–64
    token ring LAN, 162–64
End-point addressing in ATM, 45–46
    address format, 45–46
    address registration, 46
End system identifier (ESI), 45
ER-marking switching, 101fn
Ethernet, 7, 121
Ethernet IEEE 802.3, 161
Ethernet LAN, 161
Explicit forward congestion indication (EFCI), 98
Extended superframe (ESF) format, 259

F

Facility data link (FDL), 144
Fault management, 120
Fiber-distributed data interface (FDDI), 7–8

Forward Explicit congestion Notification (FECN) scheme, 98
Forwarding equivalence class (FEC), 244, 250
Frequency division multiple access (FDMA), 233

G

Generalized cube network, 59
Generic flow control (GFC), 18, 19–21
Groups, 128
GSM (Global System for Mobile Communications), 12–13

H

H.221 Frame Mux/Demux, 218
Hard handoff, 12fn
HDB3, 263
Header error control (HEC) field, 18–19
Hierarchical labels, 248–49, 255
High-bandwidth ATM backbone, 8
High-level data link control (HDLC), 4
High-speed telecommunications technology, 1
Home location register (HLR), 11

I

IEEE 802.11 protocol, 239, 241

ifOperStatus, 124
Information elements (IEs), 40–42
  generic structure of, 42
INFORMATION message, 36
Ingress, 199
Input buffering, 72–76
Input bus and output buffering, 80–81
Integrated Local Management Interface (ILMI), 46, 119, 122, 131
  protocol stack in, 135–36
Intelligent network (IN) functions, 11
Interactive distance learning, 213
Internet Activities Board (IAB), 123
Internet Engineering Task Force (IETF), 183, 252
Internet protocol (IP), 4
Internetwork layer, 199
Inverse ATMARP (In-ATMARP), 186, 189
IP over ATM, 183–96
  ATMARP, 186, 187–89
  examples of, 184
  inverse ATMARP (In-ATMARP), 186, 189
  packet transmission procedure with, 185–87
  performance of TCP/IP over ATM, 189–94
IWF, 46–47
IWF-IWF signaling, 48

L

Label, 243, 244
  hierarchical, 248–49
Label assignment, 249–50
Label distribution in ATM, 250–52
Label distribution protocol (LDP), 244, 250
Label stack, 245
Label swap, 245–46
Label switching, 5–6, 243, 248
Label-switching router (LSR), 244–45
LAN emulation client (LEC), 158
LAN Emulation Configuration Server (LECS), 164
LAN emulation (LANE) protocol, 158
LAN emulation over ATM, 157–81
  connection management, 179–80
  control frames, 171
  data transfer procedures, 177–78
    data frame format, 178
    multicast frames, 177–78
    unicast frames, 177
  emulated LAN types, 161–64
    Ethernet LAN, 161
    token ring LAN, 162–64
  emulation procedure, 168–78
  overview, 166–71
  functions performed in emulation, 164–67

    BUS, 165–66
    LECS, 165
    LES, 165
  initialization process, 171–77
    configure phase, 173
    connecting to the BUS, 175–77
    join phase, 174–75
    LECS connect phase, 172–73
    registration phase, 175
  protocol stack, 167–68
LAN Emulation Server (LES), 164
LAN emulation service data unit (LE-SDU), 166
LAN Emulation Sub Working Group (SWG), 158
LAN emulation version 2, 180
Leaky bucket characterization of traffic, 93
Link access procedures on the D channel (LAPD), 18
Link Management MIB, 132–33
Link State Acknowledgment Packet type, 255
Link State Request Packet, 255
Link State Update Packet type, 255
Local Access Transport Areas (LATAs), 8
Logical IP subnetworks (LISs), 187
Logical link control/subnet attachment (LLC/SNAP), 187, 252

Low latency, and ATM pro-
    tocol, 6–7

M

Management information
    base (MIB), 119
    ATM interface MIB, 132–
        35
        Address Registration
            MIB, 133–34
        Link Management
            MIB, 132–33
        Service Registry MIB,
            134–35
    MIB-1, 128
    organization of, 128–30
Maximum burst size (MBS),
    91
Medium access control
    (MAC) protocol, 233
Message construction, 40–
    42
Message-oriented signaling,
    262
Message-specific IEs, 41
Meta-signaling, 33
Metropolitan area networks
    (MANs), 7
Minimum cell rate (MCR),
    91, 99
Mobil Access Scheme based
    on Contention and
    Reservation for ATM
    (MASCARA), 238fn,
    240fn
Mobile communications sys-
    tems, ATM in, 10–13
Mobile switching center
    (MSC), 10
MPC (MPOA client), 199–
    201

MPLS Working Group, 250
MPS (MPOA server), 199
Multicast frames, 177–78
Multimedia desktop, 213
Multimedia services, 213–
    32
    interactive distance learn-
        ing, 213
    multimedia desktop, 213
    multimedia terminals,
        interworking of, 226
    narrow-band multimedia
        services, 214–20
        connection procedures
            for a point-to-point
            call, 217–18
        H.320 terminal archi-
            tecture, 216–17
        MCU, 218–19
        network configuration,
            214–16
        over LANs, 220–23
    over ATM, 223–26
        ATM cells for user data
            in H.321 terminals,
            224–26
        call control, 226
        terminal architecture-
            H.321 terminal, 223–
            24
    standards supporting, 214
    video conferencing, 213
Multiple layer protocol
    (MLP), 219
Multipoint Command Visu-
    alization (MCV)
    code, 218
Multipoint control unit
    (MCU), 13
Multi-protocol label switch-
    ing (MPLS), 223,
    243–57

autonomous system (AS),
    244
broadcast network, 244
forwarding equivalence
    class (FEC), 244
hierarchical labels, 248–
    49
label, 244
label assignment, 249–50
label distribution in ATM,
    250–52
label stack, 245
label swap, 245
label-switching router
    (LSR), 244–45
principles of operation,
    246–48
router, 244
routing table construction,
    252–55
upstream and downstream
    LSR, 245
VC merge, 245
Multi-protocol over ATM
    (MPOA), 197–212
address resolution, 208
components, 199–201
    hosts, 199–200
    layer 3 forwarding func-
        tion, 200
    routers, 200–201
configuration, 205
connection management,
    208
data transfer, 208–11
    incoming data, 208–9
    outgoing data, 210–11
definitions, 199
discovery, 205
Next Hop Resolution
    Protocol (NHRP),
    201–3

data formats, 205
procedures, 203–4
overview, 205–11

N

Narrow-band-ISDN
(N-ISDN), *See*
N-ISDN
Narrow-band multimedia
services, 214–20
connection procedures for
a point-to-point call,
217–18
H.320 terminal architec-
ture, 216–17
MCU, 218–19
network configuration,
214–16
over LANs, 220–23
with guaranteed quality
of service, 220
without guaranteed
quality of service,
220–23
NBMA, 199
Network management func-
tions, 119–21
configuration manage-
ment, 120
fault management, 120
performance manage-
ment, 121
security management, 119
Network-network manager
interface, 121–23
Network-to-network inter-
face (NNI), 19, 30
physical-layer protocols
for, 31
Next Hop Client (NHC),
202–3

Next Hop Server (NHS),
202–3
NHC (Next Hop Client), 199
NHRP Backward Transit
NHS Record exten-
sion, 204
NHRP Error Indication, 204
NHRP Forward Transit NHS
Record extension,
204
NHRP (Next Hop Resolu-
tion Protocol), 199,
201–3
NHRP Purge Reply, 204
NHRP Registration Reply,
204
NHRP Resolution Reply,
204
NHS (NHRP server), 199
N-ISDN, 2, 18, 47–48
multimedia services over,
214–20
signaling, 47–48
Non-associated signaling, 36
Non-real-time, variable-bit-
rate (nrt-VBR), 91,
92
Non-signaling (NS) format,
259

O

Object, 123
OBJECT IDENTIFIER,
126, 129–30
Omega networks, 54, 60–62
Open Shortest Path First
(OSPF), 248–49,
252–54
Organizationally unique
identifiers (OUIs),
186

Out-of-band signaling, 33–34
Output buffering, 76–79

P

Packet encapsulation, 186
Packet switching, 243
and cross-point switching,
57
Packet transmission procedure, with IP over
ATM, 185–87
Partial packet discard
(PPD), 193
Payload type indicator (PTI)
field, 18, 101
Payload type (PT) field, 22–
23
Performance management,
121
Permanent virtual channel
(PVC), 33
Physical medium-dependent
(PMD) sublayer, 30
Point-to-multipoint signaling, 41, 42–45, 51
adding a party, 43–44
dropping a party, 44–45
setting up the first party,
43
Point-to-point signaling, 35,
36–40
call clearing procedure,
38–39
incoming call control procedure, 37–38
outgoing call from a terminal, 36–37
restart procedures, 39–40
status inquiry, 40
Precedence levels, packets,
243fn

Primary Rate ISDN (PRI), 2
Protocol data units (PDUs), 23
Protocol identifiers (PIDs), 186
Public Packet Data Network (PPDN), 11
Public switched telephone network (PSTN), 13, 87

Q

Q.931/Q.2931, 40, 51
Quality of service (QoS), 19, 89–90

R

Rate-based control scheme, 98
Rate decrease factor (RDF), 102
Real-time transport control protocol (RTCP), 222
Real-time transport protocol (RTP), 222
Real-time, variable-bit-rate (rt-VBR), 91, 92
RELEASE COMPLETE, 36–38
RELEASE message, 38, 41, 44–45
Replicated banyan network, 64
Residual timestamp (RTS), 147
Synchronous residual time-stamp (RTS), 148
Resource management (RM) cells, 91

Resource Reservation Protocol (RSVP), 183, 250
RESTART ACKNOWL-EDGE message, 40
RESTART message, 40
Robbed bits, 48
Router, 244
Routing control (RC), 163
Routing descriptors (RDs), 163
Routing Information Protocol (RIP), 252

S

SAR-PDUs, 25–30, 146, 225, 246
    format of, 28
Segmentation and reassembly sublayer (SAR), 17
Selective cell drop scheme, 193
Selector (SEL), 45
Self-routing switches, 59–67
    banyan network, 59–60
    Batcher-banyan networks, 67–69
    blocking in, 62–64
    cascaded banyan networks, 65–67
    omega networks, 60–62
    replicated banyan network, 64
    tandem banyan network, 64–65
Service data unit (SDU), 24
Service Registry MIB, 134–35

Service-specific convergence sublayer (SSCS), 17–18
SETUP ACKNOWLEDGE message, 36
SETUP message, 36–37, 41, 43
    encoding, 50–51
Simple cell drop scheme, 193
Simple mail transfer protocol (SMTP), 17
Simple Network Management Protocol (SNMP), 119, 123–30
    defined, 123–24
    get-next operator, 126
    get-next(sysDescr.0) operator, 126–27
    get request operator, 126
    get response operator, 127
    operators, 124
    organization of MIB, 128–30
    set operator, 127
    trap operator, 127
Slotted ALOHA scheme, 234
Soft handoff, 13fn
SONET, 30, 271–75
    multiplexing multiple STSs, 275
    rates, 271
    STS-1 frame structure, 271–75
    sub-STS-1 payloads, 275
Source routing bridge, 162
SS7 (Signaling System 7), 13
Station, 199
Status inquiry, 40
STATUS message, 40

Structured Data Transfer (SDT) pointer, 26, 147
Subnetwork layer, 199
Superframe (SF) format, 259
Sustainable cell rate (SCR), 91
Switched virtual channels (SVCs), 5, 33, 186
Synchronous residual time-stamp (SRTS), 26
Synchronous transfer mode (STM), 1–2
sysDescr, 124

T

T1 interface, 259–62
Tandem banyan network, 64–65
TC sublayer, 30
TCP/IP over ATM, performance of, 189–94
TDMA (Time Division Multiple Access), 12–13, 233
Throughput, 88
Time-division switches with common memory, 69–71
Token Ring/IEEE 802.5, 161–62
Token ring LAN, 162–64
Traffic management, 87–118
  buffer utilization, 88
  cell loss ratio (CLR), 89
  congestion control, 91–102
    early work, 93–95
    preventive controls, 95–97
    reactive controls, 97–98

delays, 89
delay/throughput characteristics, 102–14
  available-bit-rate (ABR) services, 108–14
  simulation model, 102–5
  unspecified-bit-rate (UBR) services, 105–8
  variable-bit-rate (VBR) services, 108–14
quality of service (QoS), 89–90
service categories, 90–91
  available-bit-rate (ABR), 91
  constant-bit-rate (CBR) service, 90–91, 92
  non-real-time, variable-bit-rate (nrt-VBR), 91, 92
  real-time, variable-bit-rate (rt-VBR), 91, 92
  unspecified-bit-rate (UBR) service, 91
throughput, 88
Transmission control protocol (TCP), 4
Transmission convergence (TC) sublayer, 30

U

Unicast frames, 177
Unlicensed national information infrastructure (U-NII), 236fn
Unspecified-bit-rate (UBR), 88

Unspecified-bit-rate (UBR) services, 91, 92, 105–8, 240
Upstream and downstream LSR, 245
Usage parameter control (UPC), 93
User datagram protocol (UDP), 222
User-to-network interface (UNI), 18, 30
  physical-layer protocols for, 31
  out-of-band signaling on, 33
User-to-user signaling, 34

V

Variable-bit-rate (VBR) services, 26, 108–14, 240
Video conferencing, 213, 220–21
  over ATM, 13
Virtual channel identifier (VCI), 3, 5, 18, 33, 252
Virtual channels (VCs), 20, 21–22, 33, 36
  types of, 33
Virtual channel connection (VCC), 33–34
Virtual path connection identifier (VPCI), 35–36
Virtual path identifier (VPI), 5, 18, 34–36, 252
Virtual path (VP), 20, 21–22, 33, 120
Visitor location register (VLR), 11

Voice and telephony over
    ATM (VTOA), 46–
    48, 150–51
  channel-associated signal-
    ing (CAS), 48
  N-ISDN signaling, 47–48

W

Wide area networks
    (WANs), 6

Wideband wireless local
    access (WWLA),
    235
Wink, 48
Wireless ATM (WATM),
    233–42
  interface, 236–41
    limitations of wireless
      medium, 236–37

MAC-layer protocol re-
    quirements for, 237–
    38
  MAC protocol for, 234–
    35, 238–40
  networks, 235
  other protocols, 241
Wireless LANS (WLANs),
    233, 235